"Mark Elsdon has brought toge... church to face honestly and hopefully the crisis that many congregations soon must and soon will sell their property. The urging of the book is to face the crisis honestly, to plan carefully, and to utilize bold imagination in deciding new faithful futures for the congregation. The strong advocacy here is to think afresh and in concert with all sorts of potential allies, from the state to developers to philanthropists. The accent is on mission and the new ways in which faithful mission may be undertaken. This book is a welcome read, given the church's much too long devotion to buildings that may no longer serve well."

—**Walter Brueggemann,** Columbia Theological Seminary

"*Gone for Good?* is one of those books that grabs hold of you and turns you back toward the best of news: God is doing a new thing and we are invited to be a part of it. Where so many see failure, Mark Elsdon envisions possibility. He places what is often a lonely and isolated struggle into a larger context, affirming that even congregations whose buildings have become a worry and a burden may yet see visions and dream dreams. The diversity of perspectives is both inspiring and practical, challenging everyone who cares about the future of the human community to bring what we have to the table."

—**Anna Olson,** author of *Claiming Resurrection in the Dying Church: Freedom beyond Survival*

"A pastor, a scholar, a philanthropist, and a developer walk into an empty church, and what do they see? Possibility. Hope. Community. Love. Mark Elsdon has gathered voices to address the question, What do we do with the gifts, assets, and community when the pews are no longer filled? *Gone for Good?* offers a pragmatic, theological, and grounded vision for the church and its leaders to grieve the change and celebrate what may emerge if we open ourselves to imaginative futures."

—**Patrick B. Reyes,** author of *The Purpose Gap*

"Woven into the fabric of this book is a model for the work it invites. *Gone for Good?* is the result of collaboration, conversations, improbable friendships, wise and dissenting voices, and countless years of experience. Mark Elsdon and this team of brilliant, thoughtful, caring practitioners have created a powerful tool to ignite imagination around an issue that promises to both vex and propel the church for decades to come. We, in the church, cannot, must not, ignore the asset we have in our buildings and property, but we can't do it alone. We need to listen, engage, learn, and experiment across sectors. *Gone for Good?* is exactly what we need to spark a new conversation, a new imagination, for what is possible."

—Lisa Greenwood, president and CEO of
Wesleyan Impact Partners and Texas Methodist Foundation

"Mark Elsdon understands that the church, writ large, is at a tipping point. After decades of unabated decline in both attendance and relevance in the United States, we are desperate to hear the words of a present-day prophet who can lead us to new life. Elsdon is that prophet. But he doesn't stand alone atop a hill and call the masses to his door. Instead, he uses this book as a platform for a diverse group of national thought leaders to share their unique experiences and visions for the future. And while these visions are different, they are all clearly part of a wonderful tapestry that details a holistic, practical, and hopeful path forward. Elsdon issues a clarion call for churches to demonstrate courageously and selflessly how they can use their properties for good. Much more importantly, he urges them to view decline in numbers not as a death, but as an opportunity to bring new life to people and communities who are in desperate need of experiencing present-day manifestations of God's healing mercy, grace, and love."

—Dominic Dutra, author of *Closing Costs:
Reimagining Church Real Estate for Missional Purposes*

"Elsdon's book weaves together the numerous factors affecting church property and its evolving role in the lives of its communities. With a sensitivity to the complicated history of church buildings and their deep importance to the communities they serve, he brings together diverse voices to describe the decline of traditional church buildings and the essential social, economic, and spiritual functions they have provided. Crucially, Elsdon's message is ultimately one of renewal, bringing to the forefront numerous ways in which church property can continue to fulfill these functions and its broader spiritual purpose even in new forms. A seminal work in these changing times of the church."

—Audrey C. Price, associate director of
the Religion & Society Program at the Aspen Institute

Gone for Good?

Negotiating the Coming Wave
of Church Property Transition

EDITED BY MARK ELSDON

WILLIAM B. EERDMANS PUBLISHING COMPANY
GRAND RAPIDS, MICHIGAN

Wm. B. Eerdmans Publishing Co.
4035 Park East Court SE, Grand Rapids, Michigan 49546
www.eerdmans.com

Illustrations by Coté Soerens
Book design by Lydia Hall

Printed in the United States of America

30 29 28 27 26 25 24   1 2 3 4 5 6 7

ISBN 978-0-8028-8324-7

Library of Congress Cataloging-in-Publication Data

A catalog record for this book is available from the Library
of Congress.

For all the pastors and members of the churches
who made me who I am today

CONTENTS

CONTENTS

PART 2: FOR GOOD

PART 3: TOGETHER

Contents

FOREWORD

Reading *Gone for Good? Negotiating the Coming Wave of Church Property Transition* is a sobering experience. It is very much like being caught in a wave, maybe even a rip tide, but having experienced lifeguards to guide you as you are being pulled out to sea. "Don't panic, don't fight against the wave, let it take you out and then when its powerful pull begins to weaken swim not against it but across it and allow the next waves to bring you into shore." Great advice. Of course, many of us who love the water will yet seek to avoid being in the ocean when the waves are too strong or there is a warning that rip currents may occur. This coming wave, however, cannot be avoided. It was inevitable. Given a world turned into property and our lives enfolded in propertied existence, it was only a matter of time when the wave of property accumulation that established churches in the Western world would become the wave that would pull churches out into the uncontrollable sea of market-driven property relations. We are caught in something too large to control, but we can offer witness.

Offering witness is all Christians can ever do in a world intent on pushing God out to imagined margins and making moral vision an afterthought once hard cold deals have been made and monies have exchanged hands. I don't intend this as a cynical statement. It is rather a recognition that witness is important and dense work that we Christians do in the presence of other voices and procedures and operations that constantly seek to order our world for us and invite us to only respond to what has been built. These days I spend a lot of time thinking about the built environment because it has received so little thought by Christians and their theologians, ethicists, and biblical scholars. Indeed, this book presents a rare moment of Christians reflecting on place and the workings of place, but has it arrived too late and with too little? I don't think so, but it does cast light on a dilemma: how to think about church buildings and property when so few churches have thought about their life in a place and so few Christians know how to think their faith spatially.

As I have repeatedly said, we Christians do not have a real doctrine of creation. But that also means that we Christians do not have a real ecclesiology, that is, we do not have a real embodied practice of thinking and living together through place. Most Christians in the Western world live a displaced ethical life. By that I mean the actual place of gathering for their church community and its relation to their concrete living arrangements is usually inconsequential to how they understand their discipleship. The place they live and the place their church exists are simply stages on top of which they think their faith and relate to one another and to those outside their church community and outside their faith. This means that their discipleship is executed fundamentally disconnected from deep awareness of the place they inhabit. Yet the quality and character of our discipleship is profoundly affected by how we understand the places we inhabit. Most Christians, however, never got the memo on this, which means we are late to the problem of property.

Over the years, I have been amazed at the number of people who enter emotional chaos the moment I begin to talk about the problem of property. They immediately hear a call to arms in protection of their real estate, their propertied and property-seeking way of life, and a society built on the buying and selling of land. The problem of property is at heart the inability to think and live place due to the overwhelming vision of the ground as owned. That vision effectively closes off seeing the world and the places of our living as animate and communicative, as filled with histories—environmental and cultural, social and colonial—that require we situate ourselves in the long trajectories of the world's transformation. We have a responsibility to know the history that reaches back to indigenous inhabitants and forward to their current quest for reparations, as Jim Bear Jacobs so powerfully notes in his chapter in this volume. Indeed, the chapters of this volume are touching the live wires of multiple conflicts and disagreements over land turned into property.

At one level, each chapter offers excellent advice to churches, developers, community leaders, real estate agents, pastors, and everybody concerned about this coming church property sell-off. Yet at another level, these chapters open a set of deeper theological and philosophical questions about what a Christian witness might look like at this turbulent moment. There is a worrisome passivity that these chapters are working against that demands we accept the status quo of propertied relations whereby churches are at the mercy of those who wield the power to turn property toward the good. I am not denying the agency and power of churches nor lumping what I call property-workers (developers, real estate agents, planners, architects, etc.) into a big nefarious basket. We need, however, to acknowledge the colonial trajectory that we are inside as we deal with matters of church property.

Churches often do good in the places they inhabit, especially predominantly minoritized and immigrant churches and churches that serve those communities. Those churches, however, are islands, often isolated islands of care and humanization surrounded by built environments that are sometimes harmful, sometimes harmed, sometimes chaotic, and sometimes violent and oppressive. These constellations of built environments carry forward the colonial master's dream to embed his own freedom into the ground itself, allowing him to do whatever he pleases with his land and to teach his children and their children to seek to do the same with the land they obtain regardless of its history or its other inhabitants. Much of the legal system that has developed in the United States and in much of the Western world grew out of the need to organize an emerging propertied world with minimal bloodshed. We were formed in a world that was formed in the struggle over land as property, and that struggle continues.

Our witness must be greater than a successful struggle to do with the land what we want, even if it is for the common good. A church that expands its footprint of care by forming a greater island of consolation for people, builds a larger gathering place for strangers to no longer be strangers, creates a strategic place to plan for change in a city is indeed doing good work, but the witness must be wider and deeper. It must include the process itself, calling those property-workers (if they are Christian) to a discipleship precisely in and through their work, pressing them to think together with the community of faith what faithfulness to God means amid built environments that create homelessness, segregation, brutal policing, and self-centered practices of home ownership and neighborhood control. That witness must also be to people who have been schooled in the colonial practice of owning land (which means all of us) through a vision that easily turns the freedom of ownership into a weapon that unleashes race and class hierarchies and structures exclusion and hatred into the ground itself.

If we are honest, we must mourn the loss of church places, because they signal the loss of effective witness and maybe even the loss of faith. No one celebrates a dying church, and it is indeed a tragic fact that one of the tasks that is now given to those of us who train church leaders is preparing them to know how to close a church and/or consolidate congregations that have become too small to sustain their story or their mission alone. This pedagogical situation pushes against everything I hold dear because I live against the dying. Yet I know that the resurrection has transformed how we must think about dying—death the wall has now become death the door. The door that we must walk through in relation to the selling of church property leads into a new possibility of forming life in place. This means that we need to listen carefully to these authors and take note of their wisdom and experience in working at the sites of death and resurrection.

There is, however, a greater work that remains and that is to challenge the configurations of cities and towns, configurations rural and urban, that give place to death, violence, and harm, that cultivate a relentless reality of homelessness, despair, and segregation, and that teach people to turn a blind eye and closed ears to the cries of the needy all around them. For the cities and towns, neighborhoods and villages that choose to go their own way no matter the cost to human and more than human life, church communities must always offer the invitation to live and build a different kind of life, one that renders property a transparency to connected and flourishing life together. My hope is not to end private property, but to bring it to a better end: the sharing of life in the specifics of a place—its resources, its opportunities, and its relationships. Only if we turn property into a word about sharing can we give witness to the God who gives and sustains life.

This book will disappoint you if you are looking for easy answers. But it will help you if you recognize that you, along with so many others, are in need of a place to begin thinking about the property that churches hold and the mission that holds them, articulated succinctly by our savior: You are my witnesses.

Willie James Jennings
Hamden, Connecticut

CHURCH BUILDINGS SHAPE US

VILLAGE OF ELSDON

AN ORPHAN BABY LEFT ON THE STEPS OF THE CHURCH

"ELSDON"

HIS IMMIGRANT PARENTS HOSTED AROUND A JOINT OF ROAST BEEF

MARK ELSDON

WHAT HAPPENS WHEN CHURCHES ARE GONE?

CHURCHES SERVE FAMILIES

PROVIDE COMMUNITY AND COMFORT

WHERE WILL PEOPLE VOTE?

OR GET FOOD WHEN WE STRUGGLE?

CHURCH MEMBERSHIP IS TRENDING

WHO WILL I BE NOW?

CENTERS OF CIVIC POWER?

DOWN

HIGH END CONDOS?

WHAT HAPPENS WHEN CHURCHES ARE GONE?

Mark Elsdon

The question that keeps me up at night and shapes this book is this: Twenty years from now, when we look around our neighborhoods and realize that a third or more of our church properties are no longer churches, what will we have lost?

Or gained?

What will the impact be on the social fabric of our communities?

And what will each of us have done to encourage good . . . when churches are gone?

I wonder and worry about this in part because as I look back on my life I realize that churches and their buildings have played a huge role in shaping who I am today. Not just in my spiritual life, or my profession as a pastor and church leader, but in big ways and small, in the profound and the mundane. I am full of critique, skepticism, even cynicism about "the church"—but there is no denying that churches have made me who I am today and changed the trajectory of my life many times. Even before I was born.

It is likely that I got my surname from a tiny church in a tiny village in the rolling green hills of northern England. The story goes like this: In the early eighteenth century an orphan baby was left on the doorstep of St. Cuthbert's church in the village of Elsdon. The minister took the baby in and named him Cuthbert Elsdon after both the seventh-century saint who gave the church its name and the village. Thus started the Elsdon line. My family name was born out of grace in a moment of need on the steps of a church. If you visit that church today, you'll find my signature, and that of Elsdons I know, and Elsdons I don't know, in a guestbook that goes back decades.

My parents were born and raised in the Newcastle area of northeast England, not far from the village of Elsdon. When they immigrated to the United States for my father's work, they knew nobody. So one of the first places they went to was a church. One Sunday morning, after attending for a few months, they invited some of their newfound acquaintances over to their home in an attempt to make their coffee conversation partners into friends. Chatting amiably after the worship service, they offered their invitation to a handful of couples: "Would you like to come over next Saturday night to share a joint?" Their invitation was met with silence and awkward looks. My parents were confused by the lack of enthusiasm for this invitation. "Is it us?" "Our accent?" It took a little while to figure out where the misunderstanding lay, but eventually it dawned on them. "Oh no! Not that kind of joint," they said. "A joint of roast beef and some Yorkshire pudding. Would you like to come over for dinner?" Those friendships survived my parents' offer of "drugs" at church, and that congregation became a vital source of community and relationship for a young immigrant couple making a new life thousands of miles from home.

That church and others like it, as my family moved around the country during my childhood and teenage years, played pivotal roles in my life. I found my voice and independence as a toddler crawling under the pews to the front of the sanctuary; at one church, I refused to be removed from the communion rail. At another, I met my best middle-school friends and trekked mud from a nearby creek through the entire building. I would regularly bring half of my high school cross-country team to the gym of another church for a rigorous game of basketball while we were supposed to be out on long runs. We'd play until we saw the rest of the team running back by the church and then we'd slip out and join the back of the group, our coach none the wiser. A friend from yet another church invited me to go on a youth group trip to ride our ten-speed bikes in the mountains of Colorado for a week, sleeping in, yes, more churches, each night. I left that week, and the follow-up trips each summer, with an increasing love for cycling and for God. I was taught about the faith and (at least occasionally!) attended services at these churches, but church was so much more than that. It was a place to find friends, to play basketball, to get dirty, and to be reprimanded kindly.

Later, as I finished high school and went to college, churches played a more formative role in my life than even my university experience. In Berkeley, California, I became friends with people experiencing homelessness through a program my roommate and I started through a church. My sense of purpose and call to ministry and justice emerged as I encountered a much wider view of the world than what I had grown up with. My privilege was illuminated and challenged by meeting people at churches in rural Dominican Republic, in the mountains of Ethiopia, and in Black, Indigenous, and immigrant churches throughout the United States. And like so many, I owe my married life and amazing children to a church community because I met my future spouse volunteering at a church meal for people experiencing food insecurity.

While training to be a pastor in seminary, I worked with my partner at a Taiwanese Presbyterian church that afforded me the chance to see the special role churches play in the social fabric of marginalized and immigrant communities. Presbyterian churches have supported the independence of Taiwan for many decades— engaging not just in the spiritual or eternal but in the very pressing and present realities of living under occupation and threat. In the United States, immigrant churches often serve as family, community center, language training center, support group, Internet search function, and so much more.

I am the executive director of a campus ministry center and student housing community at the University of Wisconsin-Madison, called Pres House. The ministry has been around for more than 115 years. During the campus protests of the 1960s, student activists and twenty-year-old National Guard troops left their respective signs and guns on the steps outside our building. Young people from both sides of a conflict they hadn't started but were key players in would come inside for coffee and a safe pause from the unrest outside.

Today our apartment building at Pres House is home to 240 students each year. We house residents in a sober-living recovery community, provide wellness and mental health support, give out meals to students on campus who are food insecure, and serve as a home away from home for thousands of college students. I've spent countless nights sleeping on other church floors during service-learning trips with college students all over the country, and churches from all around Madison support our ministry by providing the only home-cooked meal that many students eat each week.

In 2016 my Nanna (grandmother), my last living relative in England, died. I still have family in Scotland, but the lineage that began the village of Elsdon hundreds of years ago has become a diaspora living throughout the world. At least my line has. Because my father is an only child, the Elsdon side of my family is very small. When my Nanna died, my father and I traveled back to northern England for her funeral and to make arrangements. We began planning a memorial service at the church my Nanna attended for many decades that would take place a couple of months later. In the meantime, we had a small funeral at the funeral home. We didn't make invitations, so it was attended by just three people—me, my father, and the pastor of her church, who led a short service. I'll never forget the kindness and grace the pastor of a small, aging church offered us in those quiet moments of grief.

My life has been directly impacted by literally hundreds of churches. While I imagine this is more than the average American experiences, churches and their buildings play a vital role in the social infrastructure of communities in every corner of the country. There is no doubt that churches have done more than their fair share of harm to people and communities. But they also serve many important roles in the lives of hundreds of millions of people, many of whom may not even be fully aware of it. Even many who never attend a worship service are often directly, or indirectly, touched by a church building.

So, After Churches Are Gone, Then What?

As Eileen Lindner writes in her chapter in this book, as many as 100,000 buildings, and billions of dollars of church-owned property, are expected to be sold or repurposed throughout the United States by 2030. It is difficult to get precise data on exactly how many church properties will be sold because no one is tracking that in any systematic way.

Researchers are making projections about the future of religious affiliation in the United States, however. A 2022 model by the Pew Research Center predicts that if recent trends continue, Christians will make up less than half of the US population by 2070. That number might be as low as one-third of the population, depending on how the trends evolve. There are of course new churches starting each year, but as of 2019, we have entered an era where more churches are closed each year than are opened.

The reasons for this change are beyond the scope of this book.[1] The bottom line is that fewer and fewer people identify as Christians and attend traditional church activities in church buildings. Therefore, the simple reality is that there are far more church buildings today than will be needed in the future. Some of these buildings and properties will have to become something else. Or they will end up empty and unused.

This transition is happening. We are long past the days of "revitalizing" every church in order to keep all churches open and operating buildings that are too large or needing renovation. Many church properties are going to become something different on a massive scale, whether we like it or not. The wave is upon us.

---

1. See Bob Smietana, *Reorganized Religion: The Reshaping of the American Church and Why It Matters* (Franklin, TN: Worthy Publishing, 2023), for a good collection of research on why so much is changing in American Christianity.

This transition in church property is also a once-in-many-generations shift. Churches own property in prime locations in every corner of the country. As that property is sold or becomes something else, it will not go back to being a church again in any foreseeable future.

So the question before us is this: After the wave of selling and repurposing churches crashes upon the shore, what will be left when the water flows back out to sea? What will our neighborhoods look like? If forty out of one hundred churches in a city are something else in fifteen years, what will be lost? What could be gained? As my colleague at RootedGood, Shannon Hopkins, has said, "If the projections are even partially correct, we are looking at a change to the shape of society and the Christian church the likes of which we haven't seen since the GI Bill, the New Deal, or the Second Great Awakening."

Where will the local Girl Scout troop or neighborhood association meet? Where will people go when grieving yet another mass shooting? It's at churches that millions of people meet lifelong friends and partners, get access to financial services not available through traditional banking, pick up food when bills get tight, and cast their vote. Churches are not just vital spiritual resources in a community, they provide vital social services that touch lives far beyond their parishioners.

Many of us are concerned about the increasing inequality and polarization that are tearing apart our communities, relationships, and personal wellness. Eric Klinenberg argues that "the physical places and organizations that shape the way people interact" have a direct impact on the quality of our lives and relationships.[2] He calls these places and organizations "social infrastructure." And churches are one of those key places. "Although they vary dramatically by size and resource, churches, mosques, and synagogues tend to offer all kinds of social programs in their facilities: education and

2. Eric Klinenberg, *Palaces for the People: How Social Infrastructure Can Help Fight Inequality, Polarization, and the Decline of Civic Life* (New York: Broadway Books, 2018), 5.

study groups, athletic leagues, childcare, elder support and the like
... their significance as social infrastructure is beyond dispute."[3]

As you will read in Robert Jaeger's chapter, Partners for Sacred
Places has conducted what they call a "Halo" study and found that
almost 3.7 million people visited just ninety churches in one community over a single year. Only 9 percent of those visits were for
worship. Almost half of those polled came to church to participate
in community-serving programs, and 31 percent came for education programs. This study also found that on average each church
provided more than $4 million of economic value to its commu-
nity each year. As Patrick Duggan notes, "Even in mission failure,
churches and church properties generate tremendous economic
and social value in American society."

What will replace churches on those properties? Without
thoughtful intervention, it is likely that many will end up as vacant
land or crumbling buildings; purchased by investors and resold
for significant personal profit; or as locations for new, high-end
housing units that enrich developers and investors while contributing to gentrification. After the wave has receded, will church
property have further contributed to injustice and the widening
gap between rich and poor? Or will we have put our creativity and
energy into new uses that leave communities more connected,
more just, and with new programs and support that bring light
and life into people's lives?

STONE SOUP

I've always loved the children's tale about stone soup. There are
many versions that approach the story from different cultural perspectives, but in most, the general outline of the story goes like
this: A group of travelers arrive in a village carrying only a cooking
pot. They set the pot on a fire in the middle of the village and fill it
with water. Then they drop in a stone. They begin "cooking" the
stone soup. At first the villagers just peek out of their windows, but

3. Klinenberg, *Palaces for the People*, 188.

then curiosity gets the better of them and they begin emerging to see what is happening. When they find out there is only a stone in the soup, they start to offer ingredients to make it taste better. One by one they add something. One brings some garlic. Another some greens. Another a carrot. Eventually almost everyone in the village has brought an ingredient, and the soup smells amazing. What started out as a stone in a pot has become delectable soup through the collaborative contributions of the diversity of people.

In many ways this book is a written version of stone soup. I have personally brought little to the project besides a driving question. I dropped that stone into the pot, and the authors here have contributed their incredible ingredients. Together they help us think through the important aspects of this monumental shift in church property that is taking place all around us.

As you read the following chapters, you will find that while all the authors care deeply about churches and church property, only a few of them are pastors or traditional "church leaders." You will hear from property developers, urban planners, philanthropists, real estate professionals, and more. This is intentional. I invited these different people to contribute their unique ingredients to the soup that is this book, because that is exactly how property development and reuse must happen as well. A soup made up entirely of celery wouldn't be particularly tasty. But one that includes varied and complementary ingredients can be sublime.

This book is broken into three main parts: "Gone?," "For Good," and "Together." These three parts take us on a journey of exploration and offer us hope for how church property can be used for good.

GONE?

We start out by looking at what is happening and what will be gone as church properties are sold or change use.

Eileen Lindner, a historian and sociologist, sets the stage in her chapter, "Church Property in a Diminishing Religious Footprint." She looks back at the role property has played in religion historically and describes how churches in the United States went about acquiring the property that is now in question. She explains that churches have become sellers of property rather than buyers while noting a lack of reliable data on church property transitions. She wraps up her chapter by examining what is happening in one historic mainline Protestant denomination, the Presbyterian Church (USA), as illustrative of what many denominations are going through with their property.

We then hear from Rochelle A. Stackhouse, who describes how church buildings function as community assets in her chapter, "Saving Sacred Places as Community Assets." She cautions against the twin mistakes of viewing a church property as an albatross on one hand and as a cash cow on the other, and instead offers four ways to think about repurposing church property for positive mission outcomes and the good of the neighborhood.

Stackhouse's colleague at Partners for Sacred Places, A. Robert Jaeger, describes the "Halo Effect" of churches. His chapter, "The Impact of the 'Halo Effect' on a Congregation's Community," reminds us that churches generate enormous social and economic value in their communities. The Halo Effect shows us just how much value churches create and helps church and civic leaders understand how much will be lost when those churches are gone.

Pastor and church lender Patrick Duggan emphasizes the primacy of mission in any conversation about church property. He warns against churches carelessly selling property or engaging in transactions focused solely on money or real estate in his chapter, "The Case for Missional Remaining Missional." Drawing upon the inspiring story of a church property redevelopment in Louisville, Kentucky, Duggan helps us see that while "the actual use of the property is agnostic, whatever the use is going to be must advance the mission of the church."

Planter pastor and social entrepreneur Coté Soerens asks some provocative questions about ecclesiology and economic development in her chapter, "Who Wants a Building Anyway?" While denominational leaders and others look to unload underused properties, communities of people who have been displaced or marginalized want and need property. "Where one is full of land and lacking ideas, the other is full of ideas and longing for land." Before buildings and property are simply sold, Soerens urges us to consider how land can serve a more robust place-based ecclesiology and just economic development.

FOR GOOD

While each author in part 1 offers us hope and inspiration alongside warnings, part 2 of the book focuses even more closely on what is possible. The ideas and examples expand our ecclesial and economic imagination to see more clearly what is possible with church property for the good of the other.

Churches on the brink of closure, or with buildings they can no longer afford, often wonder what to do with their property. Many consider selling. While a natural inclination, and perhaps the right choice, selling church property raises questions of justice that are an important starting point for congregations to consider. Essentially all land that churches sit on in the United States was at one point home for Indigenous peoples. Jim Bear Jacobs, church leader and citizen of the Mohican Nation, traces the legacy of sin made manifest in the doctrine of discovery that remains in play today when churches buy and sell property. He urges those who are wondering what to do with property to return that land to Indigenous tribes or organizations. Perhaps even before the church closes. His chapter, "Righting Some Wrongs by Returning Stolen Land," is an essential starting place as we consider how to use church-owned land for good.

Theologian and biblical scholar Keith Starkenburg builds upon Jacobs's reflections with a theological exploration of how land and people are intimately related in the Bible in his chapter, "Crossing the Land, Hearing the Spirit." He then connects that deep truth with implications for churches and their relationship to land that was home for Indigenous peoples. Starkenburg gives the land itself a voice in the conversation. Finally, he offers some suggestions for how American Christians can join in Christ's healing of the nations by appropriately partnering with Indigenous tribes and organizations.

The focus shifts in our next two chapters, which are both written by pastors at churches that developed affordable housing on their property. In one case the church put up housing around their existing sanctuary building and retained ownership. In the other case the church sold their property completely and now rent back space for worship in a new building that was constructed on the site. While the approaches were very different, in both cases mission has thrived, the property serves greater good, and the churches have funding for their ministry.

Pastor Joseph W. Daniels Jr. tells the story of the Emory Fellowship in Washington, DC, and their multiyear journey to build affordable housing for their neighborhood in his chapter, "Legacy Can Lead to Life." The property the church is on has a long and complicated history filled with racism and injustice as well as love and light. By staying focused on their core mission, holding fast to God in prayer, and reaching deep into the past while looking clearly into the future, they were able to redeem and reclaim a spirit of love and light on their property.

Pastor Ashley Goff, located not too far down the road from Washington in Arlington, Virginia, recounts her church's story of selling their property for affordable housing in her chapter, "When God's Call Is Bigger Than a Building." Arlington Presbyterian Church listened to their neighbors and heard God's call to let go of old wineskins—their building. They sold it to be torn down and replaced by affordable housing. In the process, they found grace in disconnecting the church from the building, and they have left a legacy of good in that location.

Building affordable housing on church-owned property is one very powerful, tangible way that churches can put their property to use for the good of the other. There is a massive need for affordable housing in many parts of the country. David Bowers is an expert in building affordable housing alongside houses of worship. In his chapter, "Lessons from Nehemiah for Faith-Based Property Development," Bowers shares nine lessons about property de-

velopment drawn from the story of Nehemiah. He acknowledges
that property development can be difficult for churches. But it is
also doable.

Much of the conversation around church-owned property is
centered around urban or suburban churches. But dealing with
church property in rural areas is just as important and pressing.
The final chapter in this section comes from Jennie Birkholz, who
works at the intersection of churches, health care, and rural communities. In her chapter, "The Value of Rural Churches and Fresh
Hope," Jennie suggests that fresh hope for rural churches can be
found in their rooted history. The central place churches hold in
rural communities, both geographically and socially, positions
them well to serve as sites for health-care services, community
centers, food production and distribution, and more.

TOGETHER

This book has come about through the fantastic contributions of
so many thoughtful people. But there is another way that this sort
of work is like the story of stone soup.

Adapting, selling, repurposing, or developing church property
is also a lot like making stone soup. It cannot be done alone. While
pastors and church members are often very well connected in their
communities, many churches go about their ministry in a relative
silo, not always deeply connected to their neighbors and neighborhoods. We often live like the villagers in the story, peeking out
of our windows wondering what is happening out there but not
really connected with organizations and people around us. That
simply will not work when dealing with questions related to church
property. The only way something beautiful and good will emerge
from the adaptation of church property is if we work together with
a wide array of partners, collaborators, and neighbors.

Making collaborative soup only works when everyone contributes something. At first we may not be sure if what we have to
throw into the pot has any value. But as we bring whatever we have
to the table, a tasty meal is created. Generosity begets generosity.

The more each party is willing to contribute, the greater the sum of the parts will be.

In the same way, churches looking at developing their property, selling it for a new "good" use, or in other ways responding to their property questions will create the best soup when they invite collaborators from neighborhood associations, city planners, community activists, civic leaders, developers, investors, other churches in the area, and more. In the final section we explore how this work happens in partnership between churches and others. Good reuse or new use of church property will only happen collaboratively. We have to do this work together.

This section starts with a look at the relationship between churches and the towns and cities in which they are located. Churches and denominational leaders may not understand the constraints cities place on the development of properties, the implications of zoning regulations, or how the property development process works. This impacts both development and the potential sale of property.

Similarly, municipalities may not understand how churches work and how they can encourage and incentivize the sort of positive development that will enhance quality of life and justice in their communities. Cities may not fully realize how much space and programming for social services will be lost if church properties become something else, and they often pay little attention to property owned by churches for a variety of reasons. But that needs to change if thoughtful redevelopment is going to take place on a larger scale than one-off projects here and there. Churches need assistance from civic leaders in order to put their changing property to the best use.

Kurt Paulsen, a professor of urban planning, introduces us to some of these ideas in his chapter, "Proactive City Planning for Church Property Transitions." He suggests that the wave of property transitions offers a unique opportunity for the planning world and the church world to collaboratively advance shared values. Paulsen provides tips for both municipal and church leaders in order to encourage "good" development on church property.

Nadia Mian, also a professor of planning and public policy, builds upon Paulsen's concepts by exploring how an organization called Yes in God's Backyard worked with a church and city planning department in California to change the zoning code in order to allow more churches to build affordable housing on their property. In her chapter, "Changing the (Zoning) Code to Build Bonds between Church and State," Mian suggests that both churches and governmental agencies need to take steps to bridge barriers between them in order to promote good development on church property at a time when such development is desperately needed.

A team of three affordable housing experts including an urban planner, Philip Burns; a real estate advisor, Andre Johnny White; and a church property expert, Jill Shook, cowrote the next chapter, "The Real Estate Advisory Team." They describe how independent advisors, who have no conflict of interest or direct financial stake in a project, are vital for churches who are looking at developing their property for affordable housing or something similar. They offer guidance and principles for selecting a good advisor and creating an advisory group in your community.

Property development is both difficult and doable. In many cases, churches that succeed in this area partner with an experienced and financially backed property developer. Tyler Krupp-Qureshi is a mission-focused, second-generation property developer. In his chapter, "Making the Most of the Church and Developer Partnership," Krupp-Qureshi reflects on the difference between property development that is profit focused and that which is prophetic. Then he offers five lessons for church-based property development based on church redevelopment projects that give church leaders insight into how the process works and what they should know when partnering with a property developer.

Addressing the speed and scale of church property transitions will require innovative philanthropic support. The final chapter in this section, and in the book, "Obstacles and Opportunities for Philanthropic Partnerships with Congregations in Transition," is cowritten by Elizabeth Lynn, a leader in philanthropy and civic engagement, and Mark D. Constantine, who has worked in foundations for thirty years. Lynn and Constantine interviewed philanthropic leaders to understand how they view the changes taking place with church property. Their responses and reflections provide important insights into the role philanthropy can play in supporting development and use of church property for the good of neighborhoods and people.

THE LIMITS OF THIS BOOK

I believe this is an important book raising the profile of one of the defining current issues of American Christianity. The diverse and interdisciplinary group of contributors have created a delectable "stone soup" that will impact church property decisions around the country on many levels. But there are always limits to a book like this. We could not "do it all" with this single volume.

First, this book is focused on Christian church property. Houses of worship in other faith traditions are also going through significant transitions. Nonprofits and businesses are facing changes in the way people work and therefore have questions about their offices and property. Some of the stories, ideas, and principles shared in this book are likely transferable to other settings, but there will be important aspects missing by focusing on Christian churches as we have done in this book.

Second, despite intentional efforts to engage a diversity of contributors across a number of spectrums, there are churches and communities of people missing from this volume. One such community not explored in depth here is immigrant churches. Immigrant churches have unique considerations, challenges, and assets that are missing from this book. I hope future writing on the subject will address this omission.

Third, for every one of our incredible contributors included in this volume, there are countless others who are not. We could have written three, five, even ten different versions of this book, each with thoughtful and knowledgeable contributors. The greatest challenge for me as an editor and practitioner in this area of work is knowing how many more authors I would have liked to include but couldn't.

Finally, there are topics and issues important to the question of church property transition that have been left out or are missing. Some I'm sure I'm not even aware of. It is my sincere hope that this book is just one voice in a larger conversation that we will have in congregations, denominations, city planning departments, seminaries, universities, and the public sphere. I hope others will pick up where we have left off and fill in where we have left gaps. May this soup be an appetizer for what comes next.

With this introduction out of the way, let's dive in and see what we have to taste, and learn about this vitally important question: Will church property be GONE for good? Or gone for GOOD?

PART 1
Gone?

1

CHURCH PROPERTY IN
A DIMINISHING RELIGIOUS FOOTPRINT

Eileen Lindner

In the biblical narrative, property plays a prominent and enduring role. It is not just the sacred vision of Eden or a promised land that the Bible deals with, but accounts of fields of grain, homes of hospitality, temples, and hillsides and plains are all pressed into service for long-remembered sermons. It is no surprise then that religious traditions that draw from this narrative have long aspired to property ownership for purposes of worship, service, education, healing, fellowship, and myriad communal activities. Perhaps nowhere has that been more fully expressed than in the religious traditions of the American people.

Yet, in the first quarter of the twenty-first century, church property ownership and stewardship have become among the central challenges and opportunities for the faithful. As closed churches are sold, sometimes at below-market prices, the church loses an important asset for ministry and diminishes the social infrastructure for the wider community.

Those seeking to address such consequences are hampered by the absence of reliable data. Still, anecdotal data are instructive. One Methodist Annual Conference (regional body) of over five hundred churches noted that three hundred of those properties were in serious or critical condition due to lack of maintenance. Many churches are expected to close and their property sold. The Annual Conference "owned $1.4 billion in real estate for 50,000 weekly worshippers; equal to $28,000 in real estate per attendee."[1]

Grasping the full nature and extent of this property crisis, even within an important subset of religious properties, say, mainline Protestantism, is not achievable given the paucity of accurate current data regarding the affiliated hundreds of thousands of church properties.

Using the Presbyterian Church USA (PC[USA]) as a lens into the broader environment, we can begin to glimpse the dimensions and outlines of the diminishing religious property footprint. While only a narrow segment of the larger religious property landscape, this denominational snapshot reveals many of the factors and dynamics that contribute to this season of rapidly increasing property transfers and may suggest potential initiatives for both church and community for responding, wisely and faithfully, on behalf of the commonweal. It also gives us a view of a "mainline" Protestant denomination whose experience will more nearly reflect the experiences of other such denominations. Further research will be needed to provide insights into the property issues of independent evangelical churches, Catholic congregations, the Jewish community, and other religious groups.

Building the Religious Real Estate Footprint

It is axiomatic to say that the establishment of church property in North America arrived with the *Mayflower*. In fact, church-owned properties preceded the Puritans. The Cathedral Basilica of St. Augustine was initiated in 1565. By 1610 the Mission San Miguel Archangel was founded in New Mexico, and St. John's Episcopal Church had secured property in Hampton, Virginia. Early land grants from European powers were often religiously based and intentional in rooting religious traditions in the soil of a new land. As central as this process was to the European colonization of the continent, it was

1. Rick Reinhard, UMC Press Release, June 11, 2021.

accomplished on a land already occupied by indigenous people. The original records and deeds have often been lost, destroyed over the centuries, replaced by more contemporary records or obfuscated by long-developed oral traditions held dear by local congregations.

Indeed, the earliest acquisition of property by a Presbyterian entity is difficult to identify even in a denomination known for its record keeping. In the spring of 1640, a group of English Puritans left Lynn, Massachusetts, to settle on the eastern tip of New York's Long Island. They had come to the New World to seek freedom from religious persecution and greater economic opportunity. The church first gathered in the Community Meeting House, built in 1640. It served as a social, civic, and religious haven for twelve years. The First Presbyterian Church of Southampton built its own, initial structure on Main Street, known then as Town Street, in 1652. By the time of the American Revolution, a third church had come to house the congregation, setting the pattern of acquiring and expanding property holdings that would continue well into the twentieth century.[2]

As the nation developed, numerous patterns of church planting evolved, often along confessional lines: Congregationalists in the northeast, Catholics in Maryland, and Lutherans and Presbyterians in the mid-Atlantic colonies. Famously, Rhode Island and Pennsylvania were developed with more diverse confessional representation—also as a matter of faith and belief. The nation's earliest cities set aside space for churches every mile or so in a prepublic transportation era.

Much later, as new communities were established in the nation's westward move, church property was secured in the center of new towns and, from the beginning, served both religious and civil society needs. Central to Alexis de Tocqueville's account in *Democracy in America* is the vitality of the civil society in America that is profoundly facilitated by religious communities and their buildings. In rural areas, towns and villages were often defined by the presence of a church, a saloon, and a mercantile. The First Great Awaken-

2. Charlene Peacock of the Presbyterian Historical Society, text to author, August 2, 2022. Original deed to Southampton Presbyterian Church (deed 1707).

ing, and later the era of robust immigration, brought many new churches and a wide diversity of religious traditions, each seeking an identifiable expression of their faith, resulting in a panoply of diverse religious architecture. Even as late as the post–World War II building boom, which created sprawling suburban housing tracts, the desirability of a church in the neighborhood was acknowledged by developers. Frequently corner lots on the main thoroughfares of new suburban communities were zoned for mixed use, and priority was given to churches and other nonprofits to maximize the livability of these "not quite towns." By the mid-twentieth century, religious organizations in the aggregate cast an enormous real estate footprint worth hundreds of billions of dollars.

THEOLOGICAL KINSHIP OF MISSION AND PROPERTY

With the world's greatest variety of Christian traditions, a wide array of understandings and theologies of *place*, *property*, and *mission* exists within the American Christian culture. The evangelical spirit so characteristic of American Protestantism has often been expressed in the conviction to "proclaim the gospel in word and deed." Thus, the property acquired by churches was not limited to chapels and sanctuaries. Churches purchased or were given tracts of land on which to build not only places of worship but also houses for clergy and often church parlors. By the nineteenth century, church offices, Sunday school rooms, fellowship halls, auditoriums, and kitchens would follow. Beyond the needs of worshiping congregations, church bodies obtained camps, conference centers, retreats, settlement houses, and schools. Hospitals and colleges were established by religious bodies, substantially expanding their footprint, but these institutions are beyond the scope of the present inquiry.

For much of the last three hundred years, the sense of calling and faithful service for many congregations has been inextricably bound up with property and mission. Moreover, the surrounding communities and developing culture came to rely on churches to provide *all* community members shelter in storms, literally, as well as to provide both location and support to religious as well as secular activities. Across considerably diverse theological conceptions, the quintessentially American and periodic spiritual "awakenings," immigrant waves, and theological impulses such as the Social Gospel strengthened the bond between property and purpose for congregations. The Industrial Revolution and movement of rural folk into urban centers provided yet another impetus to churches to maximize their outreach and service to the community, and to do it through more property. The formation of denominational centers and middle judicatory structures, and the brisk development of parachurch organizations in the nineteenth century, once again expanded the real estate footprint and the place of church within community infrastructure. Beyond religious training and worship, congregational property is commonly used to provide meeting space, food pantries, soup kitchens, clothing distribution centers, homeless shelters, English as second language (ESL) classes, senior citizen centers, and twelve-step self-help programs. Nearly one-third of all not-for-profit early childhood centers in the country are located in church-owned properties with their child-appropriate furnishings and finishes.[3]

It is not, however, only programs that serve individual needs in response to the gospel's demands of love of neighbor that are offered in church properties. Broader civil society functions, in many communities, are carried out in church facilities. Large multipurpose rooms, often based on a biblical mandate of hospitality and a sense of civic responsibility, can be used to host scouting and other youth-serving activities and to serve as polling places; parking lots can be utilized for school-sponsored sports, fund-raising car washes, and more recently farmers' markets within food deserts. Given the array of community services these spaces provide, it becomes clear that shuttering the church doors marks a consequential loss especially in inverse proportion to community wealth.

3. Eileen W. Lindner et al., *When Churches Mind the Children: A Study of Day Care in Local Parishes* (Ypsilanti, MI: HighScope, 1983).

EILEEN LINDNER

Buyers Become Sellers

The post–World War II baby boom created a generational cohort within American society that has reshaped virtually every social institution it passes through by sheer dint of its size. By the mid-twentieth century, churches were bustling enclaves in cities, towns, and suburban communities. Filled with families and age-appropriate activities at each of life's stages, congregations served as essential partners for individuals, families, and communities. Nationwide, church membership grew faster than the population, from 57 percent in 1950 to 63.3 percent in 1960. One observer refers to the fifties as "a supply side free enterprise spiritual marketplace with heady competition between religious groups and leaders with church attendance at a record high." Now, often nostalgically recalled as a normative period of church life, the midcentury mark was in fact an anomaly in American church life. The demographics of church affiliation/membership (as distinct from belief in God) during the 1950s are considerably higher than in previous generations or than they are today.[4]

By the mid-1960s, declining church membership became undeniable among the most prominent "mainline" churches. Reliable church chronicler Jackson Carroll notes that around 1964 or 1965, things took an abrupt downturn. "Membership declines that are unprecedented in the religious history of the United States have beset mainline Protestant denominations."[5] It was in 1965 that baby boomers started graduating from high school.

Throughout the 1970s a downward trend in church membership was observable across the various theological and confessional forms of church. A rich literature regarding what is often referred

4. Robert S. Ellwood, *The Fifties Spiritual Marketplace: American Religion in a Decade of Conflict* (New Brunswick, NJ: Rutgers University Press, 1997), xi; see also Carol Tucker, "The 1950s—Powerful Years for Religion," *USC News*, June 16, 1997, 17, https://tinyurl.com/ycxmvd43.

5. Jackson Carroll, "Understanding Church Growth and Decline," *Theology Today*, April 1, 1978, 70.

to as the secularization of American culture provides a number of causal interpretations but is not central to this inquiry.[6]

The decline in church membership did not immediately result in a property crisis for congregations. At first the membership decline was gradual, and congregations often had surplus budgets and endowments to account for it. Later, congregations adapted, moving from multiple Sunday services to one and reducing clerical staff by eliminating assistant pastors, paid choir members, and the like. Church property itself became a tool in staunching the membership and funding loss. By the 1980s and 1990s, congregations began seeking new revenue streams while forgoing needed building maintenance. Churches began to solicit community groups to locate weekday programs in unused Sunday school rooms, and, where possible, they invited other, often ethnic or immigrant congregations to "nest" within the buildings to share in the costs.

Denominational structures, Christian publishers, and parachurch organizations were quick to produce seminars, books, training sessions, and retreats focused on diagnosing the causes of membership decline. This literature dealt largely with strategies for outreach and evangelism, modernizing worship styles, and broadening the formats for offering church programming. Focus remained on filling the existing space, not on reducing that space. Few church publications of the era addressed the emerging crises of expensive, surplus property. By the opening of the twenty-first century, religious organizations increasingly became sellers, not buyers, of property, and the religious real state footprint began to contract.

By no means did all, or even most, of the nation's congregations experience a precipitous financial decline or organizational mortality issues. Many congregations held adequate resources to maintain their buildings, downsize their programs, freshen up their liturgical life, and continue on. Yet others, as well attested in

6. See Dean M. Kelley, *Why Conservative Churches Are Growing: A Study of Sociology of Religion* (Macon, GA: Mercer University Press, 1996). Kelley's study, first published in 1972, touched off an extended debate regarding the causes of church membership decline.

this volume, have embraced adaptive change and, with creativity and renewed commitment to mission, transformed the church's life, or even surrendered it, to a wider community good. Still others, lacking vitality, technical know-how, and needed community relationships, simply slipped away.

Colleagues in Europe, which experienced a similar decline of membership two decades earlier than the United States, report that in some postwar nations as many as one-third of the prewar congregations were no longer functioning places of worship by 1970. Since many of the churches there were demolished by warfare and simply not rebuilt, comparisons with the American experience must be done cautiously. Membership declines as recorded by the World Council of Churches *Yearbook* reinforce the belief that some of the congregations were closed and sold for lack of participation. Wander around almost any European capital today, and one will find wine bars, boutiques, bookstores, and condominiums that retain the architectural embellishments that mark them as former churches.[7]

Mapping the Topography of a Shrinking Footprint

The present challenge of finding the best and highest use of church property is made more daunting by a lack of accurate data but is also complicated by the intricacies of church governance. A modest estimate of church-owned properties of all confessions nationally would number well into the hundreds of thousands. Denominations rarely seek data on the number and types of buildings, square footage, lot size, and other particulars of local congregations. This is curious because denominations often require yearly reports of membership losses and gains, baptisms, staff members, endowments, and Sunday school enrollments. Perhaps the early Protestant confidence in a future defined by growing ever

7. Martin Robra, World Council of Churches leader, in discussion with the author, 2019. See also *World Council of Churches Yearbook* (Geneva, Switzerland, multiple years).

larger accounts for the lack of such data and for the rather delayed denominational attention to a growing property crisis.

The resultant lack of such data is ultimately attributable in part to the governance structure of many denominations. Property, while sometimes held in trust for the denomination, is, for all practical purposes, largely a matter of congregational management and secondarily a concern of middle judicatories of the churches such as presbyteries, conferences, and annual meetings. These bodies gather groups of congregations in regional patterns and are the connective tissue to the larger denomination.

The value of property held, if even indirectly, by each denomination often represents its largest financial asset. While seldom thought of in this way, the total value of all of a denomination's real property may well dwarf the value of its national budget, its pension fund holdings, its endowments, its mission funds, and its combined resources. Rethinking the importance of real property as a financial pillar of American religious life is surely worth it. One might envision a comprehensive national study of church-owned properties modeled after Mark Chaves's pioneering 1998 *National Congregations Survey*.[8] Alternatively, property data could be purchased from a third-party real estate company and then collated with census tract data to gain a clearer picture of the community. By whatever means, better and more comprehensive data will be needed if church property utilization is to be fully realized.

While churches make their most extensive contributions in the areas of worship and cultural and spiritual activities, in many settings their social service contributions remain significant. The closure and sale of a church building may remove the last food pantry, soup kitchen, or after-school program from a neighborhood. With the rising costs of property and the scarcity of community meeting space in American cities, such dislocations are not easily repaired. Especially in gentrifying neighborhoods, the closure and sale of

8. Mark Chaves, *American Religion Contemporary Trends* (Princeton: Princeton University Press, 2011), and Mark Chaves, *Congregations in America* (Cambridge, MA: Harvard University Press, 2004).

church property can quicken the process of edging long-term residents and services out of the community due to lack of available and affordable social gathering places. Sociologists have noted the role that third spaces, such as libraries, play in providing social services and a sense of social solidarity. However, churches, unlike libraries, have historically been better suited for multifunctional services such as feeding and clothing distribution and day care.[9] One study of older urban churches found that 89 percent of total visits to these institutions were to take part in something other than worship. Nearly 90 percent of the beneficiaries of these programs were not church members.[10]

One Denominational Snapshot

As a case study in what the shrinking footprint means to one prominent denomination, we now turn to the Presbyterian Church (USA), the largest of the Presbyterian denominations. Two of its national agencies recently undertook an inquiry into the escalating trend of church closings and property sales.[11] Without denomination-wide data collection, much of the exploration relied on anecdotal evidence and small electronically conducted surveys. Even though the sampling was limited, we were able to observe much about the process that leads to church properties being sold for purposes unrelated to spiritual or community needs.

According to a high-ranking PC(USA) staffer, an estimated $100 million in Presbyterian church property was sold in 2019. He

9. Eric Klinenberg, *Palaces for the People: How Social Infrastructure Can Help Fight Inequality, Polarization, and the Decline of Civic Life* (New York: Crown, 2018). Klinenberg argues that the future of democratic societies rests not only with shared values but with shared spaces like libraries and churches where crucial connections are formed.

10. Ram Cann, quoted in Karl Zinsmeister, "What to Do with Empty Churches," *Wall Street Journal*, January 31, 2019.

11. The Presbyterian Foundation and the Presbyterian Mission Agency engaged in a two-year study: Eileen W. Lindner, "Generational Wealth Transfer and Church Property Transfers" (unpublished report).

projected that in 2020 the figure might well rise to $200 million.[12] As with any partial data, this must be viewed with care. The $100 million aggregate included, for instance, a large suburban congregation that sold its property, only to purchase a larger parcel. Yet, having gathered the information largely from presbytery records, he knew this figure included dozens of small churches in urban, suburban, and rural settings that had closed and discontinued their ministry.

We explored a host of such sales and discovered some commonalities in the long, slow morbidity prevalent among small, aging congregations. Many of the churches had, several years previously, begun a downward trajectory through loss of members to death; relocation of business opportunities; the influx of agribusiness, which had emptied small farming communities; urban development that encased the church amid superhighways; and a host of other idiosyncratic causes. With faltering income and attendance, building maintenance and repairs were left undone, volunteer roles went unfulfilled, the pastor moved on to lead another church, supply preachers kept Sunday worship going but provided little else in the way of programming, and buildings crumbled further as the faithful flock grew smaller. This trajectory, or something like it, was an oft-repeated story, with most churches coming to the decision to close and sell the property three to five years following the exit of their last full-time pastor. At this juncture in the congregation's life, many elders (lay leaders) reported that they had maintained only perfunctory relationships with their respective regional governing bodies (presbyteries) and had grown weary with trying to keep the church going. At such a point, little energy and fewer resources remained for seeking an exciting and adaptive future. Largely there were sadness and sorrow and an eagerness to be done with the stress of losing their church home. At long last, with a mixture of reluctance, relief, and remorse, the remaining leaders would contact the presbytery, seeking technical assistance in closing and selling the property.

Our interactions with presbyteries revealed additional challenges. The presbyteries, with their own staff reductions in recent

---

12. Paul Grier, conversation with the author, March 2019.

years, reported being ill-equipped to manage and market unoccupied buildings. A sampling of presbyteries gave evidence of that unpreparedness. Only larger presbyteries had a written policy and procedure for dealing with such situations. Many presbyteries approached each circumstance on its own merits, often relying on volunteer church members who worked in residential real estate. Almost none of the presbyteries carried out an "impact study" to evaluate the consequences of a church closing to the surrounding community, with some reasoning that the congregation had long since lost the vitality to engage in community issues. More often than one would hope, a weary presbytery urged a tired congregation to sell the church as quickly as possible, irrespective of the purpose or plans of the prospective buyers and often without serious consideration of the potential market value of those properties. Some presbyteries found themselves saddled with three or four churches closing; that they were sold at the same time further exhausted their capacity to respond.[13]

One Presbyterian denominational office had taken notice some years earlier of the growing need for technical assistance and planning resources for presbyteries and congregations. The PC(USA) had developed considerable expertise and launched a modest program designed to work with congregations *prior* to the last tired stages of their lives. These efforts bore considerable success but were unable to keep pace with the rapid increase in congregations needing such services.[14]

Congregations in later stages of decline require even more assistance. The COVID pandemic not only increased frequency of church closings and sales but also called into question the necessity for such property holdings in the minds of many congregations. Having worshiped virtually for most of two years, some congregations are reassessing the need for all the property they maintain and whether

13. Eileen W. Lindner, presentation to the MidCouncil Financial Network of the PC(USA), 2020, audiotapes.

14. The PC(USA) developed a "Project Regeneration" to assist local churches in planning new futures, including the use of their property. The Disciples of Christ instituted "New Beginnings" in an effort to enable local congregations to envision adaptive change.

some better relationship of property to mission calling might be achieved by converting, selling, or sharing their real estate.

Denominational property initiatives confront a number of factors. First is the reality of the localized nature of property values. A distant denominational office can offer technical assistance but, without being on-site, is unable to formulate a good understanding of property values and community dynamics. A second concern is related to the governance structure of the denominations. Denominational personnel working directly with congregations could be perceived as overreach by some middle judicatories. Finally, the allocation of proceeds from sales is also fraught with opportunities for conflict between denominational, regional, and local church structures. A brief round of discussions with similar mainline denominational offices reinforced our understanding that these property challenges are now recognized by virtually all denominations surveyed.[15] Seeing the potential of new markets, several nationwide realty companies have opened "specialized church sales divisions." The use of such commercial services is sometimes very costly, and, while this may finally result in better appraisal and marketing practices for congregations and middle judicatories, it is unlikely to be sufficiently attentive to community ministry concerns and consequences, and will most assuredly favor the bottom line of those realty companies.

The anecdotal Presbyterian experience may be illustrative of broader patterns that challenge the church in its self-understanding and its witness to the world. Laments abound for the "loss" of property, for a poor selling price, for a sense of abandoning a long-treasured community, and for the lack of vision, energy, and insight that might have brought about a better future through better-considered partnerships. Those brighter futures, attested to throughout the accounts in this volume, are within the

---

15. Eileen W. Lindner and Paul Grier conducted a telephone survey in 2020 with the American Baptist Churches, the Episcopal Church in America, the Evangelical Lutheran Church in America, the United Methodist Church, and the United Church of Christ. All respondents provided accounts of closed and sold church properties and the escalating rate and complications associated with such sales.

grasp of the church writ large in America. But such futures will require an effort within and without ecclesial bodies to creatively, thoughtfully, and boldly fashion, in partnership with others, a better stewardship of real property.

A Problem—and a Possibility

The enormous real estate holdings of American churches have great potential for shaping the nation and culture in which we live. Many congregations offer vital ministries to their own members and to adjacent communities. At the same time, a growing number of church properties are underutilized, unoccupied, and deteriorating. Gaining a grip on the magnitude of the problem is elusive given the lack of data. The estimate that seventy-five to one hundred churches close each week brings an urgency to the matter.[16] Using this estimate and projecting over the fifteen-year period from 2015 to 2030, one estimates that the number of churches sold would be between 60,000 and 80,000. When ancillary buildings are included in sales estimates (such as manses, camps, conference centers, middle judicatory offices, etc.), it seems reasonable to estimate that 100,000 church properties will have been sold by the end of this decade.[17]

Few concerted, cohesive approaches to addressing this shrinking real estate footprint exist, despite the very real value of these properties within the aspirational and financial lives of American religious bodies. While these complex issues will not yield to any single national approach, neither are they fully within the scope and capability of local entities. Governmental agencies have been

16. United Church of Christ, Center for Analytics, Research and Development, 2019.

17. Such a rate of sales mirrors the European experience when acknowledging American church membership figures remain higher than those in Europe. Chaves (2020) estimated there were about 380,000 congregations in the United States. Kirk Hadaway and Penny Marier estimated there are 331,000, in the *Journal for the Scientific Study of Religion* 44, no. 3 (September 2005): 307–22. In either case, the loss of 100,000 properties in the United States begins to approach the one-third loss of church properties experienced in Europe.

underutilized as potential partners.[18] Denominations acting alone or in concert could do much to foster best practices in church dispositions, lending technical assistance, gathering and analyzing more useful property data, and working with middle judicatories and congregations in establishing procedures and practices suitable to local needs in transferring properties. Denominations might also seek out partnerships with housing advocates, early childhood organizations, and organizations addressing issues of hunger, refugee resettlement, etc., to discover new futures together. Even the possibility of a single ecumenical parachurch organization might be envisioned, addressing church property as, say, Bread for the World and Habitat for Humanity have addressed their respective issues.

All of this, at first blush, seems far afield of the calling of the church. Yet, as the nineteenth-century hymn writer counseled the church in a well-known hymn:

> New occasions teach new duties,
> Time makes ancient good uncouth;
> They must upward still and onward,
> Who would keep abreast of truth.[19]

A clear truth of the immediate and foreseeable church property crisis is that without *intention*, churches will not be gone for *good purposes*—they will just be gone.

18. This suggestion need not trigger objections of separation of church and state. As recently as June 2022, the US Supreme Court recognized in *Carson v. Makin*, 596 U.S. (2022), that the state may support shared civic endeavors and goals with religious institutions, particularly where a desired public service is otherwise scarce and a religious institution can provide that, so long as the state has similarly committed to support other such public and private programs or institutions and is not discriminating on the basis of religion. In short, the state and religious groups can cooperate to achieve common goals through sharing space or programs for a common good or overlapping values to enhance a community's well-being.

19. James Russell Lowell, "Once to Every Man and Nation," 1845, https://tinyurl.com/5337f4c8.

2

SAVING SACRED PLACES AS COMMUNITY ASSETS

Rochelle A. Stackhouse

In 2016, the Church of the Redeemer in New Haven, Connecticut, faced serious issues with funding and significant maintenance and repair expenses for buildings built in the early and mid-twentieth century. People in the congregation often joked that half of New Haven had keys to the building, because so many community groups used space for meetings and activities. That year, the buildings provided meeting space for six twelve-step groups; the advisory group for the local hospital Bed Funds; rehearsal and performance space for two community choirs, local organ students, and local piano teachers; classroom space for a local refugee resettlement agency's English class; a social anxiety group; an independent youth support group; a La Leche chapter; and disparate one-off meetings and events. Some of those groups paid to use the space, but far below "market rate" for space rental in New Haven. Others used the space for free, as part of the congregation's sense of mission to the neighborhood and city.

When faced with shrinking membership and growing maintenance costs, the congregation realized they could no longer afford to maintain the property, so the members "transplanted" to two other nearby congregations and sold the building. With about six months' notice, all the community organizations who had used the Redeemer building scrambled to find available spaces, often in other equally busy local church and synagogue buildings. The congregation sold the building to a developer who maintained the envelope and gutted the inside to create market-rate apartments. While the proceeds from the sale created a donor-advised fund in the local Community Foundation to continue to support a few of the organizations previously aided by the congregation, the property itself transitioned from serving hundreds of people weekly to becoming housing for a select few.

TSUNAMI

Similar scenarios appear throughout the country each year. The United States is in the midst of a tsunami of church closings, with thousands of churches ceasing operations or leaving their buildings each year. Not all of those congregations had purpose-built buildings; some were in storefronts, but any walk around the downtown area of a city or town of any size makes clear how many of these buildings are empty or have been repurposed.

Like New Haven, many cities and towns rely on faith communities to share their buildings to accommodate feeding programs, emergency housing, meeting space for civic groups, office and program space for nonprofit organizations, day-care and after-school services, senior citizen programs, recreation programs, arts programs, services for new immigrants, disaster relief, and a plethora of other activities for free or at below-market rates. When that space disappears, governments and nonprofits struggle to find space at affordable rates, compromising social services and civic life. While this situation is seen most easily in cities, small towns and rural areas experience the same thing, as church buildings in these communities are some of the few public spaces where people can gather. Some of these buildings carry important historical or architectural significance, either locally or nationally, and many bring beauty and stability to a neighborhood. One homeless man who regularly attended a historic urban church in Connecticut once remarked that he came to worship because it was the only time in his week that he could be some place beautiful for free and hear music to feed his soul.

Too often congregations make decisions about their property without considering that others are also stakeholders in those decisions. In urban neighborhoods affected by gentrification, church property sold to a developer can exacerbate the problem and ignores the needs of neighborhood residents. Most congregational leaders lack the expertise and experience to ensure that the history, mission, and architectural significance of their property will be respected by those who purchase it.

While many buildings are sold to developers who have no interest in using the space for "civic good," other congregations explore ways to continue the mission and vision of the congregation even while no longer owning or controlling the building. The congregation's attitude toward their property will be the determinant factor in assuring this result.

ALBATROSS OR CASH COW?

Congregations that know they need to sell or repurpose their property often see that property as either an albatross or a cash cow, and that attitude impacts how they decide to transition the property.

The metaphor of an "albatross" comes from the Coleridge poem "The Rime of the Ancient Mariner" and refers to a large bird tied around the neck. The image has come to stand for a burden that prevents someone from achieving what they hope. A congregation who spends more and more of their income or endowment, or both, just to keep the building functional, especially if they are not using much of the building, may feel that offloading the building and its costs might allow them to become vital again or fulfill their mission. The temptation in that situation is simply to sell to the highest bidder to get out from under the overwhelming burden. This too often means that the building will be turned into market-rate housing or retail of some sort (restaurant or event venue) or razed altogether. Almost always this means it is taken out of service to the spiritual or nonprofit organizations who may have been using the space.

Similarly, a congregation that sees their property as a "cash cow" decides that it only has value for the money it can produce. This may be true even if a congregation decides to stay in place while selling or leasing part of the property to someone else. The trick is the "someone else." One congregation in a large city sold a parcel it owned on a valuable street corner to get funds to keep up the rest of their property. They did not discuss this with stakeholders in the community, including their neighbors, or consider selling the property with an eye to mission. The developer who purchased the parcel built a large luxury housing unit that severely impacted the character of the neighborhood. While the church gained income (the developer gained more!), the ill will generated by this choice in the neighborhood continues to impact the reputation of the congregation years later, which the church discovered when it held a feasibility study for a capital campaign. The funds from the sale were not enough to cover the needs of the rest of the property, and the neighbors were not inclined to support the congregation.

Property as Mission

Many congregations adopt some kind of "mission" or "vision" statement for their life together, often as part of strategic or long-term planning processes. Far too often these statements are endorsed by the membership and posted on the church website or included in the annual report but fail to remind the congregation regularly who they believe themselves to be and why. Too many of these mission or vision statements consist of vague declarations of purpose—"to serve God and community," for example—without specifics of what that might look like on a regular basis in the life of the congregation.

Similarly, most of these statements completely ignore the building and property of the congregation as instruments of living out that mission. Members may consider a mission to be "feeding the hungry" and focus on volunteers and contributions but not the space they might use to do the feeding. As congregations add up the money they give each year to benevolences, rarely do they include the costs of maintaining the parts of the building used by the community and for the community. In the secular world, the property contains "civic value" to a community, providing space for services that otherwise would need to be provided by government or other nonprofit organizations. In a religious context, that "civic value" translates into property as a vehicle for the mission of serving others who are children of God.

A first step toward a mission-centered building transition, then, is clarifying how the building fits into the congregation's understanding of their purpose. Congregations might begin a transition process by envisioning how their property is a tool for their mission, how the property itself has a mission, and how the property could continue that mission even if the congregation no longer controls all or part of it. Many congregations have a history of creating ministries that are then "spun off" into independent organizations (for example, a church creates a feeding program that eventually incorporates as a separate 501(c)(3) and continues to serve people, independent of the founding congregation). Congregations can consider the next phase of the life of their property in the same way; they are "spinning it off" into continuing the mission that underlies the life and legacy of the congregation.

As part of an exploration of how mission and vision might help determine the future of a congregation's property, those who already use the property or are involved in services in the area might be consulted to surface new, innovative ideas on how the community might still benefit from the property. Before inviting potential developers to bid, a congregation might invite the current building users and other stakeholders in civic life, the arts, human services, education, or health care to imagine together how this property could continue the mission of the congregation, no matter what the future for that group holds. Sometimes congregations can only see what they don't have (money, people) and neglect to consider

the assets all around them, in their property and in the neighborhood, city, or town. Congregations may also assume that leaders
in the community already know about their buildings, while in
reality many leaders have never been inside the buildings or have
any idea how they are being used or might be used by others in
the community. Community asset mapping sessions or town hall
conversations can surface new ideas to continue to give life to a
congregation's buildings and grounds.

When Immanuel Presbyterian Church in Albuquerque, New
Mexico, invited the community to join their conversations about
the future, hoping to find partners to support their building, the
possibility of a lease arrangement with the New Mexico Philhar-
monic Orchestra arose. This had not been on the congregation's
radar screen previously, but one member of their newly created
Community Advisory Committee served on the board of the orchestra. The congregation is currently in conversation about a
long-term lease agreement with the orchestra for both rehearsal
and performance space in the sanctuary. If the conversations are
successful, the congregation will continue to worship in another
chapel space as the orchestra moves into what was the main worship space. The congregation has a new level of excitement about
how their commitment to the arts now will enliven their building
for years to come.

LEGACY

Related to mission and vision is the concept of "legacy." The vast
majority of sacred places in North America were not designed
and built by the people who currently use them. Either the building was built before the current members' lifetimes or a different
congregation took over the space, perhaps of a different denomination. "The ancestors" may be buried in an adjacent cemetery,
commemorated by plaques on a wall or in stained glass, or living
in the memory of some current members. A process of exploring
the history of the place itself and the original hopes and dreams
of the founders, as well as subsequent generations who put their

stamp on the place, can illuminate the role the building and land have played in the mission of the congregation. If the building is architecturally significant or on a national, state, or local historic register, the congregation might explore how to tell the story of the building to younger members and the community. As the current members consider the future of the building and property, they can consider the legacy they would like to leave, how to carry on the legacy they inherited, even if they are no longer in the building. The Church of the Redeemer expressed its legacy by using the funds from the sale to continue support for the caring programs it had supported during its 175-year history.

For the Chambers-Wylie Memorial Presbyterian Church in Philadelphia, the legacy blossomed in new life for people on the streets after the congregation dwindled and could no longer care for their historic and beautiful structure in Center City. The presbytery, which owned the building after the congregation dissolved, believed that the legacy of this congregation and the central tenets of their faith compelled them to reach out into the neighborhood to do something new. Today the building hosts multiple services for people in need on the streets of Philadelphia. Mailboxes, showers, clothing, food, case management, arts, and training programs as well as opportunities for worship and prayer fill the rooms of Broad Street Ministry. The building continues to serve the community, even though the original congregation no longer inhabits it.

Options for Community-Minded Transitions

After doing the work of considering mission, vision, and legacy, a congregation can consider at least four alternate scenarios that create possibilities for continuing the usefulness of sacred places to their communities, even if the congregations currently inhabiting them do not have the capacity to sustain them. Each of these alternatives to "selling to the highest bidder" requires the imagination to understand the property as part of the mission of the congregation and not simply as either an albatross or a cash cow.

Share the Property

The first scenario allows a congregation to remain in place while inviting partners in to use all or part of the property. This may be a lease agreement or an arrangement to share costs. Many congregations have buildings much larger than they need. This is often true of congregations who followed the trend of the 1950s and '60s to build separate education buildings or wings to accommodate the baby boom children. Webster Groves Presbyterian Church, a vital congregation now much smaller than it was at its peak, had an entire four-story education building that sat mostly empty. The congregation decided to seek a tenant to lease that space and use it for community good, which would also provide income for the upkeep of the congregation's two buildings. Space sharing is not a magic solution to keep a barely viable congregation alive; however, space sharing on a large enough scale can help an otherwise vital congregation to focus its finances and volunteer time on ministry and mission rather than on building maintenance. This option may require changes in the life of the congregation. For example, sharing space with another congregation may mean changes in worship schedules. An initial investment in the space to be shared may also be required; this often includes making the building compliant with the Americans with Disabilities Act or re-mediating lead or asbestos. Defining mission and vision and consulting with stakeholders in the community are critical to making this option viable.

Creative Ways to Generate Property Income

A second scenario is similar but adds to the mix creative use of the property to generate income. This might include selling air rights in an urban setting, or ground leases or development rights to part of the property. Congregations with large parking lots may discover that the land can be developed for affordable housing or leased by businesses or educational institutions that need parking. However, these kinds of projects can take years to complete and will require consideration of issues like zoning. A qualified real estate attorney, trusted developer, and detailed work with town or city planners and officials will be essential.

For example, in 2015, Cathedral of the Holy Cross in Boston utilized a ground lease to strengthen its financial footing. The cathedral signed a ninety-nine-year lease, which enabled a for-profit developer to erect a 160-unit apartment building on their parking lot, including an underground parking garage in which the church has seventy spaces. They continue to own and worship in their existing sanctuary.

Another possibility along these lines is creating a separate 501(c)(3) to raise funds only for the preservation of the building. This works particularly well for congregations with historically or architecturally significant buildings, especially since many foundations and corporations will not give grants to religious organizations but may for historic preservation or community service.

Sell, but Lease Space for Church Use

Congregations also might pursue selling the building to another owner while negotiating a lease arrangement to continue to use space for worship, offices, meetings, and education. In many cities, neighborhoods have undergone significant demographic changes throughout the twentieth and early twenty-first centuries. Majority white congregations sometimes find that none of their members live in the neighborhood, and that few of their members are willing or able to make the commute in for worship or programs. However, there may be congregations of other ethnic, racial, or religious identities seeking space for their worship and programs. Sometimes a congregation can sell their property to another congregation, often for a nominal amount, while retaining the ability to use some space for their continuing worship and programs.

Alternatively, a congregation can sell property to a nonprofit or other community-serving organization and create a deal in which they can use space for little or no rent. An order of women religious in the Midwest owns a large campus that they no longer fully utilize.

They are selling significant numbers of buildings (including a pool and wellness center, a large kitchen, and many office spaces) and using the proceeds to preserve a piece of land as park space and to build several small residences for the remaining sisters to use.

Sell and Leave the Property

Finally, even if a congregation opts to sell the entire property and cease to exist as a congregation, merge with existing congregations, or relocate, the sale need not take the property out of service to the community. The United Congregational Church of Bridgeport, Connecticut, found itself no longer able to maintain its sizable building while also continuing its much-needed social service ministries to an impoverished neighborhood. Most of its members did not live anywhere near the neighborhood of their historic building. However, many members of an Islamic community did, and they purchased the building to transform it into a mosque. The proceeds allowed the church to buy into a newly constructed office building to create a right-sized worship space and provide office and program space for their social service ministries. Thus, the original building continued to serve the community in new ways while the original congregation continued to live out its mission of service in a new location, better suited to its size and needs.

A WORD TO JUDICATORIES

While many congregations own and control their own buildings, others do not. Some denominations or regional bodies (such as Roman Catholic, Methodist, Episcopal, and Presbyterian) own the properties of their related congregations or have some measure of control over what happens to the buildings. This reality sometimes makes the news when a congregation splits from its denominational body and seeks to maintain control over the building. However, simply because the local congregation may not have control over what happens to their property does not preclude the four scenarios noted above. Assuming the congregation is still intact and using the building, representatives of the judicatory can work with the congregation on mission/vision/legacy as well as with stakeholders and community partners. A denominational office might be especially interested in how the disposition of a building impacts the neighborhood, since whatever happens reflects on the reputation of the denomination as a whole. Leaving a church empty to slowly decay is the worst-case scenario, yet this happens more often than one would hope. Of course, the ideal time to do this work is before the building is empty. Judicatories can work with congregations to anticipate futures involving transition long before transition happens, to maximize a positive result for all. Some congregations, however, live in denial of their future financial and building strains, and so they are resistant to engaging in conversations about them. Helping congregations to understand that "transition" need not mean loss of their use of the building if prepared for in advance, may alleviate some of that resistance.

HOPE FOR EMPTY BUILDINGS

Across the country, indeed across Europe as well, many church buildings already sit empty, abandoned by their congregations or in some kind of ownership limbo with a larger church body. As anyone who has worked with buildings knows well, the longer a building of any kind sits empty, the faster the building deteriorates. While it might seem that the only solution in these cases is to raze the structure altogether, some creative people are trying to salvage and restore these buildings through innovative, community-minded repurposing.

St. Liborius Roman Catholic Church, whose building was completed in 1870, once worshiped in the oldest Gothic revival structure west of the Mississippi River in a corner of St. Louis, Missouri. About twenty years ago, the congregation merged with another congregation, and the massive building was left empty. Outer buildings (convent, rectory) were sold to nonprofits, and the school became a juvenile detention facility. But the immense worship space remained empty, and the building began to crumble.

Ten years ago, a couple of entrepreneur contractors obtained the building and began to turn it into the Liborius Urban Art Studios, better known as Sk8Liborius. The founders' vision is to provide an indoor skate/bike park as well as a center for art, music, and vocational education. They describe the current "congregation" as underserved urban youth. They are working to restore the building themselves, teaching construction skills like masonry, electrical, and carpentry to the youth who make use of the skate park. Their vision is "to give people of all ages and backgrounds the chance to improve themselves and our community through new skills, vocations, and art."[1] One of the owners said he doesn't want local kids to end up in the detention center across the street; he wants them in the church building learning skills and enjoying a safe, drug- and violence-free place to skate and bike. The owners also have a love for the structure and want to see it restored to its former beauty and functionality.

While some church members and preservationists might express horror at this use for a former worship space, the mission of the owners of Liborius Urban Art Studios has not strayed all that far from the original mission of the congregation to serve the community around it. And this stunning building is being recovered from certain slow ruin.

But Before the Building Is Empty . . .

Many examples of empty church buildings being transformed into single-family houses, restaurants, bars, or event spaces exist across the country. Other congregations have taken their continuing mission, vision, and legacy to heart, and their buildings now host arts groups, affordable housing, health-care services, schools, or other community service agencies. The hope is that congregations will take on the challenge of making plans for their buildings'

---

1. Information on Sk8Liborius comes from a visit by this author to the site and an interview with the owners. This quote is from the organization's website, https://tinyurl.com/y2epya86.

future before it is too late to shape those plans to leave a legacy befitting the mission of the congregations who worshiped and served the community for many years. While one might applaud the imaginations of the owners of Sk8Liborius, one might also hope that congregations do not leave the future of their buildings to chance. Imaginative consideration of the various options for transformation of a congregation's relationship to their property can turn a hopeless task into a hope-filled future.

3

THE IMPACT OF THE "HALO EFFECT" ON A CONGREGATION'S COMMUNITY

A. Robert Jaeger

What may be lost in communities as churches are closed, sold, or become something else? Why should neighbors or community leaders care about our congregation and our sacred place? Why should civic leaders help us take care of our buildings and make the most of their potential as assets for the community?

These are perennial and increasingly urgent questions that congregation leaders should be asking as they experience change and transition, often shrinking in size and struggling to carry out the good stewardship of their buildings. They are being compelled to think in new ways about how they sustain themselves and are coming to the realization that they cannot do this work alone. Congregations are learning to reach out to their neighbors, articulate their community value, and work in tandem to sustain and maximize their buildings and other assets.

This community-minded approach to building stewardship requires a congregation to understand—and articulate in broadly understandable terms—the value it brings to the larger community. The future of sacred places will increasingly depend on a new and fuller understanding of their role as civic assets that benefit *everyone*—an understanding that needs to be embraced by neighborhood leaders, philanthropy, arts and human service organizations, and government.

The worth of sacred places can be described in multiple ways, and multiple populations have been shown to benefit from the life and work of congregations. They have an intrinsic value, of course, as places that house and express the faith of congregations that worship, fellowship, educate, and minister to members and the larger "family" of the church. But they also have a civic or public value; that is, they benefit and serve the larger community. Sacred places live out that purpose by:

- contributing to the physical fabric of the community. They have a physical presence on the streetscape that helps to define the character of the community. They are often the most visible and prominent landmarks in any given neighborhood—anchoring communities and providing a sense of continuity.
- representing the culture and history of the community. Their architecture and artistry tell the story of those who have participated in the church over decades or longer, and the immigrants and migrants who have come to the community and contributed to its vitality over many years. They tell stories of change over time, and they reflect larger demographic changes. Moreover, sacred places often contain the most important collections of fine and decorative arts in any given community, including painting, stained glass, mosaics, and carving or sculpture in wood and stone.
- bringing economic vitality to the community by hiring local workers, spending money on local services, hosting events that attract visitors who spend money locally, and incubating small organizations that need a welcoming and affordable space to do their work. This community impact includes the ways in which a congregation impacts the lives of those who live or work nearby, by serving people in need, building their capacity, and enabling them to live healthy and productive lives.

It is this last contribution—what we have termed the *economic Halo Effect of sacred places* (or Halo Effect for short)—that we will focus on here. The Halo Effect endeavors to capture the full and comprehensive ways in which congregations and their buildings support and nourish the lives of members and nonmembers alike. Understanding and communicating this value can help a congregation reach new audiences, facilitating its engagement with the community. How?

Halo can serve as a new and fresh way to help the larger community appreciate the value of a church or synagogue. It can help those who support congregation-hosted outreach see themselves in a new light. It lifts up the enormous contributions that congregations make to the health and vitality of the surrounding community.

A new understanding of the larger value of a sacred place can set the stage for new conversations with potential allies and supporters in the larger community, enabling new funding and new partnerships that can bring energy and resources to the congregation and its building.

It uses a language that can reach audiences—such as business, philanthropy, and government—that are often wary of intersecting with "religion."

DEVELOPMENT OF THE "HALO EFFECT"

The term "Halo Effect"—which attempts to capture the comprehensive, larger value of sacred places in the community—was coined by Partners for Sacred Places, and has been articulated and measured by several rounds of research conducted by Partners with the University of Pennsylvania and the University of North Carolina.

The first effort to undertake a scientific, national study documenting how congregations serve the public dates to 1997–1998 and was conducted in partnership with Dr. Ram Cnaan and the University of Pennsylvania's School of Social Policy and Practice. This study examined over 110 congregations with older buildings, randomly selected from a universe of qualifying sacred places in six cities. The findings, published as *Sacred Places at Risk (SPAR)*, demonstrated that the average urban congregation provides a wide array of quantifiable resources to the programs it supports, including space in the building (often provided free or at low cost), volunteers, staff and clergy time, cash support, and in-kind services.

SPAR's most important single finding was that *urban sacred places act as de facto community centers during the week*: 81 percent of those served by programs housed by congregations come from outside the congregation. In other words, the vast majority of those who benefit from outreach programs housed in sacred places are nonmembers.

Among the other highlights of *SPAR*:

- ninety-three percent of urban congregations open their doors to serve people in need.
- the space and resources provided to programs housed by the average congregation were valued at $140,000 annually (in 1997 dollars).
- seventy-six percent of all services provided by congregations are located in their buildings, notwithstanding support provided for missionary work or outreach taking place outside the sacred place.
- importantly, many of the programs frequently offered by congregations—such as clothing closets and food pantries—responded to basic needs for food and shelter, and children and youth were among the populations most often served.[1]

The study focused largely on the resources that congregations bring to programs they house or support but did not address many other ways in which sacred places generate economic and community value. Consequently, in the mid-2010s, Partners and Dr. Cnaan expanded their assessment of civic value, exploring other factors such as the environmental and recreational value of green space and trees, the economic impact of major building repair and restoration projects, the spending of visitors to the local community, support for local business and vendors, operational and program spending,

1. Diane Cohen and A. Robert Jaeger, *Sacred Places at Risk: New Evidence on How Endangered Older Churches and Synagogues Serve Communities* (Philadelphia: Partners for Sacred Places, 1998), 7–19.

and the role a congregation may have played in incubating new businesses or nonprofits. This study allowed Partners and the University of Pennsylvania (Penn) to test a variety of ways to capture and monetize each element of a congregation's economic impact.

A random sampling of congregations with older sacred places was chosen in three cities: Fort Worth, Chicago, and Philadelphia. The study monetized five areas of benefit: education, direct spending, magnet effect (i.e., the spending of those who visit the sacred place for programs and events), community-serving programs, and recreation space. Community development, the incubation of small nonprofits and businesses, and the impact of church leadership on the lives of neighbors were also examined but not assigned a dollar value. The results were significant and surprising: the average congregation and its sacred place provided a value of $1.7 million to its community each year.

Moreover, the study demonstrated that congregations and their leaders had an enormous impact on the lives of individuals and families. Clergy and other leaders helped people get jobs, treat their addiction to drugs or alcohol, learn English as a second language, and become healthy and productive members of the community—to name just a few types of intervention.

This study also showed that the percentage of nonmembers benefiting from programs housed in sacred places increased over the previous fifteen years, growing from 81 percent of the total to 87 percent. This trend underlined the role of sacred places as de facto community centers.

The Halo study also noted that the ninety participating congregations were visited by almost 3.7 million people over the course of one year, some coming multiple times (such as those coming for worship), and others more rarely. Remarkably, only 9 percent of those visits were for worship. Almost half came to participate in community-serving programs, and 31 percent came for education programs. Again, these findings point to the civic value of sacred places.[2]

2. Bob Jaeger et al., *The Economic Halo Effect of Historic Sacred Places* (Philadelphia: Partners for Sacred Places, 2016), 6–14.

These two studies conducted by Partners and Penn focused on urban sacred places, as did a third study, conducted by Sphaera Research in collaboration with Cardus, the City of Toronto Planning Department, Ryerson University's School of Planning and Urban Development, and the Canadian Centre for Policy Alternatives. Unlike Partners' two studies in the United States, this study monetized the "individual impact" of sacred places, that is, their role in helping people obtain jobs, learn English as a second language, become drug free, and so on, and this element of Halo pushed the average total value to over $4 million per congregation.

Recognizing that rural and small-town congregations had been overlooked to date but were likely to generate significant value in their own right, Partners collaborated with the Duke Endowment and the University of North Carolina Charlotte Urban Institute to study the impact of United Methodist Church (UMC) congregations in North Carolina's rural areas. The study examined who benefits from the presence of these congregations and what contributions these churches make to the lifeblood of their communities as conveners, trusted partners, and service providers.

Partners and UNC Charlotte conducted extensive interviews with leaders of eighty-seven rural churches and then monetized and assigned a numerical value to six areas. These areas include direct spending, education and child care, green or recreation space, the spending of visitors in the community, the church's impact on the lives of individuals and families, and community-serving programming.

Perhaps the most important finding from this study, published in 2021: rural UMC congregations indeed make great economic contributions to their towns and counties, with an average annual contribution to the economy valued at just over $735,000 per congregation.[3]

The research also showed that:

3. If extrapolated across the state, the 1,283 rural UMC congregations in North Carolina eligible for Duke Endowment's Rural Church program generate an overall economic impact of $944 million annually.

- seventy-two percent of those benefiting from programs housed in UMC churches are not members of those congregations. Rural Methodist churches, too, are community centers, just as their sister churches in cities.
- like their urban counterparts, rural churches generate value because they spend locally and hire locally; they host events that bring people to the community who spend money there; they sacrificially share space in their buildings, at low cost or no cost; and they provide needed resources and services to the community.
- many rural congregations are community hubs, providing a variety of flexible and affordable space that encourages neighbors to come together to solve problems, serve and be served, and build social capital.
- rural churches are important supporters of early childhood education and provide valuable child-care services in areas underserved by child-care centers. Congregations counsel, support, and make referrals for individuals and families struggling with a range of issues.
- small-town UMC congregations are also a magnet for visitors, attracting on average 195 visits to their towns or locales each week. Only half of these visits (53 percent) were for worship activities, while the other half were by individuals attending an event or participating in a program.[4]

In sum, the North Carolina study found that Methodist churches are not just for Methodists alone.

HOW THE HALO EFFECT CAN HELP

What then have been the larger implications of the several generations of Halo study, at both the macro and micro levels? At

4. Rachel Hildebrandt et al., *The Economic Halo Effect of Rural United Methodist Churches in North Carolina* (Philadelphia: Partners for Sacred Places and UNC Charlotte Urban Institute, 2021), 15–27.

the macro level, the nonprofit community—including Partners—has gained powerful new evidence for the public value of sacred places, which can potentially leverage new interest and support from sectors, such as business and philanthropy, that have often been reluctant to engage with religious institutions.

Civic leaders—including mayors, foundations, business leaders, arts organizations, and community groups—can now feel more comfortable engaging with and resourcing their local sacred places when they have a larger, community-serving value.

The iterations of Halo research had an enormous impact on the larger national conversation about the role of religion in society over the last two decades. The emergence of this new understanding of sacred places influenced the work of the White House Office on Community and Faith-Based Initiatives, created in 2001 by President George W. Bush to encourage support for religious programs serving a public purpose. The Office, among other early actions, initiated the creation of new faith-based offices in most cabinet-level federal departments.

At the micro level, Halo Effect findings have enabled community-serving congregations to tell their stories in new and more effective ways, encouraging philanthropy and government and civil society to be more open to supporting or collaborating with faith-based institutions. This engagement can position congregations to broaden their base of support, spreading the costs of property care among a wider array of stakeholders.

Halo Effect findings can be used by a congregation to bolster fund-raising efforts, both with members and nonmembers. The size and character of a congregation's contribution to community health and vitality can be a persuasive factor when asking for gifts or grants for capital campaigns and annual stewardship campaigns. The data can add great strength to a grant proposal, especially for funders that are not interested in religion but have a commitment to community development.

Halo findings can also raise the congregation's profile when shared with civic leaders and local media. Local leaders do not tend to think of churches or synagogues in terms of economic impact or neighborhood strengthening, so Halo can change perspectives and encourage leaders to take a fresh look at congregations and their buildings.

Halo is a vital and important component of a congregation's story of community impact. In an era when congregations need to articulate their larger value, positioning them to build new alliances and develop new financial resources, Halo can give momentum and support for new initiatives, even when they have suffered declining memberships and financial resources. In sum, Halo helps to answer those perennial questions we laid out at the beginning of the chapter:

What may be lost in communities as churches are closed, sold, or become something else? Why should neighbors or community leaders care about our congregation and our sacred place? Why should civic leaders help us take care of our buildings and make the most of their potential as an asset for the community?

The health of our communities depends on it.

4

THE CASE FOR MISSIONAL REMAINING MISSIONAL

Patrick Duggan

Steeples were designed to point to God.

The concept of architecture reflecting theology and meaning is a relic from antiquity. It came to the United States of America through Europe, who inherited it from the Roman Empire, who appropriated the concept over many centuries of interactions with the ancient African civilization of Egypt.[1] "Architecture is the built form of ideas, and church architecture is the built form of theology ... classic church architecture is not so much a 'style' as it is a 'language,' which has structure, syntax, and rules that are necessary to best convey meaning."[2]

Every element of the classic European design of church buildings in America has meaning related to the mission of the church. Stained glass windows create a "heavenly light" symbolizing the presence of God. The altar is the table where followers receive the sacrifice of Christ. The pulpit symbolizes the centrality of God's Word. For Catholics, the cross conveys the image of the suffering

---

1. Borna Fuerst-Bjeliš, ed., *Mediterranean Identities: Environment, Society, Culture* (Rijeka, Croatia: Intech, 2017), 9, https://tinyurl.com/yrnjdhz4.

2. Denis McNamara, "Built Form of Theology: The Natural Sympathies of Catholicism and Classicism," Institute for Sacred Architecture, vol. 12 (Fall/Winter 2006): 20, https://tinyurl.com/rpndexd7.

Jesus, while for Protestants a bare cross reflects Jesus overcoming death and rising to new life.[3]

The architectural elements of a classic church building are part of a centuries-old word picture summed up in the word "church." "Church" symbolizes a world of benign meaning embedded in the global consciousness as a mess of overlapping, dissonant concepts about buildings, people, architecture, theology, religion, morality, place, and institution. This word picture evokes the idea that all things related to God elevate our humanity beyond the materialistic, the secular, and the ordinary.

By "speaking" Western biblical theology to every human settlement in the world, the architectural language of classic church buildings has been one of the most effective branding campaigns in the history of humanity. Church buildings have played an important role in the emergence of the church as the preeminent institution that held sway over every aspect of Western society and culture. For centuries, church buildings have silently advanced the mission of the church everywhere they are located.

European thinkers in the fifteenth, sixteenth, and seventeenth centuries, because of their obeisance to the church, found it necessary to create the pseudoscience of race to rationalize and justify colonization, slavery, and genocide.[4] The founders of the United States of America, mostly slaveholders themselves, were able to rationalize this great evil and invoke divine imperative in the Declaration of Independence (*We hold these truths to be self-evident, that all men are created equal, that they are endowed by their Creator with certain unalienable Rights . . .*) and to delineate in the third article of the Bill of Rights that *Congress shall make no law respecting establishment of religion, or prohibiting the free exercise thereof.*

---

3. Isabelle Lomholt and Adrian Welch, "8 Amazing Things You Didn't Know about Church Architecture," e-architect (June 28, 2021), https://tinyurl.com/mw8tcrhb.

4. James H. Sweet, "Spanish and Portuguese Influences on Racial Slavery in British North America, 1492–1619," Proceedings of the Fifth Annual Gilder Lehrman Center International Conference at Yale University, 2003, 3–9, https://tinyurl.com/4fywrhm8.

In the late nineteenth and early twentieth centuries, ultra-high net worth individuals and families (sometimes called "robber barons"),[5] because of the influence of religious faith, felt a moral obligation to address unmet needs in society by founding libraries, building museums, opening schools for the blind and orphanages for children, and creating the uniquely American notion of philanthropy through charitable foundations.[6] This same moral imperative prompted the federal government to create Social Security, unemployment insurance, Medicaid and Medicare in the mid-twentieth century, and a few years later, the Great Society programs that led to civil rights legislation ending legal segregation in America.

PROPERTY AND MISSION IN DECLINE

That these heralded federal programs have suffered decades of political assault is evidence of the centuries-long decline of church influence in America, from unquestioned dominance to a quixotic shell of its former self. It is no coincidence that this decline has occurred in lockstep with the increasing number of church properties in transition. The current state of church properties is both an indicator of, and a contributor to, the waning effectiveness of the vision and mission of American Christianity.

In making the case of keeping church property missional, this is where we must begin.

1. The mission of the church as interpreted and animated by most American Christians today is at best ineffective at holding or increasing the number of adherents, and at worst is perceived as hypocritical, divisive, and a contributor to societal evils like sexism, white supremacy, pedophilia, racism, misogyny, and homophobia. This is what we mean by "mission failure."[7]

5. "America's Gilded Age: Robber Barons and Captains of Industry," Maryville University, 2022, https://tinyurl.com/4n6ybp54.

6. Marc Sollinger, "What Robber Barons Gave Us—After They Took from Us," *World*, September 23, 2015, https://tinyurl.com/2p8v9fxk.

7. "Americans Have Positive Views about Religion's Role in Society, but

2. There is no unifying vision of American Christianity that holds the imagination of all followers of Christ today.[8]

3. Reflecting and contributing to the decline in American Christianity (and accelerated by the COVID-19 pandemic), more church properties are in transition because (a) more churches are closing, (b) churches are closing at a faster rate, and (c) the number of persons attending in-person weekly worship has decreased.[9]

The language of church architecture may still speak to us, but its lofty message rings inauthentic in the imagination of most Americans. The very public ills of the church have caused the word picture to be corrupted. Rather than pointing toward God, *people within the church* perceive church real estate assets as a burden.[10]

DOES IT MATTER WHAT CHURCHES BECOME?

The word "mission," when referring to a church, is traditionally associated with the term "missionary," a seventeenth-century word for a person undertaking a religious mission[11] (e.g., when

---

Want It out of Politics," Pew Research Center, November 15, 2019, https://tinyurl.com/25ka8acn.

8. It can be argued that from the moment the church was formed in Acts 2, there has never been a single, unifying vision of Christianity. However, over the centuries diversity of Christian practice was a driver of growth. Differences among Christians in the American context today show up among Christ followers as divergence, and to the public, as disunity and discord. Jesus is loved, but his followers are untrustworthy messengers without integrity.

9. Michael Gryboski. "1 in 5 Churches Facing Permanent Closure within 18 Months Due to COVID-19 Shutdowns: Barna Pres.," *Christian Post*, August 26, 2020, https://tinyurl.com/ynv2v684.

10. In recent years, as the UCC Church Building and Loan Fund has engaged with hundreds of church leaders and dozens of middle judicatory officials, the disposition of vacant and underutilized church properties has become perhaps the single most problematic concern. These assets hold the promise of missional opportunities, but given their current condition, opportunity is inscrutable and difficult to realize.

11. Merriam-Webster, s.v. "missionary," accessed August 10, 2022, https://tinyurl.com/3kk5yep8.

Europe colonized Africa, Asia, and the Americas and the Roman Catholic Church dispatched priests to convert the so-called God-less peoples, who were subsequently colonized).[12] This is not the definition of "mission" or "missional" used in this writing.

"Mission" or "missional" is used here to refer to that which is conveyed in a mission statement, defined as "something that states the purpose or goal of a business or organization."[13] Many businesses, and most nonprofit organizations in the United States, are constituted by a mission that is expressed through the organization's mission statement. Any organization that orients its operations toward the advancement of its expressed mission is a missional organization.

The idea of missional remaining missional stands in stark contrast to the profit-oriented uses of most commercial real estate. In markets where developable land is scarce, underused church properties represent lucrative opportunities for property sales and redevelopment. From the business perspective, if churches are in possession of an abundance of underused real estate, then churches should sell these assets and let the commercial interests find new ways for these properties to realize their "highest and best use."

According to the Appraisal Institute, four qualifications determine highest and best use: legally permissible, physically possible, financially feasible, and maximally productive.[14] The Appraisal Institute, commercial real estate professionals, and every good capitalist would argue that these qualifications are objective.

Churches must take a different approach to assessing the highest and best use of real estate. The first three qualifications are necessary for the proposed use of every commercial property. However, to determine the highest and best use of church-owned property, the qualification of "maximally productive" must be driven by the

12. Erin Blakemore, "What Is Colonialism? The History of Colonialism Is One of Brutal Subjugation of Indigenous Peoples," *National Geographic*, February 19, 2019, https://tinyurl.com/d8tnzc8d.

13. Merriam-Webster, s.v. "mission statement," accessed August 10, 2022, https://tinyurl.com/6eu3wm94.

14. Philip G. Spool, "Highest and Best Use Analysis," *Working RE*, Summer 2014, https://tinyurl.com/y5xd6evf.

church's mission. Highest and best use of church property must begin with the question, What maximally productive use of this property will best advance the mission of the church?

Businesses in the real estate industry must prioritize profit over everything when determining maximum productivity of land. Churches, nonprofits, and other organizations that prioritize mission have a fiduciary responsibility to make sound financial decisions and manage their organizations with exemplary fiscal integrity. However, churches and other nonprofits cannot choose to sidestep mission when making any financial decisions, especially large financial transactions that may affect the organizations for decades. When considering the sale, purchase, development, or repurposing of property, a church must answer the question, *Does the intended use optimize the potential of the land?* through the lens of their stated mission.

This is not a matter of preference or opinion but of law. To incorporate a nonprofit organization and to secure tax-exempt status from the federal government, an organization must declare in its corporate documents that advancing a mission, not generating profits, will be its primary activity.[15] Every organization seeks to end the fiscal year with a surplus, but missional organizations must evaluate performance based on the effectiveness of the advancement of their mission.

For church leaders to assess the use of property in this way is not dismissive of the accumulated knowledge of the Appraisal Institute and the highly skilled professionals in the commercial real estate industry. It is not to claim that the industry is wrong in its manner of determining highest and best use. It is to say that owners of property are the primary decision-makers on how their property should be used within the laws of the land, and therefore can and should use metrics or methods that support and advance their purposes for owning the property. For a church to engage in a highest and best-use analysis by overlaying it with its missional

15. "What provisions must be in an organization's organizing documents for it to qualify for exemption?" IRS (2022), https://tinyurl.com/y5jf4mrh.

obligations is a smart way to use the tools of outside experts while protecting organizational integrity.

RENEWING MISSION AND VISION

Founded in 1853, the United Church of Christ Church Building and Loan Fund (CB&LF) is the first national church-building society in the United States. CB&LF builds stable, thriving communities that live the gospel by providing UCC congregations and other Christian organizations with real estate financing, operational resources, and expertise. In a typical year, CB&LF helps over five hundred church leaders renew their mission statements, discern new shared visions, and learn to fully deploy their real estate assets for mission. Inevitably, some church leaders will argue that prioritizing mission over money is not practical; that a church needs to make money to advance mission or that dwindling church revenues must be approached as a financial problem. Should these legitimate concerns be addressed in this manner?

Research suggests that churches and church properties generate significant economic and social value just as they are.[16] A 2017 Vanderbilt University study demonstrated that home values are enhanced by the presence of a place of worship nearby.[17] In 2018, the Harvard T. H. Chan School of Public Health noted numerous studies that demonstrate the value of worship in improving health and well-being.[18] In 2016 the *International Journal of Research on Religion* conducted "the first documented quantitative national estimates of the economic value of religion to U.S. society" and found that "the study's most conservative estimate, which takes

16. See also Robert Jaeger's chapter in this book, "The Impact of the 'Halo Effect' on a Congregation's Community."

17. Gabriel Kayode Babawale and Yewande Adewunmi, "The Impact of Neighbourhood Churches on House Prices," *Journal of Sustainable Development* 4, no. 1 (2011): 2, https://tinyurl.com/mx9cyyxj.

18. Harvard T. H. Chan School of Public Health, "Religious Upbringing Linked to Better Health and Well-Being during Early Adulthood," news release, September 13, 2018, https://tinyurl.com/yc769b29.

into account only the revenues of faith-based organizations, is $378 billion annually ... more than the global annual revenues of tech giants Apple and Microsoft combined."[19]

These studies were not based on the premise that "If churches did something new and different, these outcomes would occur." The research demonstrates the tremendous impact of the church and other American religious institutions *just as they are*, at the height of a decades-long increase in church closures, waning influence, and membership decline. Even in mission failure, churches and church properties generate tremendous economic and social value in American society.

Admittedly, these research findings ring hollow to the many congregations struggling through the pandemic with buildings deteriorating because of years of deferred maintenance. At CB&LF we have found that there is often a correlation between the poor condition of a church's physical plant and the lack of a renewed mission and vision. Jesus once said that you cannot pour new wine into old wineskins because the wineskins will burst.[20] Even when a church finds the resources to repair the leaky roof or replace a failing boiler, if it does not renew its mission and vision, it has only delayed the inevitable end of its organizational life. Where there is no vision, the people perish, and so will the church.

Over decades of providing capacity building, leadership development, and consulting services, CB&LF has assisted a number of churches to reverse mission failure by renewing their mission and vision. It is not an easy way forward and many churches are unable to overcome years of decline, but with strong leadership and a unified congregation a church can once again effectively ad-

19. Brian J. Grim and Melissa E. Grim, "The Socio-Economic Contribution of Religion to American Society: An Empirical Analysis," *Interdisciplinary Journal of Research on Religion* 12, no. 3 (2016): 2, https://tinyurl.com/399w75pj.

20. Ashley Goff writes about how a church in Arlington, Virginia, took this passage to heart by developing affordable housing on their church property in her chapter in this book, "When God's Call Is Bigger Than a Building."

vance mission. Because CB&LF is a missional organization with 170 years of church real estate expertise, churches that come to us to solve real estate challenges learn to duplicate our model of advancing mission through the deployment of real estate assets. Renewal of mission and vision can become the catalyst for the re-purposing, redevelopment, purchase, or even the sale of a church property. By keeping their real estate assets missional, churches can bolster their missional impact and increase their already-proven economic and social value in American society.

Church-owned property must be dedicated toward the advance-ment of the church's stated mission even when the use is not reli-gious. This is an important distinction that many churches struggle to understand. A church is not restricted to using its property exclu-sively for worship, Sunday school, committee meetings, community gatherings, prayer meetings, and other uses typically associated with religious institutions. If a church has as part of its mission, for example, "alleviating poverty and promoting abundance for all," it can make the case based on biblical theology and publicly available information that its mission calls it to help local small businesses create jobs because jobs alleviate poverty and promote abundance. This church can then create programming or launch a ministry that promotes entrepreneurship or small-business development. It can designate a part of its building as a shared workspace rentable at below-market rates for small-business owners. It can host training sessions for business owners with bankers and small-business pro-fessionals. It can host an annual business launch contest awarding cash prizes to the businesses that demonstrate the greatest impact in alleviating poverty and promoting abundance. It can use an ex-isting property or purchase a new property, develop it and build retail space leased to local businesses, then take the surpluses from that enterprise to fund other poverty-alleviating and abundance-promoting ministry work.[21]

21. Each of these programs were launched by actual churches, some of which have worked with CB&LF. Developing property and launching social enterprise can trigger questions about taxation. Every church should consult

HIGHEST AND BEST USE
THROUGH MISSIONAL REDEVELOPMENT

Ministry ideas like those described above will likely create new
uses of church property that revitalize the church and foster increased engagement with the local community. One truly transformative church-building project, the Village @ West Jefferson
in Louisville, Kentucky, is a prime example of how a church with
a renewed mission and a compelling mission can transform an
entire community when their property is fully dedicated to advancing the mission and vision of the church.

The Village @ West Jefferson is a commercial/retail facility
built in 2021 by the church-affiliated Molo Village Community Development Corporation on property owned by St. Peter's United
Church of Christ in the Russell neighborhood, directly across the
street from the former Beecher Terrace, one of the largest public-
housing developments in the country.[22] Prior to the Village @
West Jefferson, there had been for decades no bank, restaurant,
coffee shop, or sandwich shop; no day-care center, no health facility, nor other community services in the community. The community had several industrial businesses, but very few of the jobs
in those businesses were held by community residents.

St. Peter's UCC pastor, Rev. Dr. Jamesetta Ferguson, founded
Molo Village CDC in 2011 to offer a range of services, conducted
in partnership with the church, to alleviate the effects of poverty
on community residents. Dr. Ferguson was called to the church
in 2007 when the last dozen or so remaining members, all senior
citizen German immigrants who had been a part of St. Peter's for

---

an attorney or accountant with expertise in nonprofit law and accounting
expertise to ensure that their ministry and programmatic activities comply
with federal, state, and local laws pertaining to churches. For more on church
taxation, see RootedGood's tool, "What about Taxes?," rootedgood.org.

22. The redevelopment of the St. Peter's UCC property coincided
with the HUD Choice–funded demolition and replacement of the seven-
hundred-unit Beecher Terrace public-housing development. The all-new
seven hundred units of mixed-income housing include rentals and home
ownership options for low- and moderate-income families.

most of their lives, finally embraced the reality that the church needed to change or die.

When Dr. Ferguson reached out to CB&LF in 2013, she led a ministry team of five committed clergypersons with a church that had about fifty members and a budget of slightly more than $100,000 annually. This small group of people was serving one thousand people each week through meal programs, health and nutrition programs, after-school programs, Alcoholics Anonymous, services for Returning Citizens, senior citizen programs, mental health programs, and other offerings.

Dr. Ferguson requested a $1 million loan from CB&LF for the most urgent repairs needed for the 118-year-old St. Peter's UCC worship facility. Suffering from decades of deferred maintenance, the building needed $10 million in renovations to completely restore it. But the church was not able to afford a million dollars of debt, and certainly did not have the financial wherewithal to take on a full renovation of the building. Even if an anonymous donor would have appeared with a $10 million gift, restoring the St. Peter's worship facility to its former glory would not have equipped the church for the thriving ministries engaging thousands of local residents in the Russell community.

The St. Peter's church building was state-of-the-art when it was built in 1895 to serve the hundreds of mostly German immigrants who attended church every Sunday, brought their children to Sunday school, and used the church building for community gatherings. To serve the predominantly African American community now living in Russell, the old mission of St. Peter's and the former mission-advancing use of the church building were irrelevant. They no longer needed a seven-hundred-seat theater-style sanctuary with a balcony, with Sunday school rooms and parlor rooms on two floors to serve the religious, cultural, and community needs of new immigrants. To alleviate the ravages of poverty and underinvestment in the community today, St. Peter's needed flexible gathering space; office space; classrooms steeped in the latest Internet-based technology; resource rooms for education, health, personal finance, and career development; a commercial kitchen with ample storage space; and bathrooms on every floor. Even though a million dollars would have alleviated the worst of St. Peter's deferred maintenance issues at that time, CB&LF could not offer financing that would overwhelm the financial capacity of the church and not enable the church to live fully into its stated mission and vision.

CB&LF was unable to approve the loan application, but it was impossible to ignore the impact and potential of St. Peter's ministries and the transformational leadership of Rev. Dr. James-etta Ferguson. Many churches have outreach programs. Very few churches offer essential services to one thousand people a week, and even fewer do that on a shoestring budget. In addition, the church building is located on a city block less than a mile from the heart of downtown Louisville. The quality of the leadership, the vitality of the ministries, the location of the site, and the renewed mission and shared vision of Molo Village convinced the CB&LF Board and staff to invite St. Peter's UCC to participate in CB&LF's Partners in Vision (PIV) program.[23] Through PIV, CB&LF worked with St. Peter's UCC to ascertain and implement the highest and best use of its missional property.

A few months into working with St. Peter's in PIV, our team recommended to Dr. Ferguson that the maximally productive use of their church property was *not* to renovate the church building but to subdivide the property and build a thirty-thousand-square-foot commercial/retail facility on the vacant corner of St. Peter's city block. By leasing space in this facility to local business owners,[24] a credit union, a coffee shop, a day-care company, a health-care facility, and the community's first sit-down restaurant in fifty years, St. Peter's and Molo Village CDC would create over one hundred permanent local jobs and transform the community. It was also known by that time that the City of Louisville had applied to be-

23. PIV helps churches develop large, complex building projects from concept to completion.

24. Molo Village CDC's primary goal is to engage residents of the Russell neighborhood, particularly from Beecher Terrace, in holistic approaches to community development. For this reason, local business owners, and especially entrepreneurs with roots in the community who are women and people of color, were recruited as tenants rather than national chains and franchise owners.

come a HUD Choice Neighborhood grantee, which would lead to the redevelopment of seven hundred units of affordable housing directly across the street from St. Peter's.

Although we recommended to Dr. Ferguson that renovation of the church building would work better as phase two of the redevelopment of their property, she was committed to restoring the church building and did not at first agree with the idea of a commercial/retail facility. Upon further deliberation, however, Dr. Ferguson eventually came to embrace the idea. And after eight years of arduous labor, setbacks, disappointments, a pandemic, and political unrest in the community due to the Breonna Taylor police shootings, the $7.8 million Village @ West Jefferson was completed in the spring of 2021, just three months later than anticipated and on budget. Financed by $4.2 million in church building loan funds, $1.6 million in grant subsidies from two local foundations and the City of Louisville, and $2 million in equity from New Markets Tax Credits, this project was the first of its kind in CB&LF's history.

By redeveloping a portion of their site for commercial/retail use, St. Peter's is now better equipped to serve the people of Russell and provide the only retail offerings available to the residents of the new housing. They can now more effectively address the array of poverty impacts (hunger, thirst, estrangement, sickness, imprisonment, oppression) that Jesus prioritizes in Matthew 25 and Luke 4. In one of the poorest neighborhoods in the United States, a small congregation has dramatically expanded tangible access to the abundant life Jesus talks about in John 10:10. The Village @ West Jefferson is a shining example of a church using its spiritual and financial resources to deploy its assets for the advancement of its mission toward a gospel-infused vision.[25]

A View from the Mayor's Office

The editor of this volume, Mark Elsdon, interviewed former Louisville mayor Greg Fischer in the spring of 2022 to hear his perspec-

---

25. The Village @ West Jefferson lucidly illustrates the CB&LF tagline, "helping churches transform communities by living into God's economy."

tive on the Village @ West Jefferson project and the role of church property in a community. Mayor Fischer is thrilled about the impact that the project is having on an area of Louisville that the city is investing in. He is proud of the work the church has done over the years to bring this transformative development to reality.

When asked about the role of churches and church property in communities, Mayor Fischer said, "Churches represent architectural beauty *and* the soul of a neighborhood. They are more than just buildings. Churches have symbolic significance to major milestones in people's lives." He went on to say that Louisville had too many church properties for the number of people who engage in traditional church services and activities. Unless there is some intervention, some of the properties will likely end up abandoned after these congregations have closed (some already have). At the same time, Louisville needs at least thirty thousand more affordable housing units to address the housing need in the community. He estimated that $5 billion of funding is needed to address the shortage, a number that dwarfs the $1.1 billion annual budget of the city. Church property could be repurposed for affordable housing or projects like the Village @ West Jefferson.

Louisville has no specific plans in place regarding churches, a missing piece that Mayor Fischer recognizes could be helpful.[26] From his view in the mayor's office, he encourages churches to consider consolidation, to be realistic about what is happening and where they are going, and to focus on their core mission as serving the good of their neighborhood and not just gathering for Sunday services. The Village @ West Jefferson is an excellent example of what churches can do with their property to increase their impact and remain missional in a changing environment.

The redevelopment of the Village @ West Jefferson and the continuing social impact of the work of St. Peter's UCC and Molo Village CDC are a clear example of why church properties should remain missional. The former mission of the church had served its

26. See Kurt Paulsen's chapter in this book, "Proactive City Planning for Church Property Transitions," for suggestions on steps municipalities can take to encourage positive church property development.

purpose of creating a worshiping community and a bridge to assimilation for new American immigrants. The renewed mission of St. Peter's, created under new pastoral leadership, was inspired by Jesus's core purpose of liberating the poor, creating abundant life for all, and enrolling others into this divine work as explicated in Matthew 28. This mission is centered on ending poverty, creating abundance, and transforming the community that the church serves. This small church demonstrates the untapped potential within many dying congregations in American Christianity today.

St. Peter's UCC models what can happen when a church renews its mission, casts a transformative vision, and then pursues that new mission until the vision is realized. The redevelopment of this church property would not have been possible if profit was prioritized in the highest and best-use framework.[27] The Village @ West Jefferson is an example of the social impact and financial viability that are possible when highest and best-use analysis is done through the perspective of a missional owner seeking a missional redevelopment.

Even in mission failure, churches continue to generate outsized financial impact in society. If every church renewed its mission and discerned a new shared vision, how much more could Christianity impact society for good? If most missional properties remain missional, could church properties once again point people to God?

> For thus says the LORD of hosts, the God of Israel: Houses and fields and vineyards shall again be bought in this land. (Jer. 32:15)[28]

27. When St. Peter's embarked upon the redevelopment of its property, the value of all land in their community had been historically suppressed because of multigenerational disinvestment in the Russell neighborhood. As such, the St. Peter's UCC property failed the highest and best-use analysis from a for-profit perspective because a traditional development of the property at that time would not yield a profit. CB&LF's highest and best-use analysis through a missional lens determined that with subsidies from local philanthropies and the City of Louisville along with equity from New Markets Tax Credit investors, the Village @ West Jefferson was not only feasible but would transform the local economy.

28. Unless otherwise indicated, Scripture quotations in this book come from the New Revised Standard Version.

5

WHO WANTS A BUILDING ANYWAY?

Coté Soerens

"Who wants a building anyway?" asked Henry,[1] a denominational executive in my area. It was a telling statement. From where he was sitting, church buildings were a problem. They were costly and—worse—there were too many empty ones. From where I was sitting, however, we were desperate for affordable space to host community life. *We* wanted a building, and unfortunately, Henry's denomination had taken one away from our neighborhood less than a decade earlier by selling it without evidencing much thought. It was a great loss for the youth, who used to attend after-school programming there, and for our neighborhood, as we never had access to that building again.

Living in a neighborhood that lacked enough spaces for public events drew my attention to the important role church buildings play in communities and what their use, or underutilization, can reveal about how congregations understand their mission in a particular place. In theological terms, we can tell a lot about a congregation's ecclesiology by the way they use their building, how they see their purpose as the body of Christ, and who they understand themselves to be in the public life of a neighborhood.[2] Buildings,

1. Name has been changed.
2. For an in-depth look at the theology of the built environment, see Tim-

after all, are the most visible and immediately public aspect of a church's relationship to that community. And what usually gets lost on denominational executives like Henry is that, whether we like it or not, church buildings are part of a community's built environment, and any decision made over that space impacts the residents around it. Whether congregations see their building as a private or social, semipublic space has huge implications for the surrounding neighborhoods.

The same is true for church property as an asset that generates wealth. Church buildings are part of a city, and as with any property, they reflect the sins of a city's urban planning.[3] Issues such as redlining and racial covenants are reflected in the number of church buildings a denomination concentrates in different areas of a city. Are denominations critically examining real estate as a means for restoration, liberation, and reparations in their region?

Redlined Neighborhoods and Church Buildings

Consider Henry's comment, for example. Ours is a segregated town, and Henry and I live on opposite sides of Seattle. He operates in the north end, the wealthy side by decades of urban design. I live in South Park, the redlined side, where a century of disinvestment has given us a civically engaged community who can only dream of enjoying the same infrastructure our neighbors have across the industrial core that separates us from the rest of the city. Buildings are the thing we obsess about at night.

To provide some context, South Park comprises one square mile of six thousand low-income, majority immigrant, Black and brown, young residents, with a highway cutting through the middle of it. We are surrounded by industry and the Duwamish River, which was tragically turned into a superfund site after years of

othy J. Gorringe, *A Theology of the Built Environment: Justice, Empowerment, Redemption* (Cambridge: Cambridge University Press, 2002).

3. See Richard Rothstein, *The Color of Law: A Forgotten History of How Our Government Segregated America* (New York: Liveright, 2017).

unregulated industrial activity. Our neighborhood's greatest gift is our residents. What we lack in infrastructure we make up for in solidarity. But the lack of infrastructure is noticeable. There are not enough affordable buildings to host all the activities we, as a neighborhood, need to produce. And it rains a lot! Youth programming often happens in the rain. It is sad. That same youth used to gather at a church building from Henry's denomination until 2014, and that building had been serving the neighborhood for a good century before that.

And Henry is not alone in his lack of awareness. In addition to his denomination's now-sold building, there are two others that unfortunately also represent common practices for congregations all across the United States.

One church building in the neighborhood, which was perfectly located between the library and the community center, provided incredible opportunities as a place to serve the youth. I sat through many a conversation with heads of local nonprofits imagining all the ways we could utilize that building "if only it was for sale." We wanted to buy it because, sadly, and according to their own account, the congregation did not want to be in relationship with neighborhood groups, so collaboration was not a possibility. Eventually we learned that the six members of this congregation lived miles away from South Park. The building was shut all week long (while our youth groups met in the rain). Last year they put the building up for sale, and we quickly reached out to our denomination to raise the funds to purchase it. We were the only faith community in the running to buy it and wanted to use it as an arts center to host youth, parents with small children who needed a break, and the community at large. But we lost it by a marginal amount of money to a developer from the wealthy side of town. (Also in the running were our friends from a local housing-justice group.) I will forever be curious about the congregation's thought process in their decision. Although they had several offers from mission-minded groups, they chose to sell it to a small developer, whose impact to increasing density and providing housing will be mild considering the zoning and the small size of the lot. I don't think it even was about the money, as their congregation was dissolving and there was no denomination in which to reinvest it. The losses for the neighborhood, however, were much more significant because it lost one of the few buildings with potential to provide it with affordable and desperately needed public space.

Who wants a building anyway . . .

There was another building as well, which belongs to an immigrant congregation who are incredibly sweet but have a very narrow understanding of mission. That building is also empty six days a week during the day. We approached them to see if we could host community activities in the building when it was not being used. They were open to it, but when we began asking about possible uses, their response was "any biblical use." After a few follow-up questions, it became apparent that what they meant by that was Bible study and soup kitchens. Our neighborhood needed far more than that. We needed a hospitable space for folks from all walks of life to host the activities that sustain the social fabric in any community. We needed a space to practice belonging and radical hospitality that would be flexible enough to adapt to the dynamic character of people living life in a place.

A MATTER OF ECCLESIOLOGY

There is a lot of life outside the walls of any church building, life that God cares deeply about! There are families with small children whose tired parents could use a break to connect with other tired parents. There are artists looking for affordable spaces to practice their art, teach it to others, or put together shows that reflect the ethos of that community. There are food entrepreneurs looking for affordable commissary kitchens or even a space to host a pop-up! There are civic groups looking for space to host community meetings about important issues affecting that community. The list goes on.

For decades, the church in North America has been preoccupied with attracting new members into their Sunday service and programs that occur mainly inside their buildings. Millions have been spent in new facilities, staff, and equipment that resembles what is needed to put on arena concerts, such as screens, lighting, and smoke machines. We have all witnessed the many pastors striving to be the coolest show in town. While this approach might have been sensible in the seeker-sensitive context of a few decades' past, today's decline in church attendance prompts us to question how relevant such practice is to society at large. When our desire to attract people and achieve financial sustainability becomes an idol, we lose imagination and adaptability to be more open in discerning what our mission is. This may explain why denominational executives like Henry might think church buildings exist only to serve a congregation's activities on Sunday. If a congregation is dying and the building requires maintenance, it is time to liquidate it. But what if there is more to a congregation's purpose than a Sunday gathering?

Today, there is little clarity about what the church is and what it is for, which makes it particularly challenging to make thoughtful decisions about property management. We may say, "Fine, we have an empty building, are we to start a nonprofit and turn it into a wraparound service facility for the houseless? Are we to sell the sky rights and make a theater/conference room/coworking space/coffee shop in the bottom?" These are all incredibly impactful decisions not only for congregations but also for the neighborhoods around these buildings. Do we even owe a consideration to the residents of that place?[4] If we don't know who we are, what our purpose is, and who we are sent to serve, how will we strategize accordingly?

A PLACE-BASED ECCLESIOLOGY

I have found place-based ecclesiology[5] to provide a very generative framework to any faith community wrestling with property

---

4. We absolutely do!

5. While I am calling it "place-based ecclesiology," the proponents of this approach identify themselves as part of the "parish movement." For an introduction to their thinking, see Paul Sparks, Tim Soerens, and Dwight

management and land ownership because it invites the members of such congregations to adopt *place* as an organizing principle for mission, to turn their attention to their neighborhoods, and to participate in the life of the communities where they worship. Rooting oneself in place, one is invited to be engaged, and more importantly, to be curious about the ways God is moving in that neighborhood through people of peace, including folks who are not necessarily part of our church.

Place-based ecclesiology basically starts with drawing a physical boundary to define a focus for a congregation's service. By inviting faith communities to focus on *place* as an organizing principle to discern mission, place-based ecclesiology breaks open the possibilities of what a congregation's purpose can be in a neighborhood, looking at such a place as a whole, with all the intersecting issues, opportunities, and movers and shakers that converge in that particular community. To borrow from my friends at Parish Collective, when we take the mandate to love our neighbors literally, our perspective shifts from a spirituality lived in the abstract back into our immediate surroundings, our built environment, and our actual neighborhood. Our questions change, says Tim Soerens,[6] director of Parish Collective and author of *Everywhere You Look*, from "church" questions, such as building maintenance and programming, to "God" questions such as, "What are God's dreams for this neighborhood?" Which is another way of asking, "What does shalom look like here, for *everyone in the neighborhood*, regardless of whether they follow Jesus or not?" Drawing

---

Friesen, *The New Parish: How Neighborhood Churches Are Transforming Mission, Discipleship, and Community* (Downers Grove, IL: InterVarsity Press, 2014); Tim Soerens, *Everywhere You Look: Discovering the Church Right Where You Are* (Downers Grove, IL: InterVarsity Press, 2020); and Jonathan Brooks, *Church Forsaken: Practicing Presence in Neglected Neighborhoods* (Downers Grove, IL: InterVarsity Press, 2018).

6. The feminist in me is dreading the fact that I just quoted none other than my husband. But we must admit it, sometimes husbands are brilliant and come up with good stuff that is useful to our work and that is worth sharing. You are welcome. You can read more at Soerens, *Everywhere You Look*, 25.

from passages such as Isaiah 65, one can begin to see issues of racial, economic, environmental, and housing justice affecting people in those neighborhoods as relevant to God's mission, and by devoting ourselves to one place, we can build momentum to work on more impactful initiatives alongside other people of peace who are also committed to that place.

The Neighborhood as a Source of Spiritual Formation and Imagination

This shift in missional focus also has implications for our spiritual formation. As we allow ourselves to be formed by God and by our neighborhood through inescapable proximity, our heart is broken and reshaped by mutual relationships of friendships, shifting alliances, and the accountability we owe to a hyper-local democracy in which we have a role to play. I am not alone in experiencing the joy and the tears, the appreciation and defamation, that come with a life of true commitment to a neighborhood.[7] Nothing will humble you and show you the need for keeping it "Christlike" more than a neighborhood association's meeting, especially if you have skin in the game! Loving our neighbors invites vulnerability, which opens space for the Holy Spirit to be at work with its wild, creative energy. After all, as Jesus said, the wind blows wherever it pleases,[8] and it is not for the faint of heart to follow after it; our hearts must be strengthened through prayer and constant discernment. When we engage in the neighborhood faithfully, we encounter a new depth to our spiritual formation, one that challenges us to constantly be shaped in relationship to our place.

And this includes our church buildings. When we shift our orientation from our leaky roof to the neighborhood, we engage in

---

7. I find Majora Carter's book of her work in the South Bronx to provide a very honest account of the emotional cost of neighborhood engagement. See Majora Carter, *Reclaiming Your Community: You Don't Have to Move out of Your Neighborhood to Live in a Better One* (Oakland, CA: Berrett-Koehler, 2022).

8. John 3:8.

relationships of mutuality that inspire all sorts of ideas, breathing life back into our buildings and then back out into the neighborhood. Our questions shift to how is this building nurturing and sustaining the life of a healthy neighborhood. Is the shape of this building fitting the needs of this community? Do we need to make radical changes to bring about newness? How can we utilize this building to bring about God's work of restoration, repair, and reconciliation upon our common land?

The way many denominations and congregations have gone about selling and using their buildings tells me they are not considering this. Rather than a clear strategy for real estate rooted in a strong sense of identity as the body of Christ, what I have found more often instead is a reactive attitude. Instead of taking the opportunity to shape culture and lead the way in bringing about repair and racial justice through the land, we are grasping for air. When I asked Henry's denomination about the reasoning behind the sale of their building, their executive team tried to argue that they were able to support missions programming with the cash earned through the sale. But given the realities of Seattle's real estate market, it was hard to give much credence to the idea that the return on investment of a small donation to an experimental local faith expression renting a retail spot for mission would amount to the value of securing a place to host the life of the community for generations to come; a place that was safe from Seattle's speculative real estate market. From a purely financial perspective, it made me question how much this team and this denomination understood the value of their assets and how to manage them. They were either sitting on their assets by keeping buildings underutilized all over the city or throwing them away by liquidating them to the highest bidder when their limited imagination ran out. It just didn't seem right.

From an ecclesiological perspective, their behavior was even more painful to watch. While they were legally entitled to do as they wished and look at their building primarily as a financial asset, their attitude didn't break away from the traditional way of treating real estate—there was nothing particularly "Christian" about it. Furthermore, its liquidation affected the rest of our neighborhood in very concrete ways, which gets at the heart of ethical questions on the meaning of property—from the lens of love of neighbors, was it truly their building alone to sell?

EXPANDING OUR SCOPE: LAND AS A MEANS FOR REPAIR THROUGH EQUITABLE DEVELOPMENT

In the same way that we must become self-aware of our role in our neighborhoods' built environment, we must also examine carefully our role in the systemic issues related to land ownership at the regional level. Real estate is not a theologically neutral matter.[9] In the United States, land ownership is a powerful means of wealth creation with a notorious sinful origin.

I like to think of buildings as "the Ring of Power" in *The Lord of the Rings*.[10] Whenever I hear folks talking about a building they manage, I am reminded of how the ring Frodo and Gollum stewarded brought up different aspects of their personalities, depending on how healthy their attachment style and sense of self were. It looks similar when it comes to property. Whoever controls the land has power, but the land also exerts a certain kind of power upon the landowner. Without a pure, discerning heart like Frodo's, one can succumb to the temptation to hold onto the land like Gollum and lose perspective of the community around it and our mandate to work for restoration and the reconciliation of all things according to the teachings of our faith.

This is particularly relevant in the Americas. As Jim Bear Jacobs writes in this book, much like the rest of the continent, the United States was founded on stolen land,[11] and land ownership has been

9. Walter Brueggemann and Willie James Jennings have provided us with valuable theology to reflect on land ownership. See Walter Brueggemann, *The Land: Place as Gift, Promise, and Challenge in Biblical Faith* (Minneapolis: Fortress, 2002), and Willie James Jennings, *The Christian Imagination: Theology and the Origins of Race* (New Haven: Yale University Press, 2010).

10. J. R. R. Tolkien, *The Lord of the Rings* (London: HarperCollins, 1991).

11. See Jim Bear Jacobs, "Righting Some Wrongs by Returning Stolen Land," in this book.

the primary means of intergenerational wealth creation by accumulation and also by way of slave and migrant labor.[12] As Willie James Jennings notes, land has been at the center of colonization as a white supremacist project, which he describes as the practice of separating people from land and their animals for the sake of exploitation.[13] The church, and mainline denominations in particular, have benefited from their ability to acquire real estate within this system. Conversely, lack of access to land ownership is at the root of many of the issues the church seeks to help relieve. In this sense, we are pushed to examine our relationship to land ownership from the lens of racial and economic justice, and, thankfully, equitable development provides a great framework to imagine a better way forward.

As a relatively new framework[14] in community development and urban planning, equitable development has been adopted by government and community development agencies aiming at "revitalizing disinvested communities and ensuring that all residents of urban places can shape urban development and benefit from economic growth in an equitable fashion."[15] A place-based and people-based strategy, this framework adopts a comprehensive view of real estate, expanding our thinking beyond affordable housing to include racial, economic, and environmental justice, namely, promoting local businesses and access to amenities such as parks, schools, and cultural anchors in communities of color.

12. For an in-depth theological examination of the relationship between colonization, racism, capitalism, and Christian theology, see Jennings, *The Christian Imagination*.

13. Willie J. Jennings, "Can White People Be Saved? Reflections on the Relationship between Missions and Whiteness," in *Can "White" People Be Saved? Triangulating Race, Theology, and Mission*, ed. Love Sechrest, Johnny Ramírez-Johnson, and Amos Yong (Downers Grove, IL: IVP Academic, 2018), 27–43.

14. Alexander von Hoffman, "The Ingredients of Equitable Development Planning: A Cross-Case Analysis of Equitable Development Planning and CDFIs," Joint Center for Housing Studies Harvard University, accessed February 9, 2023, https://tinyurl.com/f9782trd.

15. Hoffman, "The Ingredients of Equitable Development Planning," 5.

In Seattle, the city's Equitable Development Initiative has set the ambitious goal of building the capacity of grassroots groups seeking to own land by providing grants for land acquisition and predevelopment. I have had the honor to serve on the Equitable Development Initiative board since 2017. As part of my role, I have joined others in reviewing applications by community groups requesting city funding to secure land to house creative initiatives that serve their communities in everything from housing to cultural and arts centers to child-care facilities. The Equitable Development Initiative is place-based, so groups need to be sure to serve their neighborhoods. During the same time period, I have sat through denominational meetings in which clergy and leadership complained about their underutilized, aging buildings. Where one is full of land and lacking ideas, the other is full of ideas and longing for land.

What if these denominations and these groups talked to each other? If, for example, the United Methodists were to adopt an equitable development strategy to assess their property in the Seattle region for the sake of racial justice, then they could consider liquidating some of the many buildings in the north end with a view to reinvesting that money in real estate serving redlined neighborhoods. If, in addition to securing land, the United Methodists were to adopt a place-based ecclesiology and develop means to collaborate with neighborhood groups in the south end that are full of great ideas on how to make real estate work for their community, including innovative means of ownership, I think we could witness a truly liberating partnership in many corners of Seattle. Now, if congregations were to adopt a place-based strategy and engage their neighborhoods from a perspective of collaboration and accountability to the local values, culture, diversity, and leadership, then congregations could lend their resources to facilitate community visioning of initiatives that respond directly to priorities identified by the people who live in those neighborhoods.

This is precisely what we were able to do in South Park. While we did not have a church building to put at the service of our community, we did spend many years listening to and joining in collaboration with South Park residents to identify opportunities for equitable development. In my self-imposed role as neighborhood troublemaker, I was able to host dinners and conversations with several South Park residents who cared deeply about land afford-ability. These dinners were never faith based, although it was our faith that informed the work. The goal was to listen to one another and identify goals and opportunities.

One of the main priorities we identified was the need for afford-able housing and space for the arts. I started slowly by opening a coffee shop in 2018, Resistencia Coffee, as a place-making initia-tive that would provide space for residents to connect and that would contribute to the local economy by providing a platform for local food and arts vendors. To get us started, we leveraged the resources we had within the neighborhood. Some residents con-tributed labor; others contributed financial capital. In addition, we leveraged some small grants from denominations who believed in the vision for place making as well as other grants from Commu-nity Development Financial Institutions (CDFIs).

Because from the beginning Resistencia was a "South Park by South Park" project, the coffee shop quickly became a meaning-ful place for the neighborhood, promoting connection between people and also providing an anchor for the arts. Through the re-lationships formed at the coffee shop, we were able to expand the number of folks who were part of the conversations on affordable housing and community space.

As the community grew, our corner of the neighborhood be-came a hub for the arts, community development, and food access, revealing the importance of this particular place to the well-being of our residents. With this new awareness came fear—what if this building gets sold to a random developer with no accountability to South Park? It would surely be knocked down to the ground, redeveloped at market rate, and filled with chain stores. After all, the property covered a quarter block of none other than Seattle, with its crazy real estate market!

This is when my husband, Tim, and I partnered with our friends at the Cultural Space Agency, an innovative, mission-driven, pub-lic development agency that seeks to promote access to land for the arts by communities of color in Seattle. Together we leveraged our experience and relationships in the city to raise funding to purchase this corner of South Park. When the building came up for sale in January of 2022, we were poised and ready. We put together a deal and raised the funds for the Cultural Space Agency to purchase the building and secured this piece of land for community ownership and equitable development for generations to come! The opportunities this project presents for economic justice for residents of this scrappy, young, and brown, immigrant neighborhood in Seattle is overwhelming.

But we didn't stop there. One building is not going to cut it. Our neighborhood is redlined, with a highway cutting through it. This is why I called on our friends at Placemaking US and joined the Highways to Boulevards movement by starting Reconnect South Park, an initiative to decommission the highway and reclaim forty acres of land for equitable development. The idea is ambitious, and at the beginning it was easily dismissed, but we recently secured $600,000 from the Washington state legislature for a feasibility study and community visioning. Reconnect South Park is currently led by South Park residents, and it is set up for a long and challenging journey ahead, but we are giving it our best shot.

Place-based ecclesiology can truly unlock our imagination to rethink our collective relationship to land. By understanding the important role of land and locating ourselves in our place, we are better able to think of concrete ways in which the gospel and our mission as *the body of Christ* can become incarnate in the neighborhoods we get to love. In doing so, our strategies can be guided by real people, who are part of real stories, in real places. But please note that we really can't let go of our responsibility as the church. What kind of story will we unfold for the church in North America? What will be the redemptive arc in the saga of colonization, land, neighborhood, and liberation? We get to make a dent together, if we shift our attention to God, our neighbors, and back to the land.

PART 2

For Good

6

RIGHTING SOME WRONGS
BY RETURNING STOLEN LAND

Jim Bear Jacobs

I know that one does not usually introduce oneself in a work like this. Typically, any relevant personal or professional information is reserved for a short paragraph in an about-the-author section somewhere near the back of the book. And if you're anything like me, unless a writer is really, really impressive, you probably don't take the time to seek out the relevant biographical details. But from an Indigenous worldview, this type of approach is counter-intuitive. When one is communicating, it is important to intro-duce oneself and locate oneself both physically and culturally. My name is Jim Bear Jacobs. Most people call me Jim Bear. I am Turtle Clan. I am a citizen of the Stockbridge-Munsee Band of Mohicans. The shorthand for that is simply Mohican Nation. Our current reservation is in central Wisconsin. Our ancestral home-land is the Hudson River Valley in present-day New York. I am the son of Gerald (Bear) Jacobs and Kathy Wold. I am the grand-son of Howard Jacobs and Gretta (Tousey) Jacobs. I was born and raised in the homelands of the Dakota people, in and around the Twin Cities of Minneapolis and St. Paul. And with humility and a good heart I greet you as relatives and offer some thoughts for your consideration.

WHAT RESPONSIBILITY DO CHRISTIAN CHURCHES HAVE TO THE INDIGENOUS PEOPLES OF THE LAND?

For more than a decade now there has been a growing trend within some moderate and progressive Christian faith communities to develop and utilize Indigenous land acknowledgments. These land acknowledgments are often an attempt to recognize a church's or organization's long, complicated history of colonization and ownership of land that was often swindled and stolen from Indigenous peoples. Often these land acknowledgments come out of a church's racial justice or social justice committees. And while these statements and documents are important initial steps, it is crucially important to recognize that they are in fact just that—initial steps.

Land acknowledgments are not justice. However, if done well, they can be the catalyzing spark that can lead to real justice. If current church attendance and membership projections continue as expected, over the next decade we can expect to see the closure of tens of thousands of churches, leaving denominations and congregations with a number of difficult questions to navigate. What does a good death look like for a community? How do pastors and church boards faithfully shepherd a flock through its final breaths? What is a socially responsible way to deal with billions of dollars in church real estate assets that will no longer be utilized for worship? And if these congregations have already acknowledged that their sanctuary sits on stolen Indigenous lands, what is the responsible way forward as the church wrestles to balance Indigenous land justice and ecclesial property? In an era of racial and social justice, when the cry for reparations is ever increasing, what responsibility does the church have to the Indigenous peoples of the land?

In order for churches to responsibly address the issues of how to deal with land and property that may no longer be of use to them, they must understand the legal basis for land ownership in the first place. The reality is that when it comes to private land ownership in the United States, there are no clean hands. In their book *Mine! How the Hidden Rules of Ownership Control Our Lives*,

Michael Heller and James Salzman put it into perspective: "It's no exaggeration to say that human history is a series of adverse possession conflicts writ large. Conquests, genocides, historical injustices, and dispossessions create new land claims. Over time these brutal, profoundly destructive events become the basis of ownership. It's not pretty. Nor is it fair. But it's everywhere you look. When you buy a home, your ownership is traced through the chain of title—the record of sellers and buyers of that parcel going all the way back to the origin of ownership."[1]

Damage Done by the Doctrine of Discovery

This chain-of-title process applies not only to private home ownership but is also part of church property ownership. Whenever a church purchases property, it adds its name to a story of ownership and selling. "Often that chain starts in a grant from the American government or a state following the conquest of Native peoples."[2] The authority to own title deed to any parcel of land in the United States is rooted in a series of often-forgotten papal documents from the fifteenth century known collectively as the doctrine of discovery.

As the age of European global exploration was dawning, the first of the collection of decrees that would come to collectively be known as the doctrine of discovery was issued on June 18, 1452. Pope Nicholas V issued the papal bull *Dum Diversas*. This decree authorized King Alfonso V of Portugal to seize any land already not under a European crown and to seize and enslave any non-baptized Indigenous persons inhabiting said lands. The specific language of the decree grants Alfonso the authority

> to invade, search out, capture, vanquish, and subdue all Saracens (Muslims) and pagans whatsoever, and other enemies

1. Michael Heller and James Salzman, *Mine! How the Hidden Rules of Ownership Control Our Lives* (New York: Doubleday, 2021), 54.
2. Heller and Salzman, *Mine!*, 55.

of Christ wheresoever placed, and the kingdoms, dukedoms, principalities, dominions, possessions, and all movable and immovable goods whatsoever held and possessed by them and to reduce their persons to perpetual slavery, and to apply and appropriate to himself and his successors the kingdoms, dukedoms, counties, principalities, dominions, possessions, and goods, and to convert them to his and their use and profit—by having secured the said faculty, the said King Alfonso, or, by his authority, the aforesaid infant, justly and lawfully has acquired and possessed and doth possess these islands, lands, harbors, and seas, and they do of right belong and pertain to the said King Alfonso and his successors.[3]

In this decree we see the overwhelming arrogance of the European church. Never mind that "The earth is the LORD's and all that is in it, the world, and those who live in it" (Ps. 24:1), Pope Nicholas V expanded this dominion to include all Catholic European nations in the papal bull *Romanus Pontifex* in 1455. And in 1493, Pope Alexander VI issued the papal bull *Inter Caetera*. This edict limited the notion of dominion by proclaiming that one Christian nation did not have the right to establish dominion over lands that another Christian nation had previously dominated.[4]

The effect of the doctrine of discovery on global Indigenous peoples was as inhumane as it was widespread. Barring baptism and acceptance of Christian ideals, these newly discovered people were now enemies of God. It did not enter, and indeed could not have entered, the minds of the fifteenth-century explorers that the people they encountered were the *imago Dei* (image of God). When they landed on new shores, the Indigenous people, and the lands they inhabited, were nothing more than resources

3. Indigenous Values Initiative, "Dum Diversas," Doctrine of Discovery Project, July 23, 2018, https://tinyurl.com/3pnjvtxe.
4. Indigenous Values Initiative, "Inter Caetera," trans. Sebastian Modrow and Melissa Smith, Doctrine of Discovery Project, June 13, 2022, https://tinyurl.com/2nu45yz8.

to be extracted and utilized for the glory of God and for king and crown. The doctrine of discovery became the theological foundation for the transatlantic slave trade and the wholesale genocide of Indigenous people.

The doctrine of discovery secured the authority of discovery and the domination that came with it, for the subsequent successors of the European monarchs. As the Commonwealth and eventually independent nations arose out of these European monarchies, the privileges of the doctrine of discovery were inherited by these new nations. In 1792, Thomas Jefferson, the US secretary of state, asserted that the European doctrine of discovery was international law and therefore was applicable to the newly formed US government. The United States was now one of the inheritors of a fifteenth-century theological decree.

The doctrine of discovery became codified into United States law in the 1823 US Supreme Court case *Johnson v. McIntosh*. In this case, two American men were claiming ownership of the same parcel of land. McIntosh bought the land from the federal government, while Johnson bought the land direct from the Native tribe inhabiting the land. The question was then brought to the court: Who was the rightful owner of the land? In a unanimous opinion, Marshall used historical analysis to find that only the government, rather than the Native American tribes, held title to the land. He argued that the patterns of discovery during the European colonization of the New World meant that each European nation gained sovereignty (and also title) over the land that it discovered. This trumped the right of occupancy of the Native American tribes, at least with regard to the specific colonizing power. For the United States, this right belonged to the British when they first acquired colonies. The federal government then inherited the right from Great Britain after the American Revolution. Native Americans could not sell their land except to the federal government.[5]

---

5. Johnson & Graham's Lessee v. McIntosh, 21 U.S. 543 (1823), https://tinyurl.com/5e86ck6w.

From this *Johnson v. McIntosh* decision it was established that the right of ownership and subsequently sale of land was solely held by the US government. Indigenous nations held a right of occupancy, at the will of the US government, but no inherent rights of ownership. The doctrine of discovery was cited as established precedent for property law as recently as 2005 by Ruth Bader Ginsburg in the case *City of Sherrill v. Oneida Indian Nation of New York*. In again another land dispute, Ginsburg stated that "Under the Doctrine of Discovery, fee title to the lands occupied by Indians when the colonists arrived became vested in the sovereign—first the discovering European nation and later the original states and the United States."[6] The entirety of land ownership law in the United States is founded upon the doctrine of discovery. And it is with this notion that all churches, not just dying churches, must wrestle.

To the credit of many churches, there has been widespread repudiation of the doctrine of discovery. From local congregations to national denominational gatherings, more and more ecclesial bodies are recognizing the ungodly injustice and historical trauma upon Indigenous peoples that is the legacy of a church that is wrapped up with empire. The Episcopal Church was the early forerunner in this repudiation movement when in 2009 it resolved "That the 76th General Convention repudiates and renounces the Doctrine of Discovery as fundamentally opposed to the Gospel of Jesus Christ and our understanding of the inherent rights that individuals and peoples have received from God."[7] Since that first official repudiation in 2009, several other denominations have proposed and passed similar resolutions. To date, over twenty denominations or national religious organizations, including at least one evangelical denomination and a handful of Roman Catholic organizations, have publicly renounced the

6. Dana Lloyd, "City of Sherrill v. Oneida Indian Nation of New York," Doctrine of Discovery Project, October 19, 2022, https://tinyurl.com/24rvtbzu.
7. Acts of Convention: Resolution #2009-D035, Archives of the Episcopal Church, 2009, https://tinyurl.com/4p526whr.

doctrine. These denominations have largely been in the United States and Canada; however, the list of those repudiating the doctrine includes the Uniting Church in Sweden and the World Council of Churches.

REPAIR AND RIGHTING OF WRONGS

In the wake of all these churches repudiating the doctrine of discovery, one must ask, What is the point? In what ways do these eloquently worded resolutions of repudiation and repentance mitigate the harm to Indigenous people? How does this move the church closer to living out the call of the gospel? The short answer is, they don't. Grandiose proclamations don't in any way benefit the lived experience of Native people. Following the surge of repudiations, many local congregations and even denominations have developed curricula to allow their members to become more aware of and better educated about the doctrine of discovery. Again, this does nothing to help Native people. Many of these local congregations and denominations have gone on to develop land acknowledgment statements. These statements are often printed and posted or read before events and worship services. They often acknowledge the Indigenous people that once inhabited the lands that the congregation currently occupies. They will usually recognize that the land was acquired from Indigenous people through unjust and immoral means. More often than not, they will express deep gratitude and acknowledge the Native tribe for stewarding the land and being an example of how to live in right relationship with creation. (I am being somewhat hyperbolic in this summation, but not much.) Again, in terms of the repair to Indigenous people and communities? Nothing.

Jesus teaches us how we, as people of God, are to act when there is a relationship that needs repair. "So when you are offering your gift at the altar, if you remember that your brother or sister has something against you, leave your gift there before the altar and go; first be reconciled to your brother or sister, and then come and offer your gift" (Matt. 5:23–24). During Jesus's earthly ministry, bringing your gift or offering to the altar was the central act of worship. It was a public symbol that one was a person of God. In this passage Jesus is essentially telling his audience that if they are not going to be about the repair of fractured relationships, then they should dispense with the empty theater of pursuing righteousness. God does not want your offering until you are in reconciled relationship with your brother or sister. In other words, unless your repudiation and acknowledgment move the church to actual repair of the generations of trauma within the Native community, it is nothing more than a meaningless, unacceptable offering.

It is the responsibility of all churches, and indeed of all humanity, to be agents of justice in a broken world. Any work of justice that intersects with Indigenous people will have to contend with the issue of stolen land. Christians love to use the word "reconciliation." Indeed, even in the foregoing Matthew passage Jesus speaks of reconciling with our brother or sister. Osage author and theologian George Tinker speaks of reconciliation this way:

"Christians like to talk about reconciliation . . . *re-concile*, to concile again. And Indians won't have it. We aren't conciled. We were pushed and pushed out of our lands, our people killed, our cultures and languages destroyed. When they talk about reconciliation, what Christians are really saying is, 'Can you forgive us for when we took the land?' The bottom line is, 'Can we keep the land in good conscience?'"[8]

In 2012 I had the pleasure of sharing space with George Tinker, and his words were very clear. "Accept no apologies, without the return of land!"[9] As the church continues to decline, and more and more congregations wrestle with how to face a communal death

8. Quoted in Terra Brockman, "Decolonized Sacred Land: How a Church Became the Home of an American Indian Organization," *Christian Century*, March 11, 2020.

9. Mahle Lecture in Progressive Christian Thought, Hamline University, St. Paul, April 17, 2012.

in a dignified way, they will have to come to terms with what to do with their land and buildings. I would like to suggest that one option that should be at the top of the list is to return the land to Indigenous tribes or organizations. Given the immoral legacy of how the land came to be "owned" in the first place, through the doctrine of discovery, and the current trend of recognizing and acknowledging that the land is in fact stolen, "land back" or land return can be the only real viable option for communities that truly want to lean into the gospel.

In 2015 George Tinker oversaw just such a land return. For decades prior to the property return, a church building in Denver, Colorado, was co-utilized by the Rocky Mountain Synod of the Evangelical Lutheran Church in America and the Four Winds American Indian Council. The building was legally owned by the Rocky Mountain Synod. Four Winds used the building as a hub and community center to serve Denver's nearly forty thousand American Indian residents. As the community around the church began to change and it was no longer viable for the synod to continue to own the building, decisions had to be made about what to do with the building. From a capitalistic perspective, the obvious choice was to sell the property to some developer and, with your final breath as a congregation, make as much money as the market would allow. This, however, would jeopardize Four Winds and almost certainly require the Native community center to uproot and relocate. The optics of Native Americans being dispossessed of their home and forcibly relocated were not lost on anyone involved. Rather than pursuing avenues of capitalistic self-advancement, the Rocky Mountain Synod declined to sell the property, even turning down an offer of one million dollars, and instead chose to turn over the land and the building to Four Winds. This allowed the Native community center to remain in its location and boldly state that their facility is not an abandoned church: "This is decolonized land. This is a liberated zone."[10]

10. Brockman, "Decolonized Sacred Land."

Followers of Christ everywhere should all be able to agree, if our gospel does not cause us to follow the example of Jesus and turn away from self-preservation, and passionately work toward liberation and justice, then it is in fact not gospel. It is not good news. Over the last few years, across Indian country we have seen a handful of land-return gestures. From governments both state and federal, to civic organizations and some churches, it seems that the idea of returning land to Indigenous hands is taking root in the collective imagination. And even though I legitimately applaud all these efforts, I think that the church can do better.

I long for a day when land-back justice would not be reserved for the last breath of dying churches. Don't get me wrong. I celebrate anytime land is returned to Indigenous people. But returning land that is used up and buildings that might be crumbling is not really the gesture that works to undo systems of historic oppression. It does not move the needle of social justice as much as we might think it does. It is my hope that everyone that is reading this and associated with a church would consider carefully returning land to Indigenous people long before the writing of their own demise is on the wall. When the apostle Paul speaks of the *kenosis* of Jesus in Philippians chapter 2, he implores believers to empty themselves of power. I would suggest that returning land to its rightful inhabitants, as a last act of life, is not emptying. It is not *kenosis*. Instead, I want churches to consider true vulnerability, true *kenosis*, true emptying of power.

Imagine vibrant, living churches forming meaningful relationships with Indigenous-led organizations. Imagine that these relationships move beyond the usual missional and transactional superficialities. Imagine that the church opens itself to truly receive the teachings and wisdom that come from Native communities. Now imagine that out of this relationship the church—this still-living, still-thriving, even still-growing church—out of an urgency for justice, puts action to their faith and returns the land they occupy. Then with all of that vulnerability, all of that emptying of power, the church humbly asks permission to continue to utilize the land and building. Can you just imagine how palpable the

Spirit would be at that sacred ceremony of healing? This is what our repudiations, our acknowledgments, our apologies, must lead us to. This is the gospel of healing. May the church heed the call of the gospel. May the church put action to their repentance. May the church restore that which has been stolen and work to heal that which has been broken. May it be so. May it forever be so.

7

CROSSING THE LAND, HEARING THE SPIRIT

Keith Starkenburg

I was recently at a forum dedicated to the care of Mato Paha as it is known in Lakota, or Noavose as it is known in Cheyenne, or Bear Butte, which is a part of Bear Butte State Park outside of Sturgis, South Dakota. The park manager distributed a map showing that a third of the land around the mountain has been bought by representatives of the Lakota, Cheyenne, and Arapaho nations, costing millions of dollars over the last two decades.[1] The park manager, who is Lakota, mentioned that, although these nations have many other pressing needs, they want to protect the mountain. These nations purchase these parcels of land to care for the land and to protect it for prayer and ceremony. One of the Lakota participants mentioned that he thought it was strange that the Lakota were buying land that, according to the Fort Laramie Treaty of 1868, belonged to them. He was smiling but also quite serious. This sentiment is not unique. If you are around representatives of the Lakota and other Indigenous nations, and you are listening, these kinds of experiences will not be uncommon.

---

1. Clara Caufield, "Tribal Purchase at Bear Butte 'Noavose' (no-wah-wiss)," *Native Sun News Today*, January 9, 2019, https://tinyurl.com/yc7aen6t; "3 Native American Tribes Buy Bear Butte Land for 1.1M," Associated Press, November 19, 2016, https://tinyurl.com/48k7yjtw.

My task is to consider what these land claims mean for congregations who are struggling with what to do with their land. Non-Indigenous will tend to hear these claims as simply a matter of property rights and the execution of the stipulations of treaties or contracts as well as the enforcement of federal, state, local, and tribal laws. That is indeed part of the story. For many non-Indigenous folks, however, a fuller understanding of these claims requires a closer look at both the sacred narrative of Scripture and the history and experience of Indigenous nations.

This chapter has three parts. First, I want to set out a theological account, in biblical terms, of how nationhood, people, and land play a role in the economy of God's work in creation. In terms of my own history, this is an account of the gospel in biblical terms that I have come to embrace after I learned to listen to Indigenous people—both Christians and non-Christians—describing their situation, their history, and their desires for the future. Second, I want to show how this theological account can help us understand the current situation of Indigenous nations in Turtle Island/North America. Third, very briefly, I want to add a few comments in support of what Jim Bear Jacobs asks of congregations in this volume.

THE HEALING OF THE NATIONS

The gospel is an announcement of the healing of the nations. The book of Revelation has a multifaceted vision of the end of creation in Revelation 21-22 that depicts this healing: "Then the angel showed me the river of the water of life, bright as crystal, flowing from the throne of God and of the Lamb through the middle of the street of the city. On either side of the river is the tree of life with its twelve kinds of fruit, producing its fruit each month; and the leaves of the tree are for the healing of the nations" (22:1-2). In these sentences, the seer describes a future in which God in Christ's presence and de facto rule allows the nations to be healed. To understand this reality more deeply, especially in light of Indigenous histories and habits, I pose and answer these questions:

What are the nations? Why do the nations need to be healed? How are they healed? What does healing look like?

What are the nations? It helps to begin with the picture of creation provided in the earliest chapters of Genesis. In the garden of Eden, humanity and the land are who and what they are because of their relationships to one another.[2] Adam bears essentially the same name as the land: "the LORD God formed [Adam] from the dust of the [Adamah (the ground)], and breathed into his nostrils the breath of life" (Gen. 2:7). From the perspective of the human being, to be Adam is to be from the *adamah*. Humanity's purpose is to enjoy God's presence in the park in which humanity is placed (2:8), and that enjoyment includes the task of serving and protecting the ground from which he comes (2:15). From the perspective of the land, to be the *adamah* is to be a host to Adam. Just as human beings are to care for the ground, the land also cared for them. Before there was rain from God's hand, a stream rose from the land to water the ground (2:10). When God called, the *earth* responded and brought forth vegetation that human beings could eat (1:12, 29). Human beings and the land come from each other and care for one another. Their names, and thus their identities, include that relationship.

How do the nations fit into this? The first uses of the Hebrew word for nation—*goy*—appear in Genesis 10, the Table of Nations. The Table of Nations is a set of genealogies of the descendants of Shem, Ham, and Japheth—the progenitors of all of humanity in the wake of the great flood in Genesis 6–9. The table is a way to note that the nation of Israel shares a common history and ancestry with all of humanity, even as it is called to be the nation that blesses the other nations of the earth.[3] Each genealogy in the table ends with this formula (with some variation): "These are

2. See Mari Joerstad, *The Hebrew Bible and Environmental Ethics* (Cambridge: Cambridge University Press, 2019), 49, and H. Daniel Zacharias, "Graceland: The Land as Relational Gift in the Bible," *Journal of NAITTS: An Indigenous Learning Community* 17 (2019): 160–62.

3. See J. Daniel Hays, *From Every People and Nation* (Downers Grove, IL: InterVarsity Press, 2003), 56–63. Richard Bauckham highlights the impor-

the descendants of . . . in their lands, with their own language, by their families, in their nations" (10:5, 20, 31). The nations are distinguished by kinship relationships between humans, by their language, but also by their land. The text recognizes the tie between the land and people insofar as the names of these nations signify both the land and the individual to which a nation is related. Cush, Egypt, and Canaan are obvious examples.[4] Adam and *adamah* are identified by their relationship. Just so, the identity of peoples includes their belonging to a particular land, and the identity of lands includes hosting particular people. This is part of what it means to be a nation.

In describing Israel's history with God, Walter Brueggemann writes that "The Bible is the story of God's people with God's land."[5] This is true not only for Israel but also for other nations in some way.[6] On the one hand, God gives land to peoples. Deuteronomy reports that Israel was instructed in the wilderness not to take the land of Esau's family (2:5), the Moabites (2:9), or the Ammonites (2:19). Just as the nations are given the land as a "possession" (2:5, 9, 19), just so Israel is given land as a "possession" (4:20-21). On the other hand, God gives peoples to lands. The relationship between the land and people is so interwoven that the land's cleanness depends on the people's cleanness (Lev. 18:28). If the people become too unclean, the Lord warns that the land will vomit out Israel just as the land vomited out the previous inhabitants (Lev. 18:27-28; 20:22).[7] People and land are given to one another and thus depend on one another as agents of God's pro-

---

tance of Gen. 10 for Revelation in ways that cannot be fully explored here (*The Climax of Prophecy* [Edinburgh: T&T Clark, 1993], 327-37).

4. Victor Hamilton, *The Book of Genesis: Chapters 1-17* (Grand Rapids: Eerdmans, 1990), 332.

5. Walter Brueggemann, *The Land*, 2nd ed. (Minneapolis: Fortress, 2002), 12.

6. See Walter Brueggemann, "Exodus in the Plural," in *Texts That Linger, Words That Explode* (Minneapolis: Fortress, 2000), 89-103; Christopher Wright, *Mission of God* (Downers Grove, IL: IVP Academic, 2006), 462-67.

7. See Joerstad, *The Hebrew Bible*, 75-77.

vision, as participants in God's care. That mutual dependence is part of what creates the identities of the nations that emerge from that relationship.

Nations, then, emerge from relationships between specific peoples and lands as they are given to each other by God for each other's benefit. The nations, in sum, are gathered groups of creatures who find a shared identity in mutual giving and receiving before the God who brought them into being.

Why do they need healing? The nations tend to worship creatures rather than the Creator, and the book of Isaiah calls out the ramifications of this misdirected worship. Assyria is arrogant and idol making (10:10-13) in its ravenous desire to conquer others (10:7). Babylon cuts down trees with abandon (14:8) and is given to arrogance and self-worship in its military and political dominance (14:13-14). Philistia's policies mean that the poor do not eat and cannot be safe (14:30). Moab oppresses (16:4), and Ethiopia conquers (18:2). Israel worships idols (2:7-8) and over-develops the land such that the poor cannot glean from it (5:8; cf. Lev. 23:22). The nations, peoples, and lands as gathered bodies do not know how to live with one another before God in peace.[8] In short, the nations need healing from their spiritual, social, economic, and ecological sin.

The nations also need to heal from multifaceted suffering, including the dismemberment of the nations, the tearing apart of lands and peoples. In Lamentations, the people of Israel plead with God in exile,

> Remember, O LORD, what has befallen us;
> look, and see our disgrace!
> Our inheritance has been turned over to strangers,
> our homes to aliens.
> We have become like orphans, fatherless;
> our mothers are like widows. (Lam. 5:1-3)

---

8. Wright, *Mission of God*, 457-58.

The lament is that they have lost their *relative*. The land is their father, their spouse. The family has been dismembered. From the perspective of the land, 2 Chronicles notes that the land has finally received a Sabbath rest (2 Chron. 36:21; cf. Lev. 25:1-7).[9] Yet, in this rest, the land is also said to mourn and lament. Indeed, the opening lines of Lamentations describe Zion's loss from the perspective of the city itself:

> How lonely sits the city
>> that once was full of people!
> How like a widow she has become,
>> that was great among the nations! . . .
> She weeps bitterly in the night,
>> with tears on her cheeks;
> among all her lovers
>> she has no one to comfort her. (Lam. 1:1-2)

The exile is, for the land too, the dismemberment of something like a marital relationship. The people *and* the land are both widowed in the exile. This suffering happens in other nations as well.[10]

How are the nations healed? In short, the nations are healed by God's entrance into creation in Jesus Christ. As the apostle Paul teaches, "Through him God was pleased to reconcile to himself all things, whether on earth or in heaven, by making peace through the blood of his cross" (Col. 1:20). How does this work? In Jesus's life and death, God enters and becomes a member of what is broken: Israel and the nations. Christ is the oldest brother "within a large family" (Rom. 8:29) of both Jews and gentiles (11:23-24). As Christ identifies with Israel and thus with all gentile nations (given Israel's vocation as stated in Exodus 19:5-6 and elsewhere), somehow, when something happens to him, it happens to the whole of reality. As the apostle Paul says, "I have been crucified with Christ" (Gal. 2:19). Jesus's death, then, is a dismemberment, a dis-

---

9. Zacharias, "Graceland," 167.
10. See Isa. 13:18-20; 16:9; 23:4; 34:10-11.

placement, a loss of inheritance (Mark 12:7; Luke 15:13). But, that dismemberment, that displacement, that loss of inheritance, that brokenness is made whole in the resurrection. As such, when Paul writes that Jesus Christ is the "firstborn of all creation" (Col. 1:15) and "firstborn from the dead" (1:18), he indicates that when Christ is raised, heaven and earth are raised with him.[11] When Christ is raised, he himself becomes the inheritance, the site of all the blessings of the Spirit—holiness, adoption, redemption, forgiveness, the revelation of God's will, and the worship offered to God, among many other realities (Eph. 1:3-9, 11). Even more, when Christ is raised, he inherits the cosmos along with those who are united to him by the Spirit (Rom. 4:13).[12] The nations, in Christ, as Revelation states, "will inherit these things" (Rev. 21:7) in the new Jerusalem. In his life and death, Jesus Christ suffers the displacement of the nations. In his resurrection, he brings an inheritance—a new sharing in God's life and the perfected cosmos—that can never be lost.

What, then, does healing look like? In Isaiah, for example, God promises to the exiled people of Israel a homecoming to the land (43:5) and that the land will receive its people in songs of praise (49:19; 55:12). Isaiah also includes other nations in this declaration of homecoming, unveiling that the nations will be at home in their lands while also being at home with one another. Isaiah articulates this in an oracle about Egypt, Assyria, and Israel:

> On that day there will be five cities in the land of Egypt that speak the language of Canaan and swear allegiance to the LORD of hosts. One of these will be called the City of the Sun. On that

11. See Keith Starkenburg, "What's Good for Christ Is Good for the Cosmos: Affirming the Resurrection of Creation," *Pro Ecclesia* 30, no. 1 (2020): 71-97.

12. For biblical scholarship on a Pauline theology of inheritance, see Mark Forman, *The Politics of Inheritance in Romans* (Cambridge: Cambridge University Press, 2011); Esau McCaulley, *Sharing in the Son's Inheritance: Davidic Messianism and Paul's Worldwide Interpretation of the Abrahamic Land Promise in Galatians* (Edinburgh: T&T Clark, 2021).

day there will be an altar to the LORD in the center of the land
of Egypt, and a pillar to the LORD at its border. It will be a sign
and a witness to the LORD of hosts in the land of Egypt; when
they cry to the LORD because of oppressors, he will send them
a savior, and will defend and deliver them. The LORD will make
himself known to the Egyptians; and the Egyptians will know
the LORD on that day, and will worship with sacrifice and burnt
offering, and they will make vows to the LORD and perform
them. The LORD will strike Egypt, striking and healing; they
will return to the LORD, and he will listen to their supplications
and heal them. On that day there will be a highway from Egypt
to Assyria, and the Assyrian will come into Egypt, and the Egyp-
tian into Assyria, and the Egyptians will worship with the Assyrians. On that day Israel will be the third with Egypt and Assyria,
a blessing in the midst of the earth, whom the LORD of hosts
has blessed, saying, "Blessed be Egypt my people, and Assyria
the work of my hands, and Israel my heritage." (Isa. 19:18-25)[13]

This is an end to idolatry, to dismemberment, to desolation,
and to isolation from one another. Egypt will be Egypt. Assyria will
be Assyria. Israel will be Israel. Lands and peoples are not given
up, nor are they isolated from one another. Assyrians, Egyptians,
and Israelites are both within their land and within the lands of
others. To be in is to be out, and to be out is to be in. Nations—
peoples and lands—will be distinct in culture, with borders that
allow for the differences to be crossed through the act of worship.
Their lands and people are connected, crossed by a highway worn
into place by pilgrimages between them. If peoples and lands
make nations, then nations cannot be made whole without land
and people being brought back into relationships of mutual gift-
giving and harmony before their Maker.

13. A key article on this text is John F. A. Sawyer, "'Blessed Be My People Egypt': The Context and Meaning of a Remarkable Passage," in *Word
in Season: Essays in Honor of William McKane*, ed. Philip Davies and James
Martin (Sheffield: Sheffield Academic Press, 1986), 57-71.

These prophetic declarations become, in Christ and the Spirit, indicators of an eschaton—an end to creation—that is currently under way in anticipation of Christ's return.[14] In Revelation 21-22, in depicting that end of creation, the new Jerusalem is one land, but it is a land that gathers the nations as they walk by the light of God in Christ (21:24). In a sense, the new Jerusalem is both a home and a highway, a place where all belong and a place that unites all other places. As Revelation reveals, "the kings of the earth will bring their glory into it" (21:24) and "people will bring into it the glory and honor of the nations" (21:26). But how will they worship, how will they bring their glory? In a similar description of the final gathering of nations, Isaiah writes that

> The glory of Lebanon shall come to you,
>> the cypress, the plane, and the pine,
> to beautify the place of my sanctuary;
>> and I will glorify where my feet rest. (60:13)

When the nations worship, they bring their lands with them to contribute to the sacred art of the temple, just as Israel brought the fruit of its fields in festival to Jerusalem.[15] The new Jerusalem is a place where the nations are healed because it is a chance for all of them, in differentiated unity, to give the mutual creations of their lands and peoples to the One who has given them to each other. The new Jerusalem is the place where all nations, all gath-

---

14. Richard Hays, in describing Paul's hermeneutic of Scripture (including Isaiah), writes that "He calls his converts to understand that they live at the turning point of the ages, so that all the scriptural narratives and promises must be understood to point forward to the crucial eschatological moment in which he and the churches find themselves" (*The Conversion of the Imagination* [Grand Rapids: Eerdmans, 2005], 11).

15. As Greg Beale writes, "the depiction is that of nations now bringing everything they possess to God"; *Revelation: A Shorter Commentary* (Grand Rapids: Eerdmans, 2015), 295. Beale does not mention the fruits of the land being brought forward, but that would be the implication of his insight if the creation is brought back to life.

ered fellowships of land and people, cross over into one another as they offer themselves to their Creator in Christ, by the Spirit.

DESCRIBING THE SITUATION IN NORTH AMERICA IN LIGHT OF THE HEALING OF THE NATIONS

In 1980, the United States Supreme Court ruled that Lakota people deserved compensation for the loss of the Black Hills due to its seizure in 1877. In the decision, the court quoted an earlier court's description of the case: "A more ripe and rank case of dishonorable dealing will never, in probability, be found in our history."[16] The Lakota nation was awarded $102 million, but they refused it. They still refuse the money to this day.[17]

How do we interpret this situation? Is it a matter simply of theft or robbery? It is that, but there is much more to see. Consider how Frank Fools Crow, an important leader of the Lakota and a committed follower of Jesus, testified to a congressional subcommittee in 1976: "The Black Hills are sacred to the Lakota people. Both the Sacred Pipe and the Black Hills go hand in hand in our religion. The Black Hills is our church, the place where we worship. The Black Hills is our burial grounds. The bones of our grandfathers lie buried in those hills. How can you expect us to sell our church and our cemeteries for a few token white-man dollars? We will never sell."[18] The Black Hills is a church and a burial ground that has been taken. That would be enough to say. Yet Fools Crow's reference to the Sacred Pipe indicates more.

The Sacred Pipe refers to the ceremonial pipe given to the Lakota in the Black Hills by the White Buffalo Calf Woman, a figure who plays an important role in the formation of the Lakota nation. According to the account of Nicholas Black Elk (another commit-

16. *United States v. Sioux Nation of Indians*, 448 U.S. 371 (1980).
17. See Jeffrey Ostler, *The Lakotas and the Black Hills* (New York: Penguin Books, 2010).
18. Thomas E. Mails, *Fools Crow* (Lincoln: University of Nebraska Press, 1979), 212.

ted Christian), she gave the pipe as a sign of all creatures. The bowl, carved with an image of a buffalo, comes from the earth. The stem represents that which grows from the earth, and the attached feathers signify creatures of the air. As a result, this happens in ceremony:

> All these peoples, and all the things of the universe, are joined to you who smoke the pipe—all send their voices to Wakan-Tanka, the Great Spirit. When you pray with this pipe, you pray for and with everything. . . . With this pipe you will be bound to all your relatives: your Grandfather and Father, your Grandmother and Mother. This round rock, which is made of the same red stone as the bowl of the pipe, your Father Wakan-Tanka has also given you. It is the Earth, your Grandmother and Mother, and it is where you will live and increase.[19]

In terms of western European culture, smoking the pipe is something like a marriage-renewal ceremony before God. The pipe ceremony recognizes and deepens familial bonds between all the creatures involved. In addition, the pipe was smoked at the Fort Laramie Treaties in 1851 and 1868, further binding the Lakota to the Black Hills.[20] Fools Crow, speaking forthrightly to a non-Lakota audience in terms they could at least find plausible, was articulating that the Lakota nation is a body identified through place, made of a people and land. Before God, the Lakota are the Black Hills, and the Black Hills are the Lakota. To give up the Black Hills would be to give up their family. To give up the Black Hills would be to give up themselves. To give up the Black Hills would be to give up their Creator.

This means that the loss to the Lakota and to the Black Hills, just as it was for Israel in exile, is the dismemberment of a family. This has happened for many other nations in North America. The

19. Joseph Epes Brown, ed., *The Sacred Pipe* (Norman: University of Oklahoma Press, 1989), 5–7.
20. Ostler, *The Lakotas and the Black Hills*, 39.

Odawa, the Potawatomi, the Keetowah, and many, many others have been dismembered or at least maimed. The Lakota can visit the Black Hills, can purchase land in the Black Hills, and can visit the uniquely sacred sites. However, they do not have a full share in the caretaking of those sites or other federally owned land in the Black Hills. They need the permission of federal or state government officials to care for or enact their lives on this land. The land, for its part, is at the mercy of federal and state governments in its yearning to host its peoples. Yet, the Lakota and the Black Hills still exist, even if at one time the United States did indeed try to "Kill the Indian and Save the Man." Their national body has been maimed, not destroyed. Many nations are in a similar position. Some fare better, and some have been destroyed through displacement and assimilation.

What is the situation of the church in all of this? When it comes to the dismemberment of Indigenous nations, the nations that derived from European settlement are chiefly responsible for what has happened, including the United States. As institutions, churches did what they could at times to resist this or alleviate this, but they also cooperated and benefited from this dismemberment, as did many other institutions.[21] Residential schools are perhaps the worst example of how many churches in North America cooperated with this dismemberment.[22] At this time, given the history

21. For example, the American Board of Commissioners for Foreign Missions, Jeremiah Evarts, Samuel Worcester, Elizar and Esther Butler resisted the removal of the Keetoowah/Cherokee from Georgia. See John Andrew III, *From Revivals to Removal* (Athens: University of Georgia Press, 1992).

22. See David Wallace Adams, *Education for Extinction: American Indians and the Boarding School Experience, 1875–1928*, 2nd ed. (Lawrence: University of Kansas Press, 2020 [1995]). How did the church come to cooperate with the colonial project? Jim Bear Jacobs, in this volume, points to the doctrine of discovery, a theological-legal-cultural practice of European civil and ecclesiastical powers that justified European lands claims through discovery (see Robert Miller, *Native America, Discovered and Conquered* [Lincoln: University of Nebraska Press, 2008]). The evil cultural habit of colonialism in

of the United States, I believe that owning land in most places in the United States is part of the dishonoring of Indigenous people and the land itself until the United States and other institutions—including churches—can find ways to repair their relationships with Indigenous nations.

However, even if we could somehow make a case that church institutions were only resistant to the dismemberment of Indigenous nations (which is not true), the church is always and everywhere a church of nations, as the book of Revelation attests. The highway crossing of the nations is a sign of the church that, somehow, we already have among us. The new Jerusalem is a gathering of nations. Yet it is gathering for a purpose. As a sign of that new Jerusalem, the nations are gathered into the church by the Spirit to be healed not simply at the end of time but even now. At the end of Revelation, the Holy Spirit and the church ask Jesus Christ to come, to return, and ask others to join them in this prayer. The author then adds:

> And let everyone who is thirsty come.
> Let anyone who wishes take the water of life as a gift.
>
> (22:17)

It is the water of life that waters the tree of life—all images of God's life—and that water is available even now. Revelation presents both a future impossible to achieve without a new divine act and a future in which the church is invited and called to participate. The church is meant to be a place where the nations heal as they partake of God's life.

---

relationship to Christianity includes other factors as well, and reflecting on this should include thinking about the dynamics of white supremacy and supercessionism (for example, see Willie Jennings, "Can White People Be Saved? Reflections on the Relationship of Missions and Whiteness," in *Can White People Be Saved?*, ed. Love Sechrest et al. [Downers Grove, IL: IVP Academic, 2018], 27–43).

KEITH STARKENBURG

How to Follow the Spirit in Relation
to Indigenous Nations in North America

How can churches follow the Spirit and participate in the healing of the nations?

The most important thing is to consider very carefully what Indigenous leaders such as Jim Bear Jacobs articulate. Researching the history of land in which your church is situated is a key first step. If no one within the church body can undertake this kind of search, then sponsor someone who can do it for you. In part, the goal of this exercise is to listen to the land through its history, to gain a sense of what the Spirit has done in and through this land. The goal is to see and confess the truth, including what has been done against others and what the church failed to do. The church will be both uplifted and sobered, both grateful and remorseful. If it is at all mature, it will desire to do something about its relationship with the Indigenous nations who belong to that land.

All of this will mean many other practices as well. This will include befriending the peoples that belong to the land. It will involve being patient and humble about inevitable blunders and missteps with Indigenous partners. The most important thing is to listen intently, to allow relationships to unfold even when it is difficult. Yet also anticipate the potential gift of new relationships in which humor and encouragement can arise.

Most importantly, follow the advice of the apostle Paul. Allow your church to be emptied. As does Jim Bear Jacobs, Indigenous nations may ask that you place the care of the land in their hands. They may suggest that care of that land would be shared. They may ask for something else, including money. Be willing to do as much as is possible, given what the history of the land unfolds. Even if there is a relatively just history with Indigenous nations, there is still the matter of the church's witness to the other institutions in the United States, including in our more local communities. Giving up the care of the land to an Indigenous people is a sign of the healing of the nations.

Finally, some may fear that the implication of this chapter is that all land in North America needs to be placed into the exclusive care of Indigenous nations. As many Indigenous leaders have taught me, that would be to use injustice to cure injustice. While there may be some radical activists who think that a full relinquishment of land to Indigenous peoples is necessary, it is not a significant number. However, some land in the United States must be relinquished, especially uniquely sacred places such as Bear Butte. In other cases, Indigenous peoples should be given the right of first refusal to buy certain lands. In the end, most land will mostly likely continue to be held by non-Indigenous people and institutions—until, that is, dealings in just partnership allow for a more broadly shared indigeneity.[23] However, we do not control the future. Churches only need to seek truth telling and mutual relationships with Indigenous partners, and let the Spirit lead them into what healing will require.

23. I do not mean to overdraw the distinction between Indigenous and non-Indigenous. Barbara Kimmerer suggests that settlers or immigrants aim to become "naturalized" to their place (*Braiding Sweetgrass* [Minneapolis: Milkweed Editions, 2013], 214), which is the best articulation I have seen of what becoming Indigenous means for settlers and immigrants. Honest and open reflections about these dynamics must continue.

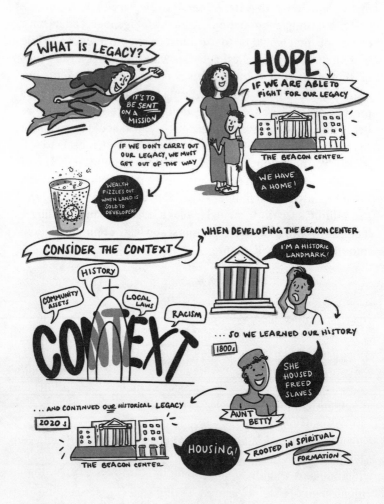

8

LEGACY CAN LEAD TO LIFE

Joseph W. Daniels Jr.

Legacy. It is a word that I've been dealing with a lot as I move beyond my thirtieth year of pastoral ministry in one place. And it is a word resonating with me as I, like many clergy over these past few years of the COVID-19 pandemic, seek to navigate the changing landscape of church in our present-day society.

Legacy. It is also a word I consistently ponder as my passion continues to grow around the issue of churches preserving and using their property to revive and revitalize neighborhoods and communities. It is a passion born out of my own journey. A long journey of leading a congregation of fifty-five people once on the brink of closure—worshiping in a decrepit building in such bad condition that congregants had to go across the street to the police station to use a decent bathroom—but now finding itself as a four-hundred-plus-member, predominantly black, working-class congregation. A congregation with twenty different nationalities from across the world, having repurposed its church building and property to build a $60 million, ninety-nine-unit, fully affordable rental housing and commercial development project called the Beacon Center in Washington, DC. Yes, in the nation's capital we did this—arguably the hardest city in which to do development because of the layers of bureaucracy and politics that occur.

Legacy. It is a word, but even more so a reality for me that at sixty-two years of age sits center stage in my forward movement as

I approach, as author Robert Wolgemuth appropriately titled one of his books, the *Gun Lap: Staying in the Race with Purpose*. I am particularly concerned about the legacy of church property and what is going to happen to churches finding themselves fighting to survive let alone thrive in the midst of crumbling edifices, shrinking congregations, irrelevant ministries, disintegrating budgets, enormous financial pressures from inside and out, the evolution of technology and hybrid worship, and alternative venues for the "fellowship of believers" to gather. If you are reading this chapter and this book as a church and civic leader, I know you are concerned, too. You are pondering legacy.

If you are not pondering it, I hope you would. For in my opinion, too many churches are abandoning their legacy for a dollar. A dollar that doesn't last nearly as long as many developers might persuade you to believe. As a former district superintendent in my denomination, the United Methodist Church, who pastored at the same time, I'm concerned that too many denominations are selling off property to keep their internal, outdated structural and staffing models sustained. And too many churches, desperate to get out from under the financial strain of keeping a dying ministry alive, are selling God's mission out to money-craving developers. Developers who cannot possibly know the history and context of a historic place like a church and community—unless they've dwelt in or been woven into the fabric of that community and church for any significant period of time.

So, the word "legacy," for these and other reasons, has been swelling in my soul over these past several years, and over the time in which I've been asked to write this chapter for this very timely book. Through it all, I've come to believe strongly that legacy can lead to life!

THE PERSONS DELEGATED

The word "legacy" comes from a late Middle English, Old French, and medieval Latin term meaning "person delegated." If I go a little deeper, "legacie" describes a "body of persons sent on a mission"— ambassadors, envoys, or deputies charged with a commission. Those appointed by someone else in a last will, yes, but the persons charged with a commission to tell those of us with still much living to do that we are being delegated with fulfilling that individual or group's wishes. We are the persons delegated to carry out a mission. A mission we are called to continue until God calls us to delegate it to others coming behind us.

Little did I know on that bright sunny day in the spring of 1994, standing in the cleaners across the street from the church I pastor with a pile of shirts in my arms waiting to be cleaned, looking out the window and seeing the entire 6100 block of Georgia Avenue, NW, that God would begin pouring out a vision and mission that would really take off fifteen years later. Because I was one of the "persons delegated" to carry out a legacy. And little did the congregation of Emory United Methodist Church, affectionately known as the Emory Fellowship, realize that they were among the "persons delegated," the "body of persons sent on a mission" charged with a commission, of fulfilling a legacy, the depths of which at the time we did not know. A legacy of ensuring that marginalized and disenfranchised people in our neighborhood and community had a safe and affordable place to lay their heads.

From the start, as church and civic leaders, when we talk about church property and preserving the use of it for the common good, we've got to ask ourselves, "Am I the person delegated?" And our congregations or organizations have to ask ourselves, "Are we the persons delegated?" The people delegated to ensure that a mission given to a church or organization to bless its community in positive, life-transforming ways continues. If we are, we need to fully embrace the process. If not, we need to get out of this game and join another game. If we embrace it, however, do know that legacy can lead to life.

It was hard to see that when we first started together as pastor and people at Emory Church, needing to revitalize an entire ministry, let alone the mausoleum-looking 1922 church building that sat atop what was known as "Vinegar Hill." White flight had left the congregation and property in a bad way. A white church that had once boasted 1,500 members in 1950, Emory had dwindled to 30 people, predominantly black, by 1976. The Brightwood neighborhood, which was all-white and did not welcome black visitors back in the 1940s and 1950s, had become predominantly black. With the civil rights movement of the 1960s, or what the late representative John Lewis of Georgia called "the Nonviolent Movement of America," in full swing, upwardly mobile and economically stronger black families began to move "uptown." Whites began fleeing to the suburbs. Government policies that made it easy for white families to purchase houses in the suburbs became the norm. Businesses moved where their primary clientele lived, and the Brightwood neighborhood, once strong and vibrant with activity, was left a shell of what it once was.

I came to Emory as a part-time pastor because once the full-time white pastor left in 1976, all the church could afford were part-time pastors for the next sixteen years. And upon arrival, the conditions of blight were real. Chipped paint all through the sanctuary, signs of water damage in many sections of the roof, wooden pews not shellacked in years, red carpet ripped to the floor, nasty-looking bathrooms, a one-hundred-year-old piano with four working keys. Fortunately, we had a good organ. And we had the foresight to use the asset of our property, even with its issues, to lease out space to a school. As many churches can relate, the income literally kept us open.

That was inside. Outside, blight was all around us. Broken alcohol bottles and crushed beer cans buried themselves into the grounds around the church. Used condoms and used syringes were found weekly in the church's stairwells, the visible witnesses of marginalization and disenfranchisement. Combine that with trash bags filled with dirty clothes and stinky blankets, the smell of urine on the front steps, and two or three persons who were homeless always found sleeping inside or outside of the church, and a strong segment of what would become Emory's mission was before us on a weekly basis. Uplift the marginalized and disenfranchised of our community. Provide them an affordable place to live, food to eat, opportunities to get well. Be the living gospel of Jesus Christ for the congregation and community. Very quickly I found myself as the "person delegated." And, as I preached and taught revival and resurrection every Sunday in those early years, a remnant of faithful believers rose up to embrace the fact that they were the "persons delegated," a body of people being sent on a mission to provide hope for its community. We were the legacy that could lead to life!

A Messy History

It was a legacy that had its roots in a messy history. A history entrenched in racial injustice, segregation, slavery, and war. Yet a history that always had a glimmer of hope if the "persons delegated" had the courage to fight for it. Legacy can lead to life when church and civic leaders take the necessary time and make the necessary investment to contextualize church property development. What we will find is history informing our legacy, not dissuading it—even when the history is messy. Because it is the history of our congregations and communities, the history behind why our church property is where it is, that God uses to speak to us the legacies that can bring life in the present and future.

My Old Testament professor, the late Dr. Gene Rice at Howard University School of Divinity, was brilliant in teaching us this fundamental truth, through his instruction on exegeting biblical texts. He instilled in us the understanding that every biblical text is written in context. As students, we would be anxious to string multiple biblical texts from all over the Bible together for preaching purposes. But Dr. Rice would insist that we "stay in the text," because every text is written in context, and if we stay in the text, God will speak from that one text everything that needed to be spoken. It was Dr. Rice's admonition that would lead some of us to adopt a phrase later that goes "every text is written in context. And a text without a context is a pre-text for a 'con.'"

I've learned that the wisdom and instruction that Dr. Rice gave me in studying context in biblical texts can be and needs to be applied to the development of church property. In fact, our task as the "persons delegated" is to do this very thing. For many development projects have left communities with a "con," and many developers have "conned" church and civic leaders because all of us have either not known how or have refused to put "text" in "context." We've not done the historical contextual work that is vital and necessary for church property development. We have even succumbed to "revisionist history," a history told by one segment of the population, not all. But when we are faithful to the process of excavating historical context, we can uplift a history that may be messy and ugly, but a history that informs us that legacy can lead to life and that our property can be maintained for good.

Like that of your church, Emory's history has some mess in it. White folks begin the history of Emory in 1832 when the Emory Methodist Chapel started in a redbrick house just one hundred yards from the church's present location. The church got its name from a noted Methodist bishop, John Emory, who believed one could be Christian and own slaves. He is the same Emory who was the founder of the university by his name in Decatur, Georgia.

Unlike today, Emory was an all-white congregation back then; its members, like the bishop it was named after, were slave owners and slave masters. In 1844, the denomination split over the issue that has haunted the United States of America since its inception—slavery. That year witnessed the formation of the Methodist Episcopal and Methodist Episcopal South churches. Emory became part of the latter, and this division in the church reflected the division in society—a division that would lead the nation into civil war.

Emory Church soon found its history interwoven with the Civil War because of its geographic positioning on Vinegar Hill—the highest point overlooking the city from the north. It soon found itself next to a Union fort—Fort Massachusetts. That fort would later be named Fort Stevens—the primary fort defending the White House and preserving life on the northern side of the city.

During the war, Emory served as a place of worship, a barracks for soldiers, a hospital for the wounded, and even a jail. But even more so, Emory was a last line of defense for preserving life and the hope of justice for multitudes of people, particularly for the marginalized and disenfranchised in society—at that time, slaves.

History like this is vital to any church development project. It helps mold and shape the direction a congregation should take to use its property to serve its community, how it goes about doing it, and how it can partner with the private, government, and public sectors to maximize that use for the common good. Out of this, legacy can lead to life.

Why Don't We Build Right Here?

Through our own ministry to people hungry and homeless on the streets around us, we had used our property to do transitional housing. We housed families in our church building as we built relationships with the private and governmental sectors to refurbish our former church parsonage to expand the ministry. Seeing that we were just scratching the surface in meeting the need, we looked to acquire more property in our neighborhood to house transitional families.

At the same time, through our community-organizing skills, we began a one-on-one relational meeting campaign to listen to neighborhood residents about what they'd like to see the Brightwood community become. Overwhelmingly, we heard "affordable housing." That it was becoming too expensive for longtime residents to stay in the neighborhood because of rising property taxes—a result of gentrification in downtown Washington, three miles south of us, and downtown Silver Spring, Maryland, two miles north of us.

As our history informed us yet again, we were being called to be a last line of defense, preserving life for those in the margins of society. Some were seeking to move from homelessness to permanent residency, while others were being priced out of the neighborhood in which they'd invested their entire lives. We had senior citizen church members who were having to move to the suburbs, simply because they could not survive in a community becoming too expensive.

JOSEPH W. DANIELS JR.

The call to preserve the well-being of people was so strong that one day, one of our members, after three failed attempts to buy property in the community, uttered the words that would change our lives forever: "Why don't we just build right here?" We owned our property; it never dawned upon us to build on it.

And right there, the vision of what would become the $60 million Beacon Center project was born. An example of what churches can do when they are willing to become the "persons delegated" to further a legacy born in a deep history that informs future growth.

To our knowledge, never before had a church in Washington, DC, let alone a black church, undertaken a project this size—a project driven by the mission of a congregation as opposed to a congregation selling its mission to a developer. With that came obstacles. Church and civic leaders contemplating church development need to know and not be afraid of the fact that there will be obstacles when you are the last line of defense, called to preserve life and justice for the marginalized. But if you remain faithful, and lean into your history, your legacy can lead to life!

Obstacles

The obstacles were many. The annual conference in our denomination threw up roadblocks and did not support a black church doing something its predominantly white churches had not done. The city elected four different mayors over the course of our project. With every new election came the need to build new relationships, which meant time and money lost.

Money became an obstacle. On one occasion, we ran out of predevelopment money. By the grace of God alone, one of our development partners, Gina Merritt, worked for free for two years, at times sacrificing her own financial needs for our project's well-being—because she believed in us and what we were doing. When you stick to your mission, God will send you angels unaware.

There was the pressure of high expectations. The eyes of pastors of other black churches, and city leaders, were particularly on us, because no other black church had pursued a project of the size and scope that we had. As one influential pastor in town told me: "We're all watching you, Joe. Because if you can do it, you give all of us hope that we can, too."

Furthermore, our congregation was becoming development-weary. People were giving constantly to the church's building efforts but not seeing substantive progress. Church folk began to doubt and doubt seriously whether such a project would come to pass.

What is important for church and civic leaders seeking to re-purpose church property for the common good—"persons delegated" faithfully to build a legacy that leads to life—is that these and other death knells will arise seeking to stop our efforts and crush our spirits. But when you are on a divine mission, I'm a witness that nothing or no one will stop you, even when times get very tough.

Our congregation believed this, which is why there must be congregational development along with building development. Many churches ignore congregational development, preferring instead to focus on the financial windfalls of property development. However, it is congregational development that builds the will of a people and can push a project to the finish line. Without our congregation devoted to what we called "the three *p*s"—persistence, patience, and prayer—as well as other spiritual disciplines, we would not have made it.

HOLD FAST TO THE MISSION

But at the same time, if we are faithful to the history of our property, legacy will prevail. Our greatest obstacle ironically became historic preservation. Three weeks before our first settlement, we were served with a landmark designation by a quasi-historical preservation group in the city, effectively shutting down our project.

Sitting on a historic site, the first thing we did in development preparation was to address all issues of historic preservation. But what we didn't know was that the preservation laws in Washington are different from those elsewhere in the country. In the fine print of the laws in the District are the allowances of other preservation groups, many of whom are unknown. These groups at times emerge to file landmark applications in an attempt to protect history and shut a project down.

Such is what happened to us. If you don't learn anything about developing church property, you *must* learn all the intricacies of historic preservation. It can, and will, make or break your project. It almost killed ours. I knew things were bad when, early in our effort to get through the landmark process, I ran into a former DC mayor who was doing a development project himself. Both of us ironically were at the Office of Planning that day. I knew him well, and said, "Mr. Mayor, what are you doing here?" He said in disgust, "These folks have landmarked my project. I can't believe this. It's such a stupid law."

I said to myself two things that day: (1) if they will "landmark" a former mayor, they will landmark anybody, and (2) Mr. Mayor, why didn't you change the law while you were in office?

It is important to note that oftentimes landmark decisions have racial undertones. They can often be vehicles by which whites seek to preserve control over various parts of a city inhabited by people of color. In our case, we had people in and out of town seeking to control what we had the right to build—even when we owned our own property!

When a project is landmarked, everything ceases. Work stops completely until there is a hearing by the city's Historic Preservation Review Board as to whether the landmark is honored or denied.

The hearing, held a month later, was critical to our project. Either the landmark was rejected or our project, and perhaps even the future of our congregation, was down the tubes. If the landmark was approved, we would owe contractors hundreds of thousands of dollars for settlement fees that we did not have. If the landmark was approved, we would be stuck in the school, with no place to go because our church building was in no condition to return to. If the landmark was approved, our congregation's financial future would have been "toast."

When in doubt, stick to the mission. Legacy can lead to life!

In the heat of the battle, we recalled that we were doing this project in defense of justice, for the preservation of marginalized lives, for people being priced out of the city and neighborhood where they'd spent all or a significant part of their lives. We pursued this project for the preservation of our church in community, long after many of us would be dead and gone. And so we turned to the One we knew could get us through—God—and we turned to the vehicles in which we could get God's attention—persistence, patience, and prayer!

The day of the hearing came, and we packed the hearing room, something never done before. In addition to church members, we had people from the community, private industry, and government present in support of us and prepared to testify.

Civil War buffs whom we'd never met came from Florida and Georgia to testify against us—some even telling revisionist history in their testimony. Columns appeared in the *New York Times* and *Los Angeles Times* prior to the hearing, raising questions about the wisdom of development near federal forts.

LEGACY LEADS TO LIFE

We testified, however, having a new piece of history: no one had mentioned the full story of Elizabeth Proctor Thomas.

In our "patience, persistence, and prayer," we learned more about Ms. Thomas, a woman everyone used to call "Aunt Betty." Everyone who told the story of Emory's history always started with the Civil War. But Emory's history didn't start there. Neither did it start in 1832 in that little redbrick house. It started with a "free" and courageous black woman in the middle of slavery days by the nickname of "Aunt Betty."

Through a conversation with the National Park Service, we discovered that eleven acres of land, of which a small portion included Emory Church and Fort Stevens, had been owned by Elizabeth Proctor Thomas and her family all the way back to 1800.

And this free black woman used the land during slavery days to house runaway slaves and free blacks who had no place to go and no place to lay their heads. These were individuals who worked at the federal forts in Washington but who could not live in the forts because of the laws of slavery and inequality. According to the Park Service, the government called these individuals "contraband." They couldn't tell who was slave and who was free, and so everyone was labeled in a derogatory fashion.

But "Aunt Betty" knew who they were. They were people, they were her people, and they were just trying to find justice, fairness, and life on Vinegar Hill, where light shined out of darkness. And, to get right down to it, she was their last line of defense, preserving their lives justly. She was simply trying to "house" them affordably!

We told the board that this was all we were trying to do, with a divine mission given to us as the "persons delegated" with a legacy. A legacy we discovered that had been passed down to Aunt Betty some 215 years prior. To deny our efforts was to deny history. And that wouldn't be right. Furthermore, we discovered that President Lincoln evicted Aunt Betty from her home to build Fort Massachusetts, promising to rebuild her house and give her land back after the war. However, Lincoln was assassinated before the war was over, and Congress reneged on Lincoln's promise: a grave injustice.

The board adjourned to make its decision. And it came back with a unanimous one against us. Our project appeared done.

Walking out of the hearing room wondering what was next, we were confronted by the chair of the review board who came to our development team in tears. She said she was devastated that the board had to rule against us, what a wonderful project the Beacon Center was, and how much the city really needed projects like it. But she said the board had to reject us because the landmark met all the legal requirements for shutting a project down.

But then out of nowhere as we prepared to exit, she said: "I think there may be a way forward, if you are willing to negotiate." I said, "We're all ears; we don't have any options at this point." She said, "Meet me in my office next week and let's see what we can do." After three more sessions with her and two board members and miraculous last-minute adjustments to our architectural design, we came back two months later for a hearing before the board. Packed out the hearing room again. Continued to labor 24/7 in prayer. And at the end of the day, the board unanimously approved us.

Legacy had led to life!

At the ribbon cutting, with Mayor Muriel Bowser intentionally at the center of it all, and Aunt Betty publicly recognized, revered, and redeemed, we all celebrated. For a legacy grounded in a mission, preserved through history, that traced as far back as 1800, had been fulfilled through us. "Persons delegated" to bring new life!

We moved into the Beacon Center in March of 2019. All ninety-nine units occupied, a wait list of five hundred people—which has swelled to eight hundred today. And soon thereafter, the topic that began dominating affordable housing in the city—and that has now swept through our own annual conference in the United Methodist Church—is: How can we develop more church properties for community mission and benefit?

How? Legacy. "Persons delegated" across the private, government, and public sectors to fulfill a mission. Legacy that is guided by history. Because legacy can bring new life!

9

WHEN GOD'S CALL IS BIGGER THAN A BUILDING

Ashley Goff

Jesus asked his disciples, have you heard about the new wine and new wineskin? If so, why do you keep saying the old is good? The church you have grown accustomed to is an old wineskin. The wine inside the wineskin? It is old, too.

I have a holy story to tell. This is one of Arlington Presbyterian Church (APC)[1] listening to neighbors, hearing God's Word, responding to God's Word to transform itself for the sake of God. APC relinquished the old to create the new. In 2016, the church demolished its building, its old wineskin, along with the old wine. Called by God to do something about the affordable housing crisis in Arlington County, Virginia, APC let God create a new wineskin for the sake of the neighbor.

Jesus uses the parable of new wineskins in the fifth chapter of the Gospel of Luke as a way to teach his disciples that a new age is upon them. To take on this new age, to see the radical newness appearing before them, Jesus's followers would need to concede to the ways they had interpreted the traditions, God-talk, and rituals of the faith.

---

1. Arlington Presbyterian is a member congregation in the Presbyterian Church (USA) and National Capital Presbytery.

Jesus called loudly, "Father, I place my life in your hands!"
Then he breathed his last. (Luke 23:46)[2]

What would it mean if we trusted God's promise that resurrection follows death?

From what we know of the gospel stories, the resurrection doesn't appear to us in the familiar or status quo. We know this because of the gardener, the locked room, Emmaus Road, and that breakfast on the beach. Jesus's parable of old and new wineskin has something to say to us about our cemented loyalty to our congregational buildings and property. So do the stories in the fifth chapter of Luke that precede the parable.

I use these stories, along with the parable, as a framework to tell the story of Arlington Presbyterian Church and its call to demolish its building for the sake of its neighbors, God's beloved ones. Throughout this chapter are quotes from APC folks, those who lived through this story. I came to APC in 2018 just as the story was entering a new chapter. These quotes help me tell the story with integrity and from the lived experience of those whose DNA is now full of the ups and downs of this journey.

The Wineskin of a Congregation: The Context

Arlington County, on the land of the Piscataway people, is a metropolitan suburb that shares the Potomac River as a border with Washington, DC. Within the past two decades, Arlington County has undergone a dramatic transformation, becoming one of the most expensive places to live in the United States.[3]

Since April 21, 1908, Arlington Presbyterian has been in the Alcova Heights neighborhood on Columbia Pike, one of the main arteries through Arlington County, affectionately called "the Pike." The four-mile radius that encompasses the zip code of the

2. Biblical quotations in this chapter are from *The Message*, unless otherwise noted.

3. "Arlington Rents Continue to Reach into the Stratosphere," *Inside NoVa*, July 29, 2022, https://tinyurl.com/mr4cu89e.

church, 22204, has become home to almost fifty-four thousand people. APC's neighborhood has been called the "word in a zip code" because 130 different languages are spoken within this tiny geographic area. The average median income for a household in Arlington County is $122,000, yet half of those who use the Arlington County food bank come from our 22204 zip code.[4]

As the demographics of the neighborhood changed, so did the size of Arlington Presbyterian. Like many PC(USA) congregations, APC's membership had been in a steady decline. Within the decline was the congregation's detachment from the pulse of life in the neighborhood. In symbolic irony, the heavy, red, main entrance doors to the building had become a burden to open and would lock themselves at unexplainable times.

All the while, between 2000 and 2013, Arlington County lost 13,500 housing units that were affordable to lower-income individuals and families. Arlington County was in, and continues to be in, an affordable housing crisis.

Like so many congregations, the land APC was on, along with the brick-and-mortar building, held the tender, fierce, devastating stories of people displaced and of a congregation: the displacement of the Piscataway people, Black enslavement, a fire in 1924, a complete rebuild finished in 1930, wedding ceremonies, funerals, baptisms, confirmation classes, and the work for racial and LGBTQ equity in a southern commonwealth.

And the congregation began to ask itself: "Is the old good?"

Pushed Out into Deep Waters

APC's discernment process called them into deep waters, recognizing they needed to shift away from the inertia of traditional church programs and the building itself. These deep waters proved, over time, to be many things: chaos, the unknown, fullness, and incomprehensibility. APC kept trying to be new wine as

4. Lily Duran, director of client services, Arlington Food Assistance Center, discussion with Ashley Goff, August 3, 2022.

they continued to be entrenched in historic models of what church was supposed to be.

In 1999, APC's session, its governing body, voted to engage in the Transforming Congregations project of National Capital Presbytery, a three-year program to help congregations name ways to connect with their communities and create a new congregational vision. APC did the obligatory steps: they brought in a consultant, worked through core values, created a vision statement. The desire for transformation was there within the congregation. The church spent five years working through the Transforming Congregations process with "little to show for all the expense and effort."[5]

Once when he was standing on the shore of Lake Gennesaret, the crowd was pushing in on Jesus to better hear the Word of God. He noticed two boats tied up. The fishermen had just left them and were out scrubbing their nets. He climbed into the boat that was Simon's and asked him to put out a little from the shore. Sitting there, using the boat for a pulpit, he taught the crowd.

When he finished teaching, he said to Simon, "Push out into deep water and let your nets out for a catch."

Simon said, "Master, we've been fishing hard all night and haven't caught even a minnow. But if you say so, I'll let out the nets." It was no sooner said than done—a huge haul of fish, straining the nets past capacity. They waved to their partners in the other boat to come help them. They filled both boats, nearly swamping them with the catch. . . .

Jesus said to Simon, "There is nothing to fear. From now on you'll be fishing for men and women." They pulled their boats up on the beach, left them, nets and all, and followed him. (Luke 5:1–11)

In 2009, at Visioning Retreat, leaders were invited to cast their nets wide and far, letting their prophetic imaginations run wild.

5. Jon Etherton, "APC Old and New Wineskin Questions," interview by Ashley Goff, August 1, 2022. "APC Old and New Wineskin Questions" refers to a Google form to which members of the congregation responded electronically.

They had a strong hunch they needed to toss their nets on the other side of the boat, jettisoning long held expectations, assumptions, and long practiced ways of being church.

How do we tell the story of our future, no holds barred?

One group imagined an act of God destroying the building and replaced it with affordable housing and new church space and a coffee shop. This vision of the future excited us and energized us. We imagined it was possible![6]

In 2010, APC's session discerned a proposal to create affordable housing.

At the session retreat many of us discerned a call from the Holy Spirit to do something radical: untether ourselves from the building and do something different. We did not know the path ahead and our original thoughts were not where we ended up.[7]

This was a turning point. APC allowed themselves to go into deep, holy waters when they realized something radical had to be done with the church building. Their attachment to the crumbling, physical structure limited their power, their ability to act, as followers of God's way.

We [made the turn] when we accepted that the physical church itself could not stand anymore.[8]

We were endlessly dealing with a building that demanded all our time and most of our monetary resources.[9]

6. Susan Etherton, "APC Old and New Wineskin Questions," interview by Ashley Goff, July 30, 2022.

7. Jon Etherton, "APC Old and New Wineskin Questions."

8. Kendra Parham, "APC Old and New Wineskin Questions," interview by Ashley Goff, August 1, 2022.

9. Don Peebles, "APC Old and New Wineskin Questions," interview by Ashley Goff, August 1, 2022.

A three-part vision emerged: nurture disciples of Jesus Christ, be a place of crossroads and connections, and use the property to provide affordable housing for the South Arlington community. Out of deep waters came that prophetic call and imagination. Like those ancient fisherfolk, Jesus showed APC something new and amazing out of what was right in front of them—neighbors struggling to live and work in Arlington County.

Simon, Andrew, and John upended their way of fishing. They left everything at possibly the height of their fishing careers, renouncing the ancient world's view of prosperity and success to follow Jesus.

> We chose to dynamically break open old models. As a community, we were asking questions about new ways and new directions. I felt the Holy Spirit calling me and I felt that I needed to stretch myself. I needed to risk. It felt as though I was being asked to come and join in the boat.[10]

Invitation to a Changed Life

As the visioning of the congregation continued, APC members connected the crisis of their own congregational life to the life of the surrounding community. In 2012, APC realized they needed to set their priorities within their call from God to the neighborhood.

> We really needed to stop asking ourselves questions and start knocking on our neighbors' doors in a sincere, committed, and organized effort.[11]

It wasn't enough to do the intellectual discernment processes or for the congregation to assume they knew the needs of the neighborhood.

10. Parham, "APC Old and New Wineskin Questions."
11. Laura Gehrenbeck, "APC Old and New Wineskin Questions," interview by Ashley Goff, August 2, 2022.

We were challenged to pay attention not to what we thought
needed to happen, what we imagined the community needed,
but to listen to what our neighbors had to say—to get to know
and be in relationship with our neighbors and hear them.[12]

Congregants rode buses up and down Columbia Pike. They
talked with local business owners, teachers, domestic workers, any and all who make up the infrastructure of Arlington
County. On Saturday mornings, church members set up tables
in the church's parking lot, located right next to a bus stop. They
used the community-organizing strategies of listening sessions
and one-on-one meetings to listen to the deep wisdom of the
neighborhood.

One day in one of the villages there was a man covered with
leprosy. When he saw Jesus, he fell down before him in prayer
and said, "If you want to, you can cleanse me."
Jesus put out his hand, touched him, and said, "I want to. Be
clean." Then and there his skin was smooth, the leprosy gone.
(Luke 5:12–13)

APC listened. They heard of people covered in debt and ex-
orbitant rent. They heard of people longing to be healed from
weary commutes, financial uncertainty, and living away from
family and kinship. They listened as neighbors shared hopes,
dreams, and ideas for their future, a future they wanted to be in
Arlington County.
This relational work allowed a guiding question to emerge for
APC: *What is breaking our hearts in our neighborhood?*[13]
The stories of the neighbors broke the heart of APC, binding
the well-being of APC up in the well-being of the neighborhood.
Jesus pulled the congregation into the neighborhood streets, and

12. Susan Etherton, "APC Old and New Wineskin Questions."
13. Peebles, "APC Old and New Wineskin Questions."

they practically tripped over the need for affordable housing as they listened to story after story.

> We heard a longing for connection from our neighbors. We sat with them, we ate with them, we listened. We offered community and communion.[14]

The stories signified the emerging incompatibility with the old and the new: as we began to think about jettisoning our 1950s building, we also started to rid ourselves of the 1950s version of Christianity that had captured our thinking. Our ministry shifted from if "we build it, they will come" to "we will go to the neighbors and build."[15]

It wasn't about what we could do for our neighbors, it became about how we heard God's invitation in their stories. How their stories became our stories together.

COME ALONG WITH ME: BUT FIRST DEMOLISH YOUR CHURCH BUILDING

At this point in the journey, there was increasing clarity in APC's call from God to create affordable housing. There was also anger, frustration, and inflamed grief within the congregation. Some congregants were livid over the idea of demolishing the building for affordable housing. Worldviews, the understanding of church, the clash between letting go and certainty bumped up against each other. Death and resurrection were intermingled. Proposals for what was next were put forth only to be met with nos from within the congregation and National Capital Presbytery itself.

Decades of unaddressed conflict rose up as the conversations continued around affordable housing. Everything was stretched out and laid bare—grief, emotions, hopes, dreams, systems, congrega-

14. Susan Etherton, "APC Old and New Wineskin Questions."
15. Peebles, "APC Old and New Wineskin Questions."

tional traditions, and even long-standing relationships. At one point, a fraction of the congregation tried to get APC's building designated as historical to keep the building from being demolished. The quest to get the building named as historical was an act of preservation.

Preservation and sustainability run counter to who we are as humans created by God. Our incarnate bodies are not here forever. We die. All of us. Yet we lock down our pews, glorify our stained glass, wait around for the next church flood hoping insurance will pay for the damages. The way we relate to our church buildings runs counter to who we are in the way God created us.

> Our Church had become a fortress behind nearly impenetrable red doors. We had started worshiping programs and a building instead of doing justice and walking humbly with our God.[16]

Might it be idolatrous to assume that church as we know it is the future God intends?[17] What if God is calling all of us to radical transformation because God wants nothing more for us, as Christians, than to be resurrected?

At the hearing before the Arlington County Historical Affairs and Landmark Review Board (HALRB) vote, those in favor of demolishing the building proclaimed, "The call from God to do something about affordable housing is bigger than our church building itself, so the building must go."[18] The HALRB voted against the designation, sparing APC from being declared "historical" and restricting its transformation.

On November 2, 2014, the members of Arlington Presbyterian voted to sell their building and land for $8.48 million to Arlington Partnership for Affordable Housing (APAH), a nonprofit developer

---

16. Peebles, "APC Old and New Wineskin Questions."

17. Anna B. Olson, *Claiming Resurrection in a Dying Church: Freedom beyond Survival* (Louisville: Westminster John Knox, 2016), 7.

18. Jon Etherton, speaking before the Historical Affairs and Landmark Review Board, January 2, 2014.

ASHLEY GOFF

committed to creating affordable housing in the county. In January 2015, National Capital Presbytery resoundingly voted to approve the sale of Arlington Presbyterian to APAH with no dissent. In December 2015, the Arlington County Board, the elected governing body of Arlington County, voted to approve the proposed development, 5-0.

By this point, one-third of the congregation had left over the decision to sell the property.

As APC let go of the building and relationships, they also had to shed their relationship with all the stuff. Calling it the "ministry of stuff," with incredible intentionality, the congregation found a home for all the stuff in the building. From the letting go of church music, Sunday school curricula, the pews, and pipe organ, like at the tomb, the death and resurrection of the building, APC renounced it all in order to follow their call from God.

In July 2016, the heavy equipment made its way to Columbia Pike and demolished the building. The cross that was affixed to the top of APC's steeple was allowed to tumble to the ground during the demolition. It was pulled out of the rubble with dents, cracks, and a deep bend that occurred when it hit the ground with force.

Some friends arrived at a house carrying a paraplegic on a stretcher. They were looking for a way to get into the house and set him before Jesus. When they couldn't find a way in because of the crowd, they went up on the roof, removed some tiles, and let him down in the middle of everyone, right in front of Jesus. (Luke 5:18-20a)

After this [Jesus] went out and saw a man named Levi at his work collecting taxes. Jesus said, "Come along with me." And Levi did—walked away from everything and went with him. (Luke 5:27-28)

To center themselves in front of Jesus, APC walked away from all the material stuff to follow. What APC took with them, like Levi, like the disciples in the boat, was their full selves, their newfound freedom, wisdom, and feistiness. To faithfully respond to God's call, APC demolished its perception of church, security, and its heavy grasp on its future. The old and the new were incompatible with each other, and that meant the building had to go.

> We realized the impermeable stone walls and opaque windows of the APC church building would have to come down.[19]

> The rooms in the old building. The tenants. It was all in a set configuration. It held us back in trying to do something new.[20]

APC learned that this leaves a community in a very precarious position. What was the future of the congregation? Would the congregation die from this call to enter deep waters and follow?

> Were we truly being the feet and hands while occupied with endless meetings about roof repairs?[21]

LETTING GO OF THE OLD TO LIVE INTO THE NEW: THE STORY CONTINUES

After the sale of the building was approved by National Capital Presbytery, APC recommended to APAH the building be named Gilliam Place, after Ronda A. Gilliam (1906–1970), the first African American ruling elder at APC and a long-standing visionary within the South Arlington community.

In November 2019, after spending almost two years in a small, traditional chapel in a United Methodist building just up the street, APC took the cross and a few other remnants of the old building and completed a three-thousand-square-foot build-out on the ground level of Gilliam Place for its worship and office space.

19. Peebles, "APC Old and New Wineskin Questions."
20. Michelle Lanier, clerk of session, Arlington Presbyterian Church, discussion with Ashley Goff and APC Stewardship Team, July 21, 2022.
21. Gehrenbeck, "APC Old and New Wineskin Questions."

To really live into the transformation, we couldn't go back into a familiar type of church building. It all had to be new for us to be new. Otherwise, if we built a new, traditional looking church space, we'd just act like we did in the old building.[22]

When we left the old building and moved into the Methodist chapel, I think some of us still wanted some semblance of the "old" as uncomfortable as it was there. We couldn't imagine the new and so we tried to keep one foot in what we knew. We were finally cut off—from the old, and from the certainty of the new. And we had to do that to be truly free. We had to take that leap into the unknown, trusting what might be.[23]

[Jesus] also told them a parable: "No one tears a piece from a new garment and sews it on an old garment; otherwise the new will be torn, and the piece from the new will not match the old. And no one puts new wine into old wineskins; otherwise the new wine will burst the skins and will be spilled, and the skins will be destroyed. But new wine must be put into fresh wineskins. And no one after drinking old wine desires new wine, but says, 'The old is good.'" (Luke 5:36–38 NRSV)

What was happening around Jesus to push him to share this parable? Maybe Jesus was increasingly hearing his followers say, "But, Jesus, the old is good. Aged wine is pretty good, too." Maybe Jesus used this parable because the disciples weren't ready for new wineskins. Maybe Jesus was seeing the disciples underestimate their own prophetic imaginations and the possibilities of life with God.[24] Time and time again, throughout the call to become a new wineskin, APC tried to be new wine in its old building.

22. Don Peebles, member, Arlington Presbyterian Church, discussion with Ashley Goff, November 9, 2019.
23. Peebles, "APC Old and New Wineskin Questions."
24. "In the Midst of New Dimensions," Unitarian Universalist Santa Fe, YouTube, April 23, 2017, https://tinyurl.com/vdpkjz2e.

I think we tried to fit our old wineskin and God's new thing together for a long time. The best of both, I think we imagined.[25]

Yet the power of the call, the power of the new wine, would not allow such a compromise with the old and the new. New wine was fermenting and breaking the old wineskin.

The old wineskin was holding us back from what God would have us do in that space and time. I knew that if we tried to put the new wine into the old skin, we would end up trying to preserve the skin and not drink the wine. The purpose of wine is to be drunk and shared not bound up in a skin carried from generation to generation.[26]

What is APC's story now in this new wineskin? How do we pull forward the parts of the Gilliam Place story that need to come with us into this new wineskin? What parts of the story do we need to let go of? How do we continue to ferment new wine in a new wineskin?

If we've learned anything, it's that a call never stops. Deep waters are always around us. We are constantly invited to let go and follow. Deep waters. Let go and follow. Old and new wineskins.

These dynamics crashed into us in March 2020.

As the pandemic hit, we began to hear more stories about food insecurity, job loss, and struggles to pay rent in Gilliam Place and in South Arlington. We had $6.5 million left from the proceeds from the sale, and people in our local community needed $500 to cover household rent.

As we heard and felt the stories about the death-dealing ways of White Supremacy through the murders of George Floyd and Breonna Taylor, we knew we needed to have deep conversations about our faith and wealth.

We needed a new money story.

25. Gehrenbeck, "APC Old and New Wineskin Questions."
26. Peebles, "APC Old and New Wineskin Questions."

We had been like a traditional Presbyterian church. Throughout the decades, even during the discernment process, we had seasons of stewardship, capital campaigns, and wealth that had accumulated over time. However, our main stories about money concerned budgets, management, and investments. Old wine was in a new wineskin. We knew this would be hard work. We knew we needed help.

This meant working with a consulting group, Vandersall Collective,[27] to get to the roots of our money stories, both individually and as a congregation. We explored wealth and poverty in the biblical stories and God's desire for alternative economies. We took a hard look at ourselves and asked ourselves to integrate our collective money narratives.

Turns out our money stories hold shame, disconnects, relationships, joy, security, and harm. We bring all of this to the table, consciously and unconsciously, in our conversations about wealth and possessions.

Our wineskin around money was designed around transactional practices. There was a small number of us who knew how our money worked and was organized. Our budget process was scarcity-driven. All of these dynamics were frustrating and harm inducing, particularly considering the new wineskin we were inhabiting. We found we were having conversations about how to hold on to our money and keep the money in our bank accounts. We were treading in shallow waters. With our money, we were tossing our nets to the same side of the boat over and over and over again.

As part of the ongoing new wineskin work, we created, through storytelling, a set of core values: place based, justice focused, transformational, prayerful, communal, inclusive, and rela-

27. The Vandersall Collective offers a radically human approach to reaching people, raising money, and reimagining the future for congregations and nonprofits.

tional. Yet again, we found freedom in creating new wine for a new wineskin.

> The new wine made us not afraid. Not as much fear of dying, of going away. Not as much fear to say, "Hey, let's share what we have because we're not afraid of it all going away."[28]

If God's call for us is to step into deep waters, renounce and let go, demolish structures that limit full participation in life and relationships, shouldn't our money follow that call? How can our money story disrupt cycles of power and privilege in church and society? How can it be one of mutual dependence without an expectation of return? What if we put all our money where our values are?[29]

In 2021, we created a new, participatory budget process. In essence, we decentered ourselves from our budget. We wanted a neighbor-driven annual budget. Whose budget is this anyway?

To center our neighbors in the budget, as APC did with the call to Gilliam Place, we realized we need to go back into the neighborhood and ask questions based on strengths and assets rather than just needs and deficiencies. We set up one-on-one meetings and asked: Where do you see the common good happening at Gilliam Place? Is there something we could be doing together? What's important here? Is there anything we could be doing together? What are the gifts, what is the power, the ability to act, in our neighborhood?

These stories shaped the spirit and intent for our budget. We interpreted the first draft of the budget through our core values. We created a visual to represent the connection between our money story, budget, and our core values. The conversation

28. Lanier, discussion with Ashley Goff and APC Stewardship Team.

29. Edgar Villanueva, *Decolonizing Wealth: Indigenous Wisdom to Heal Divides and Restore Balance* (Oakland, CA: Berrett-Koehler, 2018), 10.

about finalizing numbers came last. At that point, the numbers fell into place.

For More of the Story, Go around the Corner

There is a plaque on the outside of Gilliam Place, created by an unknown entity, that says here once stood the Arlington Presbyterian Church. The plaque names how APC played a significant role in the life of the South Arlington community. The end of the plaque reads, "In 2016 the church sold its building to Arlington Partnership for Affordable Housing. In 2017, the building was demolished."

The end. It reads like a church obituary.

Not to be outdone by a building plaque, several APC folks want to put up a sign at the bottom of the plaque that reads, "for more of the story, go around the corner . . ."

Creating new wine for a new wineskin hasn't been easy, and God isn't finished with us. Right now, APC stands in the tension between our previous stories and the ones we hope will guide us forward. As we claim these new stories, we see ourselves sharing life and evolving with those in Gilliam Place.

> I now realize how our new space has allowed us to begin living a new future together with our neighbors that would have been inconceivable in the old building.[30]

> We are still dynamically breaking open those old models of church. We stand in the community, asking questions about new ways and new directions.[31]

We commissioned a new hymn to honor this new era of APC at Gilliam Place. We sing these words often in worship:

---

30. Jon Etherton, member, Arlington Presbyterian Church, discussion with Ashley Goff and APC Stewardship Team, July 21, 2022.
31. Parham, "APC Old and New Wineskin Questions."

We have been called to listen and called to act, we have been called to tear down and called to build, and we're still people on a journey, our work isn't done. Keep us faithful in the way of love.[32]

This hymn is a reminder that God is not done with APC even after this miraculous story. We're still people on a journey, drinking new wine in a new wineskin. For all of this—for the old wine and old wineskin, for the new wine and new wineskin—we give God never-ending thanks.

32. Paul M. Vasile, "Keep Us Faithful," November 2019. This is a song Vasile wrote for the congregation.

10

LESSONS FROM NEHEMIAH FOR FAITH-BASED PROPERTY DEVELOPMENT

David Bowers

Many houses of worship have underutilized land and air rights. Those resources can often be activated for community benefit via the development of affordable housing or community facilities. Development can be difficult. Development is also doable.

The biblical story of Nehemiah is inspiring and instructive. A conquered people living in distress for over one hundred years. A son of the people moved to action by the condition of his kin. A series of bold and strategic actions taken by Nehemiah to initiate a rebuilding project that helps strengthen a city. The trials and tribulations brought on by naysayers. The ultimate success of the project. The lessons inform the work I do with Enterprise Community Partners' Faith-Based Development Initiative (FBDI). Since 2006 the FBDI has provided training, financial or technical assistance, or both, to hundreds of houses of worship seeking to meet community needs via the development of affordable housing or community facilities.[1] Here are nine

---

1. See https://tinyurl.com/52pe9523.

lessons from the book of Nehemiah that can inform community development efforts undertaken by houses of worship.

LESSON 1: BOTHERED AND COMPELLED BY THE NEED (NEHEMIAH 1:3–4A AND 2:2–3)

If houses of worship want to get engaged in community development, it helps if they are bothered by the needs of people in their community. We must give a damn. Nehemiah was bothered by the struggles of his people. While serving as the king's cupbearer, Nehemiah inquired about the well-being of his fellow Jews living in Jerusalem. He received word that their condition was tenuous. He broke down and wept and shared with the king the source of his sadness. Such is the dissonance it caused him that he replied to the king with a sense of incredulity and righteous indignation. "Why should my face not be sad, when the city, the place of my fathers' tombs, lies waste and its gates are burned with fire?"

Today many congregations exist in areas with people living in "great distress and reproach"—much as Nehemiah's kin were living. As of January 2020, over 580,000 people in the United States were living unhoused.[2] One of every five renter households devotes more than half of its income to housing costs.[3] For those families that want to build something today and leave something for the next generation, there is this reality: Black households' median net worth is roughly $24,000, compared to roughly $188,000 for a White family.[4] Meanwhile, home ownership rates for Black households is 44.7 percent, compared to 74 percent

2. National Alliance to End Homelessness, "State of Homelessness: 2022 Edition," accessed February 10, 2023, https://tinyurl.com/42m9unz6.
3. National Low Income Housing Coalition, "The Gap," accessed February 10, 2023, https://tinyurl.com/ym8kr7dy.
4. James H. Carr, Michela Zonta, and William Spriggs, "2021 State of Housing in Black America: Emerging from the Covid Pandemic Recession," commissioned by National Association of Real Estate Brokers, accessed February 10, 2023, https://tinyurl.com/yk7dp6a7.

for White households.[5] Over 13 million Americans live in a food desert.[6] Forty percent of counties are pharmacy deserts, and 9 percent are primary-care deserts.[7] Half of Americans live in a child-care desert.[8]

Many houses of worship exist in a sea of need where members of the congregation or the larger community, or both, are living in distress, facing toxic choices while wrestling with issues including access to affordable housing, child care, health care, and healthy food. These are real people with real needs. Some congregations in urban settings are dealing with issues of market-induced displacement of low- and moderate-income residents from areas where housing prices have escalated. New residents, higher incomes, and more amenities make for higher prices. Demographic shifts—ethnic and economic—make for changing needs around a house of worship. In some cases, a reverse dynamic occurs where suburban houses of worship are seeing demographic shifts with more low-income residents moving to suburban areas. The needs of those residents are often new for an area that may have been used to certain demographics for generations.

LESSON 2: PRAY (NEHEMIAH 1:4–11)

It may seem obvious, but when confronted with a challenge, people of faith should pray. When Nehemiah is brought to tears upon hearing of the distressed state of his people, he immediately prays,

---

5. Census Bureau, "Quarterly Residential Vacancies and Homeownership, Fourth Quarter 2022," January 31, 2023, https://tinyurl.com/799m97pw.

6. Ann Wright, "Interactive Web Tool Maps Food Deserts, Provides Key Data," US Department of Agriculture, April 30, 2021, https://tinyurl.com/yhshfwcz.

7. The Good Rx Research Team, "Mapping Healthcare Deserts," September 2021, https://tinyurl.com/4m2cekuu.

8. Rasheed Malik et al., "The Cornonavirus Will Make Child Care Deserts Worse and Exacerbate Inquality," Center for American Progress, June 22, 2020, https://tinyurl.com/5n7a4rz4.

fasts, and makes confession for his sins and those of his people. Nehemiah ask for forgiveness, and for God to remember God's commands and promises to the people.

Speaking to God should never be perfunctory for people of faith. When taking on the challenge of doing a ministry of community development, a congregation should ground its response in an intentional, open dialogue with God. In earnest fashion seek God's attention, forgiveness, mercy, guidance, and provision. Before learning about the real-estate development process, there is a fundamental question: What is God calling us to do and to be in relation with our community and the world? Prayer can be a grounding point of an intentional discernment process for any congregation. In addition to providing guidance, the spiritual discipline can equip the members for challenges. Some challenges will be innocuous and simply part of the process. Some will be mean-spirited and designed to undermine the efforts.

A resource on the early discernment process can be found at Incairnation.org, a ministry of Arlington Presbyterian Church.[9] As Pastor Ashley Goff describes in her chapter in this book, Arlington Presbyterian Church transformed their property for affordable housing through a remarkable process. One of their resources, called "Walks-Talks-and-Dreams," references the daily prayer and regular Bible study that became part of the church's discernment work.[10] There is quite a backstory to what is today a successful mixed-used development built in collaboration with the developer Arlington Partnership for Affordable Housing. An intentional discernment process that included prayer and listening was essential to turning around an initial no.

9. See https://tinyurl.com/yxs8nsy3.
10. "Walks, Talks, and Dreams," Incairnation, January 26, 2021, https://tinyurl.com/2cp4m75u.

LESSON 3: MUST BE MOVED, NOT JUST TOUCHED
(NEHEMIAH 2:4–5)

The world needs more people moved to action, not just people that are touched. When confronted with human needs, it is easy for people to simply be touched. "Oh, what a shame, look at that homeless person lying on the street. So sad." This is what I call "barbershop and beauty salon talk." We lament the sad situation of people who are suffering and then go right back to our daily routines.

Nehemiah could have easily taken this position. He was eight hundred miles away working for the king. He could have been touched by the distress of his people and gone right back to living his life. Instead, he was moved to action. He prayed and fasted, then said to the king, "Send me to Judah . . . that I may rebuild it." Nehemiah realized the challenges his people faced. There was action *he* needed to take.

Consider this question: What relevance does our congregation have to the needs of the people who live in its community? If someone came up to us and said they were suffering from thirst—would we offer them a glass of water? How do we respond when we know that people are in need and we have a resource that could help? It is easy to shut down because we do not believe we can solve the problems. We can't fix everything, so we often fix nothing. The suffering becomes the backdrop for our comings and goings that never impede on our sensibility to engage in a transformational manner. Because of fear, apathy, or laziness. Perhaps disdain for the other. Or feeling we do not have the time. Sometimes we just feel overwhelmed.

Nehemiah heard of the need and was moved to action. "Send me."

LESSON 4: GOVERNMENT SUPPORT IS OKAY
(NEHEMIAH 2:7–8)

Nehemiah received government assistance for the building project. He was given papers that allowed for his safe passage and an earmark of critical timber. Some modern congregations are understandably weary of working with the government. Some have hesitation because of government bureaucracy. Some have distrust based on instances of historic government disinvestment in certain communities. But government assistance is not only okay—often it is essential.

There are multiple ways the government may play a role.[11] Zoning approvals, alley closings, utilization of air rights, setbacks, density adjustments, and building codes are just some of the issues that may be in play. If you are building housing—depending on the household incomes you want to serve—there is a strong chance the project will need some financial subsidy. Much of the rental housing affordable to low-income households in America is built utilizing Low-Income Housing Tax Credits. These federal tax credits typically flow through state housing allocation agencies. Increasingly, state and local governments need to provide financial support that will allow affordable housing developments to serve our neighbors with the lowest incomes. Local housing trust funds and rent supplement programs are just two examples of local tools.

Be okay with government assistance. Government resources are our resources. And look for ways in which your project may be in line with local government priorities.

Lesson 5: Survey the Need (Nehemiah 2:11–15)

While Nehemiah sensed the need, before embarking upon the work, he surveyed the wall. Today this equates to the fundamental need for a market study/feasibility analysis. While congregational leaders may have had a vision, it is important to hire professional help that can do a formal study to determine community needs and demand.

11. See Kurt Paulsen's chapter and Nadia Mian's chapter in this book for more on the relationship between churches and municipalities.

One of the success stories for the Enterprise FBDI was when a church in Montgomery County, Maryland, made a "no-go" decision. They owned several acres of land and wanted to build affordable senior housing. They believed there was a need. But the market study came back saying there was an oversupply of senior housing in their region. The church decided to hold off on any building project. A success story because the church made an *informed* go/no-go decision.

Today many houses of worship are commuter institutions. Members may not live in the neighborhood in which they worship. Nehemiah did not live in the community where the building project would take place. This may be the same reality today for many congregation members. And even if they do live locally—there may be plans at the local government planning office that the average resident would have no idea about. Having a professional do an analysis of what is needed in the neighborhood and surrounding region, as well as what is already planned and approved for development, will help ensure that a project is meeting actual demand.

It is wise to have the firm completing a market study also do a feasibility analysis. This provides not only a sense of what could be built that meets a demand, but also an analysis of how feasible it is to build that type of project. A feasibility study will look at questions like: Is there a demand for affordable rental family housing? Is the land zoned for such a building, or will a variance be needed? If a variance is needed—how likely is it to be granted? What type of financing will be needed for the project? How "easy" is it to secure such financing? How much subsidy may be needed and how much may be available from local philanthropy or government? Is approval needed from any neighborhood associations? How long on average does it take to complete a project in your jurisdiction? Understanding the level of time and effort that may be needed for a project will help a house of worship make an informed decision.

LESSON 6: CAST THE VISION AND GET THE PEOPLE ENGAGED TO BUILD (NEHEMIAH 2:17–18)

Instructive is the role of the leader of the congregation to cast a bold vision and get congregational buy-in. Nehemiah starts by speaking to the need—"the distress" the people are experiencing. He challenges the notion that the people must continue to live in such a manner—"that we may no longer be a reproach." As my late father used to say, "*surely*, we can do better." And Nehemiah connects himself to them by saying "we." It would have been easy for Nehemiah—who worked for the king eight hundred miles away—to say "look at the distress *you* are in . . . *you* need to get to work." Instead, he makes the connection with his fellow Jews and makes it a "we" proposition. "We" are doing badly. "We" must do the work of building.

Modern-day houses of worship are well served when their leaders cast a vision for a better reality for the "we" that includes parishioners and those in the surrounding community. There are likely congregational members struggling with the same issues that impact residents in the region. And even if they are not directly impacted by the issues that may be addressed with an affordable housing or community facility development, it is crucial for leaders to speak to the interconnectedness of humanity. The COVID pandemic has shown the ripple effects when one group of people are not okay. If any part of the body is hurting, the entire body is not able to optimally function.

Nehemiah also speaks to the connection he has with God and the government. The spiritual leader of the house sets a tone for the membership by being in relationship with God and government officials. Nehemiah was intentional on both fronts.

Be mindful, however, that houses of worship operate with varying cultures. Congregations that belong to a denomination with a connectional polity operate differently than those that belong to a denomination with a congregational polity. Some congregations have a "buck starts and stops with the pastor" culture, and some have a culture where congregational trustees "run the show." There may be a bishop to consult for approval. Whatever the reality, there should be a process by which the leadership engages members of the congregation in a manner that secures buy-in and helps people set their hand to what they believe is indeed "this good work."

LESSON 7: PUBLIC/PRIVATE PARTNERSHIPS:
UTILIZE A TEAM (NEHEMIAH 3:1, 14, 32)

Nehemiah 3 records an ancient reflection of what is often called today a "public/private partnership." It is a beautiful scene of people with various talents working on the building project. The king made an earmark of government resources. The first verse of the chapter notes that the chief priest and "his brethren" were involved. Throughout the chapter we see references to government officials involved. The chapter ends with a reference to goldsmiths and merchants. Simply put, the rebuilding project Nehemiah spearheaded involved government, the temple/religious folks, and the business community.

This is a model for what is needed today. Over the years I have encountered government officials that did not see houses of worship as community development partners. This government attitude of "this is not what they do" or "they don't have the expertise" prevents them from engaging with mission-aligned partners that control valuable land. Recent examples of progress in this arena by local governments include Washington, DC, and Alameda County, California, investing money to support faith-based development efforts that provide training and technical support to houses of worship looking to do development.[12] We are also seeing examples of local and state governments examining

12. Executive Office of the Mayor, "Mayor Bowser Unveils New Tools to Add Affordable Housing," news release, December 16, 20211, https://tinyurl.com/2p84aajs.

how to enable land-use and zoning policy adjustments to make it easier to support affordable housing development on land owned by houses of worship. In response to a state law, in 2021 Seattle enacted legislation that provides a density bonus for development of affordable housing on land owned or controlled by religious organizations.[13]

It is important to put together partnerships and a strong team. As the introduction and part 3 of this book make clear, all are well served when an intentional approach is taken that recognizes the benefits that a range of people including residents, government leaders, development professionals, members of the house of worship, and affiliated religious bodies bring to the table.

If needed at the early stage, a trained professional can assist a congregation through the discernment process about who God is calling them to be and what God is calling them to do. If a yes decision is made about exploring a development project, firms that do market study/feasibility analysis are an important resource. A real estate/land-use lawyer that represents just the interests of the house of worship is an *essential* resource for the congregation. A real estate development consultant for the house of worship can help in fully understanding the implications of the market study/ feasibility analysis findings, as well as help a congregation navigate the road to selecting a development partner if a go-forward decision is made.[14] To help avoid potential conflicts of interest, it can be important for the early-stage consultant to be paid but not have any potential financial interest in whatever development deal unfolds.[15] This is so the congregation can be comfortable they are getting unbiased advice from the consultant. The lawyer and development consultant are critical members of a team that can

13. "Affordable Housing on Religious Organization Property," City of Seattle, accessed February 13, 2023, https://tinyurl.com/yey4wct3.

14. See chapter 14 below, by Philip Burns, Jill Shook, and Andre Johnny White, on how to use, and create, advisory teams for this purpose.

15. Burns, Shook, and White have an explicit conflict-of-interest clause in their agreements with churches to address this concern.

help a church get connected with a good development partner and make sure the interests of the church are reflected in any final partnership agreements.[16]

The religious community should also consider how denominational entities can support a project. Mark Elsdon wrote about this powerfully in his work *We Aren't Broke*. Denominations are wrestling with how to support congregations that have declining memberships, reduced financial support, and facilities in need of investments for safety and operational and energy efficiency purposes. Denominations should think of how they can provide financial and technical support to assist congregations. Grant dollars or low-cost, long-term loans (with forgiveness clauses if projects cannot proceed) for early predevelopment costs can be catalytic for projects. Assistance with navigating required denominational approvals related to the land can help save time and money and reduce stress. If religious institutions sell the land they have stewarded for generations, they should be mindful that they will no longer be able to utilize it for community impact. It is important for denominations to consider how the money or professional support they can provide could help leverage land for missional impact in the community, while allowing the institutional church to own/control the land for future generations. In some cases, a development may also provide an economic benefit to churches and their affiliated entities over time. There are also examples of individual congregations supporting the building efforts of other religious entities—some bring cash or technical experts while others have the land. The key here is for religious entities and people to think about what resource they can bring to the building effort.

16. See the chapter by Tyler Krupp-Queshi for insights on church development from a property developer.

Lesson 8: There Will Be Naysayers
(Nehemiah 2:10, 19; 4:1-2, 7-11)

As stated earlier in this chapter—"Development can be difficult. Development is also doable." Part of that difficulty will come from naysayers. Opposition may come from members of the congregation or the denomination. Some may come from people in the community you are trying to help. From people who look nothing like you, or from people who look just like you. From folks who benefit from the dysfunction and despair of the people, or from folks you think would be with you. Naysayers can come from all angles.

It is fascinating to chart the progression of the opposition in the book of Nehemiah. Sanballat and Tobiah are disturbed someone is seeking the well-being of the children of Israel. Know this—everyone won't be pleased when someone comes looking to offer real transformational and empowering help to people in need. Fear, disdain for the poor, racism, hatred, apathy, self-interested greed from those who benefit from the status quo—a range of reasons drives the naysayers' disturbance at someone seeking the well-being of the people.

The progression continues—like the stages of grief. The opponents go from being disturbed to laughing and despising Nehemiah and the building crew. Then they ask if Nehemiah's crew is against the king (government leaders). Then they get furious and mock the Jews. As progress is made with the rebuilding, the anger increases and the naysayers start conspiring to attack and create confusion in an effort to halt the work. This is serious stuff. The opposition can flow across spiritual, reputational, economic, legal, and, in extreme cases, physical fronts. Congregations and their leaders need to be prepared for opposition.

Enterprise FBDI partners have stories of buildings that no one cared about suddenly becoming candidates for historic preservation status. Traffic studies become a topic of hot debate. Zoning and density debates become very heated. In the same way people tell modern-day athletes to "shut up and dribble," there are those who will tell the church to "sit down and pray." They will question why this "spiritual" body is looking to build housing or a health clinic or affordable child-care space. They will question why the church is concerned about the jobs that will be created and how money during and after the development process can be directed to and through professionals and institutions run by people of color or women. I have heard partners describe examples where local community residents that utilized church space for meetings turned up at the eleventh hour threatening to oppose projects. Opposition will sometimes be vocal, sometimes protracted, sometimes hateful, sometimes expensive, sometimes subtle.

Therefore, the lessons outlined in this chapter are so important. Prayer is necessary. The story of Emory Church that Joseph W. Daniels Jr. tells in this book is a vivid reminder of the power of prayer in the face of obstacles and naysayers. When opposition comes, having a spiritual grounding and covering is foundational. Having a strong team of public and private-sector partners, as well as congregation and community support, will help when the naysayers are looking for avenues to exploit to undermine your work. First Baptist Church of Clarendon, in Arlington, Virginia, was faced with multiple lawsuits when they set out to build affordable housing, but they had support from the local government and ultimately prevailed.[17] Having the spiritual grounding and a strong earthly development will help you complete what has been purposed for your work.

17. Michael Pope, "Virginia Church Reinvents Itself as Affordable Housing Developer," WAMU, June 19, 2015, https://tinyurl.com/2va9nbyu.

LESSON 9: REMEMBER WHO YOU ARE WORKING FOR
(NEHEMIAH 4:13-16)

I have heard many inspiring stories from faith leaders about how congregations persevered in the face of naysayers, delay, opposition, heartache, surprises, and frustrations. The responses echo the essence of what is noted in Nehemiah 4. Leadership is strategic when it places people in the work, and it reminds people to remember the divine source of their strength and calling. "Remember the Lord, great and awesome . . ." As noted in the section on prayer—this may seem an obvious "card to play"—sometimes the obvious is overlooked. People of faith by definition believe in someone or something greater than themselves. This is part of what makes a faith-based development deal unique. It has been said that "hope is not a strategy." Perhaps. But hope grounded in a faith in the Divine that is "great and awesome" can propel people to press through obstacles and hard times. As I remarked at a grand-opening ceremony, "When the underwriters said no, God said yes." The source that we look to for lesson 1 is the same source we look to in this lesson. God. Members of houses of worship are well served to remember the source of their faith as naysayers and setbacks arise.

Nehemiah encourages the people to remember God. The people are told to fight for their families. For the people. To serve God through service to the people. The naysayers were "deeply disturbed that a man had come to seek the well-being of the children of Israel." Well, that is what people of faith are called to do. Seek the well-being of the people.

SO WHAT, NOW WHAT?

Amid expanding needs in many communities, what are people of faith called to do with the resources we steward?

For many, the answer can be found in the land below their feet and the air above their heads. There is vast potential to build "out and up" on undeveloped or underdeveloped land owned by congregations. There is financial and missional value in the land and the air rights above it.

Several studies have examined the amount and potential impact of land owned by houses of worship in America. A 2020 policy brief by the Terner Center for Housing Innovation at UC Berkeley noted that over 38,000 acres of land in California are used for religious purposes. Of this, in five counties accounting for 31.5 percent of this land, there are 12,254 total potentially developable acres on 6,298 potentially developable parcels.[18]

Peter Tatian of the Urban Institute looked at property data for Washington, DC; Arlington, Virginia; and Montgomery and Fairfax Counties and found nearly 800 vacant parcels owned by faith-based institutions, making up almost 726 acres.[19] Most of these parcels are zoned as residential, and if we assume multifamily housing could be built on that land, depending on the density of housing, it could support the construction of between 43,000 and 108,000 new housing units.[20]

The work by the Urban Institute and the Terner Center provides examples of increasing analysis being done to quantify how much land is owned by houses of worship and the potential impact that could be activated by various types of community development. Referencing research done by the Interfaith Alliance of Colorado, a 2018 headline in the *Denverite* captured it this way:

18. Daniel Garcia and Eddie Sun, "Mapping the Potential and Identifying the Barriers to Faith-Based Housing Development," Terner Center for Housing Innovation, May 2020, https://tinyurl.com/mwmd2z8z.

19. "Three Things We Learned from Cleaning One Million DMV Property Records," *Data@Urban* (Urban Institute blog), December 3, 2019, https://tinyurl.com/b62mccfr.

20. Peter A. Tatian, "How Faith Communities Are Addressing the DC Region's Housing Challenges," Urban Institute, December 10, 2019, https://tinyurl.com/y7pmktyd.

"Denver Has a Housing Crisis. Guess Who's Got 5,000 Acres and a Moral Mission?"[21]

This movement can be grounded in what I call "*radical common sense.*" There is compelling human need in communities across the country. There are houses of worship in these communities. These congregations often own/control a resource that could be activated to help meet some of that compelling human need. Resource, meet need. Need, meet resource. Need and resource—allow me to introduce you to opportunity. Opportunity abounds for big churches or small temples; for those that own a couple of lots in a city or thirty acres in the suburbs; and for those with denominational polity or congregational polity.

Before the COVID pandemic, the reality was that many churches were places that people traveled miles to for worship, meetings, and ministry activities, and then returned home. On the journey to and from the church, in many cases congregants were passing through communities with residents living in distress. Passing by walls burned down. Passing through communities where people need real, life-changing transformational engagement. In some cases, we were sitting next to that person in need during service and had no idea of their struggles. During the prevaccine period of the COVID pandemic, many congregations saw the land of the sanctuary and temple sitting unused.

So what, now what? People of faith remember—we are called to be do-gooders. We are called to care and concern for our blood family, for our family of faith, and for the stranger. People are in need. We have critical resources: land, people who care with gifts and talents, in some cases money, relationships with influential neighbors and government officials, and most of all belief and faith in "the Lord, great and awesome." It is time for us to do more good. Let the naysayers know that we aren't gone yet. We are still breathing and still serving God through work that will help make

21. Andrew Kenney, "Denver Has a Housing Crisis. Guess Who's Got 5,000 Acres and a Moral Mission?" *Denverite*, May 10, 2018, https://tinyurl.com/hwyr7x73.

life better for people in our community through the faithful stewardship of the land God has entrusted to us.

In several instances in Nehemiah 3 there are references to people repairing the wall in front of their house. For houses of worship existing in a sea of need—be mindful of the multiplier effect. You do not have to build it all or solve it all by yourself. Build on your land. On your block. In your neighborhood. The call for us is to get many houses of worship doing appropriate development at the same time toward meeting clearly identified community needs. Put your brick on the wall. If you do it by your house and I do it by mine—over time the wall gets rebuilt.

11

THE VALUE OF RURAL CHURCHES AND FRESH HOPE

Jennie Birkholz

My dad was born and raised in a small, rural town in Wisconsin. With a population of around three hundred, it was a tight-knit community where everyone knew everyone and some more. The town was mostly made up of immigrants or close descendants of immigrants from Germany and Bohemia, which influenced the culture. The language, food, and traditions were brought from their native land and preserved and passed down within the community. In the center of the town was the Catholic church in which much of the community's social and spiritual life was anchored. The priest and nuns were assigned full time and lived and served the residents of the community. They too embodied the community culture by providing services in German and celebrating Bohemian and German traditions.

The church provided space for much of the rhythm of community life with communal meals, social activities, and life celebrations. A private school, run by local nuns, was housed within the church that my father attended. Even though public school was available in a nearby town, this school was preferred by locals because it was within walking distance, it preserved the cultural beliefs of the people, and its employees were known and trusted. This was important to the people of the community, who thrived on relationships and trust to survive in the new country.

JENNIE BIRKHOLZ

In this rural community, my father could not identify one person or family that was in need because everyone lived in community, with one another taking care of each other. When someone died in the town, the church bell would be rung for the number of years that the person was alive. Everyone in the town knew when someone had passed away and would honor that person's time on Earth. Lives in this small town were closely knitted together with the common bonds of social belonging, spiritual fulfillment, and community well-being.

This is not an uncommon story in the history of early American, small-town churches. Early in America's history, 95 percent of the population lived in what is now considered rural America.[1] When new immigrants came to colonize the land, they often would collectively settle and create small towns where they created a sense of continued belonging through preservation of culture. Since the people brought with them their religion, churches were one of the first structures built and were often placed in the center of town. These strategically located churches would be built with spaces for congregating that allowed them to serve as multipurpose centers for the community. Churches became central hubs for the community, providing space not only for religious activities but also for social activities, community organizing, and civic events. The social fabric of the community was knitted together by diverse gatherings that would take place at the church such as meals, celebrations, and recreational activities. Churches also served as a safety net in times of crisis, transforming into hospitals, community shelters, and emergency organizing hubs.

In many small and rural towns today, we find relics of this piece of American history. These churches and generational congregations have remained while businesses, hospitals, and people have come and gone. While the structures may still stand, these once-vital, thriving centers of communities now largely stand empty

1. Tim Slack and Leif Jensen, "The Changing Demography of Rural and Small-Town America," *Population Research and Policy Review* 39 (September 14, 2020), https://tinyurl.com/h37s62wc.

and lack a purpose. However, the unique attributes that once made these churches vital parts of the community remain today.

TODAY'S RURAL AMERICA

Throughout the decades, rural America has experienced changes that have caused despair and hopelessness in these once-thriving communities. Population decline, economic changes, and increased social isolation have all negatively impacted the well-being of these communities. Rural land accounts for more than 70 percent of America, and 46 million people (15 percent) live in rural areas. Rural America has higher population rates of the elderly, persons with disabilities, and veterans than other parts of America.[2] Recent studies have revealed that residents living in rural areas are not thriving. They have a greater risk of death from heart disease, cancer, stroke, lower respiratory disease, and unintentional death, which has led to an overall decrease in life expectancy. These disparities are even worse for persons of color.[3] Deaths of despair such as suicide or drug overdoses have ravaged these communities. Financial distress, lack of infrastructure or social services, deteriorating sense of community, and family fragmentation all contribute to high rates of these diseases of despair.[4]

At the center of all of this is the unraveling of the economic, political, and social fabric of rural America. The impact of the weakening of social connectedness has hit rural communities hard. Recently exasperated by the global pandemic, social isolation has increased and feelings of belonging to a community have decreased, creating an epidemic of loneliness and isolation. Some persons have turned to belonging on the Internet, where extrem-

2. "Rural Health," US Food & Drug Administration, June 22, 2021, https://tinyurl.com/bdd8jwnk.

3. "Rural Health Disparities," Rural Health Information Hub, accessed February 13, 2023, https://tinyurl.com/a9pamx36.

4. Daniel R. George et al., "Perceptions of Diseases of Despair by Members of Rural and Urban High-Prevalence Communities: A Qualitative Study," *JAMA*, July 23, 2021, https://tinyurl.com/2mu248ep.

ism and hate groups have taken advantage of this vulnerability and used it for evil.

The population in today's rural areas is changing as well. With the exception of communities near metro areas, rural population is in decline and losing more persons than are gained. What re-population that is occurring in America's rural areas is culturally diverse in nature. Rural areas are becoming a preferred place of settlement for immigrant populations. These new people bring with them their own cultural beliefs and practices, which mirrors the history of early rural America.[5]

The Rural Church

Today, church membership rosters may be small in rural churches, but opportunity for community reach is large. In small towns there are limited resources, so faith communities continue to fill in those social services gaps. They are central distribution centers, emergency shelters, and child-care centers.

Rural churches have aging congregation members, and their once-robust attendance numbers have dwindled over the years. The inability to attract new members to refill the pews has been attributed to a few factors, some of which are national trends and others are unique to or more severe in rural areas. In rural communities, the overall population decline and increase in age mean there are fewer families in the community to engage.

Many small towns have multiple churches of different denominations, each with a small number of aging members. These churches are mostly facing the same challenge of dwindling church rolls and operate in silos. They often compete for "new members," hold separate community events, and support different missions. For example, I have worked with one small community that has ten different physical churches, but each one has

5. D. W. Rowlands and Hanna Love, "Mapping Rural America's Diversity and Demographic Change," Brookings, September 28, 2021, https://tinyurl.com/3f7xuc4p.

fewer than twenty members. While one church contributes $50 a month to missions within the community, another church chooses to send all missional funds outside of the community. They each hold separate children's summer events but have low attendance and struggle to find volunteers. Each church has struggled financially to keep up with building repairs and everyday utilities. Many have a member (or two) that funds the entire church, so when that person passes away, the church will too.

Since the number of members in these churches is small, there is often a dearth in formal leadership. Most of these churches do not have full-time pastoral leadership assigned to them. The pastors are either bivocational, lay leaders, or "on rotation" from the denomination. Without consistent leadership and spiritual care, the church is left in the hands of the few remaining congregation members. These volunteers often lack the capacity or time to dedicate to strategic planning or program development.

Many small-town and rural churches tell the same story of how COVID-19 impacted their community. Before the pandemic, church pews were filled on Sunday mornings, members went to lunch together afterward, and had Bible studies during the week. When the churches temporarily closed for safety, the technology to continue to connect was not available at the church or in people's homes. Persons became increasingly isolated and out of touch with their communities. Emerging from the pandemic, the churches' attendance dramatically dropped, and persons have not returned.

In some churches, differing opinions over public health precautions such as masking or the closing of the church during the pandemic created disagreements within the congregation. These have revealed deep political divides within churches and even denominations. This has caused members to leave the church altogether or practice in different ways. Younger generations have turned away from formal church settings and may seek community in other places or practice their spirituality in alternative ways.

Much of the new population within rural communities are from culturally diverse groups of people reflective of the history of rural

America. There is growth in rural areas adjacent to large metros because of the lower cost of living, opportunities for a slower lifestyle, connection with nature and creative ventures. Despite these opportunities to breathe life back into vacant church buildings, established churches largely remain static or steadily declining. Observing this phenomenon firsthand, I have seen that many historical churches are not inclusive and welcoming to all members of the community. There is often an expectation for "others" to acclimate to the existing culture of the church, as opposed to the church acclimating to the needs of, or identifying with, the existing people of the community. This "othering" carries over into any missional work that the church does and ends up separating congregational members from those persons suffering in the community. Missions that are provided within the local community are largely transactional in nature as opposed to relational.

FRESH HOPE

Like Christian beliefs of the death and resurrection of Jesus Christ, the church too will go through cycles of death and resurrection. This will take faithfulness, hope, and persons watching for the resurrection. What may seem dead, hopeless, and abandoned can be resurrected with life-giving, grace-filled revival. Fresh hope for rural churches can be found in the rooted history of these community churches.

But time and space must first be made for grief. The recognition and release of the deep grief that congregation members are holding will make room for hope. Simply looking at current assets or possibilities without recognition of the losses ignores and invalidates the pain and grief congregations and their members are going through. Examining the losses and staying in the ashes allows members to understand the true pain of the loss and that it could be reenvisioned. Jumping immediately to fixing does not provide time to dig into the roots of the life-giving ministry and instead can create a pattern of recrafting the same programs that have failed.

A rural church that had eight members remaining stepped through this process. They were asked to bring an object that represented the best and worst of times in their congregation. Objects such as a face mask worn during COVID and choir sheet music were shared. These objects symbolized good times and bad for each person. Taking time for this exercise helped the leaders remember where they had come from and be ready to move forward.

In a paradoxical way, fresh hope for the future of rural churches can be cultivated by allowing them to draw upon their existing strengths and commitments from the past and applying those gifts in new ways. While they may not have used these terms, rural churches have strength in connecting spiritual health with human wellness, self-organizing for change, and building community partnerships. All three of these approaches provide fresh hope for a new future for rural churches.

CONNECTING SPIRITUALITY WITH WELLNESS

By combining their focus on spiritual fulfillment with social determinants of health, churches can provide a unique role in the community that other institutions cannot. The US Department of Health and Human Services defines social determinants of health as the conditions in which people are born, grow, live, work, and age.[6] These conditions are shaped by the distribution of money, power, and resources in a community and are not individual behaviors. A key component of social determinants of health is spirituality and social connectedness. Research has revealed that persons participating in spiritual communities live healthier, longer lives, experience less behavioral health challenges and lower incidences of death by suicide.[7] Spirituality creates a connection with a higher power and with those around us that then influences behaviors and mind-set. Faith communities offer structure and opportunities to learn and practice spirituality both individually and in community.

6. "Social Determinants of Health," US Department of Health and Human Services, accessed February 13, 2023, https://tinyurl.com/zw2rfecd.

7. Tracy A. Balboni et al., "Spirituality in Serious Illness and Health," *JAMA*, July 12, 2022, https://tinyurl.com/kt58sn3j.

By continuing to serve as a community center for spiritual resources, churches can again serve as one of the weavers in the
social fabric of society and offer the needed antidote to social
isolation and improve disparities in health outcomes. The church
assets that gave it this historical role remain: central location, public gathering space, and people commonly rooted in community.
Leaning into this role will improve the well-being of the community, congregation, and the church.

SELF-ORGANIZING FOR CHANGE

One of the greatest challenges that plagues rural churches is the
available hands and feet for the work that needs to be done. Full-
time assigned paid clergy leadership is rare in rural churches, which
leaves congregations to lead themselves. Administrative decisions
are left to long-standing committees often made of persons that
have been serving for decades. While these persons are historical
assets, many have expressed a desire for a break and spiritual rest.
The resurrection of faith communities will take a different structure that leans into the deepest roots of the church. Deconstruction
of committees and moving into self-organizing strategies decen-
tralize power structures and decision making. This makes way for
efficient use of everyone's assets and rapid implementation.

Self-organizing is one of the earliest ways that the church was
birthed. Jesus sent out the disciples, with their unique gifts and
talents, to spread the news and create clusters of communities.
He did not have planning committees, develop a strategic plan, or
have job descriptions. When there was a question in early groups
of Jesus followers, it was often responded to not with a direct
command but with storytelling, teaching from people, or a self-
reflecting prompt. This same structure of self-organizing has been
seen in rural America with barn raisings, community responses
to tornadoes or other natural disasters, and responses to modern
tragedies such as school shootings. By self-organizing, members
represent the church in community partnerships and are empowered to follow their unique gifts without having to run it through
a committee that meets once a month.

COMMUNITY PARTNERSHIPS

Churches can no longer be insular institutions and instead must open hearts and buildings to others in the community. A key role that churches can play is that of a convener. Rural churches, like the one my father grew up in, have existed at the literal and figurative intersection of rural communities since they were founded. They can bring people together across the community that normally don't interact. Partnerships between faith communities, nonprofits, health systems, and the community are key to understanding how the church fits into the community today. It also allows for these partners to understand the value that churches can offer, including physical and spiritual assets.

By building upon community partnerships, churches that want to go deeper with their impact can focus their work on breaking down systems of power that cause oppression. This can create a pathway for equitable health, well-being, and a community where everyone flourishes. Faith communities can move their work or funding of work that is charity or transactional to systems that provide liberation of people. Much of this is achieved through community-centered strategic planning, with community members driving the process.

REVISIONING SPACES

Churches in rural communities hold spatial capital—buildings and land situated in accessible, central locations in the community. Reenvisioning those spaces is beneficial to both the church and the greater community. When land is reimagined by churches as a resource instead of as a burden, new community can be formed. Developed and accessible public, or quasi-public, land and spaces are a valuable resource in rural communities.

Many rural churches remain located in the center of towns or on main traffic routes, so they are already in areas that people access for shopping, schools, or business needs. Allowing the church property to be used as a modern public space that serves the greater needs of the community will not only support the vitality and growth of the community but provide exposure and potential income to the church. There are many potential uses for church land and buildings. When repurposed thoughtfully and integrated with the spiritual assets of the church, property can positively impact the health and well-being of the community.

Here are a few examples of ways churches can reuse their property for church and community good.

Community Gardens and Farmers' Markets

Even though many rural communities are surrounded by agriculture, often crops do not stay in the local community for personal consumption. Paradoxically, these communities are very often food deserts and lack access to fresh food such as fruits and vegetables. What is available is often expensive and distant, requiring transportation, which many do not have access to. By efficient utilization of the land that churches own, they can address this nutritional community need and provide opportunities for socialization and economic stability.

Church property can be transformed into mini-farming communities with vegetable gardens, orchards, and small farm animals such as chickens. Fresh food can fill the pantry of those in need and provide a critical nutritional need in the community. The church can then take advantage of its central location by hosting regular farmers' markets where the remaining food can be sold to raise funds for the church. Creating a community garden or orchards and holding farmers' markets also provide community social opportunities through volunteerism.

Recreational Space

The availability of recreation infrastructure such as sidewalks and bicycle paths is particularly limited in rural areas, which contributes to a higher prevalence of poor health outcomes among rural residents.[8] Research has suggested that in rural areas, access to

8. Stephanie S. Frost et al., "Effects of the Built Environment on Physical

indoor recreational facilities is most impactful on physical activity for adults.[9] Parks and low-cost recreational sites require public land and infrastructure that are often not available in rural areas. Using church property to provide opportunities for community recreational activities would meet a need for physical and social connection in the community while also bringing persons in proximity to the church. Going beyond the traditional playground with an all-abilities park or a skate park on church property would reach out to a wide spectrum of people to create intergenerational bonds across the community.

Community Center Space

Urban areas have libraries, community centers, health clinics, and dedicated spaces that exclusively house charities or social services. Rural and small-town communities lack the physical spaces to house these essential services, and investing in new buildings for those services is often not viable. Facilities that do exist in these communities, such as schools, are not open to all persons during school hours and are closed for long holidays and the summer. Church buildings are an existing asset that can be repurposed or updated to provide space for those needs.

Church buildings are often accessible, located in the center of towns or on main traffic routes; have large gathering spaces; and may be the only public buildings open to all residents. Furthermore, church buildings are often empty most days of the week, so there is available space. The COVID-19 pandemic forced many churches to adopt new technology to offer remote services or classes. This investment makes the facility even more appealing to organizations looking for spaces to use. Rather than rural communities building new facilities, underutilized church buildings

---

Activity of Adults Living in Rural Settings," *American Journal of Health Promotion* 24, no. 4 (March-April 2010), https://tinyurl.com/f5mu65n.

9. Christiaan G. Abildso et al., "Environmental Factors Associated with Physical Activity in Rural U.S. Counties," *International Journal of Environmental Research and Public Health* 18, no. 14 (July 2021), https://tinyurl.com/yatk76xy.

could be adapted for community-center space. It is much more affordable and efficient to update an existing, underutilized church building than to construct a new facility from scratch.

Health-Care Space

Rural health disparities have been linked to a lack of access to health care and geographic isolation.[10] Even though there is a shortage of health-care and specialty-care providers in rural areas, it is difficult to recruit persons to practice there. Often there are no hospitals or clinics with modern technology; there is limited opportunity for professional growth; and the workload is high and the pay is low. Health-care and social-support services all require specific physical spaces in the community, which are limited in rural areas. All of this contributes to a lack of access to quality health care in rural areas. Churches can address this need by offering space and resources for health-care providers. A rural church's location, available space, and infrastructure can make it a good candidate to serve as a satellite site for health care.

"Community resource hubs" is a model that allows for a "one-stop shop" for all social-service and health-care needs. These hubs are open to the public for a variety of social and educational activities, such as exercise groups, adult education classes, support groups, culinary classes, and senior day activities. The advantage to having these services under one roof is better coordination of services, whole health care (physical, mental, and spiritual), and the efficient use of transportation resources. Church buildings in rural areas could be repurposed as community resource hubs.

Community resource hubs are created by bringing together social-service organizations that do not already have a presence or have a limited presence in the community. They are given offices to provide services such as health care, public assistance, and even legal assistance. Nonprofits and community support such as food pantries and diaper banks that are scattered throughout the

10. "Rural Health Disparities."

region can be relocated to a central location to reduce the burden of transportation and increase efficiency of time. Providers receive space in the community and also have access to volunteers; technology; emergency resources, such as food pantries; and spiritual-care coordination.

When access to a higher level of care, such as a mental health professional, a physician, or a specialty-care consultation, is needed but not available, telemedicine can be utilized. Since COVID-19, many rural churches have invested in technology and video-conference infrastructure. This technology combined with available private office spaces, a central location, and wraparound social supports, including spiritual practices, makes churches an ideal telehealth or in-person medical provider site.

Ancillary health-care providers such as nurses or community health workers are essential resources in rural communities that lack medical providers. Faith Community Nurses and Faith Community Health Workers are professionals that are housed out of churches that provide health-related support to not only the congregation but also the community. At the core of their services are group events that promote socialization and incorporate spiritual practices. Some activities are yoga classes, walk-to-Bethlehem programs, nutritional eating classes, and faith-based fall prevention classes, all of which support health and wellness in a social and spiritually framed atmosphere. Emerging research has revealed that Faith Community Nursing is an effective strategy to improve health outcomes and health behaviors.[11]

FUNDING RURAL INNOVATION

Resurrecting the rural church will require transformation of both the hearts and minds of the congregation to want to thrive again. The practices of isolationism, silos, hierarchical power structures, and charity-driven missions will have to be broken. Rural churches

11. "Faith Community Nursing," University of Wisconsin Population Health Institute, updated June 3, 2020, https://tinyurl.com/2v45f6sx.

will move forward best within community networks, woven together by common threads of trust and missional alignment. Churches can create meaningful relationships by reaching beyond their walls to listen to the community story. When partnering with other churches, nonprofits, and community groups, they can create a larger pool of people and physical and financial capital.

Funding of rural churches varies from congregation to congregation but mostly centers on giving from individual congregation members. Some are surviving off the donations of one or two members while others rely on full congregational giving. Starting new capital projects for land or property modifications will take up-front capital. Other projects, such as the housing of a nurse or community health worker, will take ongoing funding to keep them going. A little money may be raised through internal projects, such as the selling of foods grown on-site, which can be used to sustain missions long term.

Recently, rural health and well-being have become a significant funding focus for foundations, the government, and health-care systems. These entities have allocated funding, coaching support, and other resources to implement programs in rural communities; however, a general lack of trusted institutions and nonprofits in these areas has created a challenge for them to get the resources to the communities in need. Many of these organizations have turned to faith communities, sometimes the only institutional pillars in the community, to partner with to house or even run new programs. Churches wanting to provide or support programs that will improve the lives in the community can reach out to these entities to see what is available to them.

Health-Care Partnerships

Funding for health-care systems is often tied to patient outcomes or is a result of cost savings derived from prevention. For example, health-care systems can be penalized by insurance companies if patients are readmitted to in-patient care under certain conditions. Patients who do not have insurance and frequent the emergency room for their care, known as high utilizers in the health-care field, are costly to health-care systems because they do not receive any reimbursement for the services. These patients often do not get better because they have no source of follow-up care or social support systems to assist them in the community. In urban areas health-care systems can use the public and nonprofit social services resources in the community to provide interventions. Rural areas are more challenging because they do not have a strong social services network or many local health-care providers for follow-up.

Some health-care systems have turned to churches in rural communities to provide the follow-up support needed to successfully keep residents safe in their homes. Health-care systems have established faith-based programs and partnerships in which they train church members to visit patients and provide a ministry of presence. The church member is thus able to help the patient with prescriptions, housing, or food if needed. Congregations find this program beneficial because it provides a reach-out to persons in the community that they have never had contact with before and creates a pathway for the patient to a relationship with God and the church. Health-care systems have found significant savings with these programs and continue to expand and support them across the country.

Foundation Partnerships

There are many foundations across America that focus on improving population health, improving community well-being, and reducing health disparities. Because rural areas disproportionately have poorer health outcomes and health disparities, foundations have begun to focus funding, programs, and support in this target area. Foundations are partnering with churches in rural communities because they are trusted anchor institutions that are centrally located. For example, some foundations are funding community nurses that are located within churches, so all programing and costs are not the responsibility of the local church. The nurses provide community outreach and conduct health screenings and wellness classes that bring people into relationship with the church. This is mutually beneficial to both the church and the larger community.

Foundations are also providing funding for churches to create their own health and wellness programs. With this unrestricted funding, rural churches can plan and implement projects they believe will support the spiritual, mental, and physical health of their congregation or community. Some program examples include planting orchards, providing extended ministry programs, and hosting community training such as Mental Health First Aid. This allows churches to unleash their imagination to find new, meaningful ways to connect with the community and create fresh hope for the church.

Foundations that choose to support rural work will find that these communities need longer-term commitments and multiyear funding. Creating trust and empowering the people to decide what is the best solution for their community are especially critical in rural areas. So many activities have been forced upon them that to have control over their own story and solutions is key to sustained transformation. To achieve this, funders that shift away from traditional grant making to trust-based philanthropy and participatory grant making will find greater success.

Rural America is the historic soul of our nation. The once-thriving heartbeat of American culture is dealing with sickness and despair. The anchoring churches in these communities can play a vital role in transforming despair into hope and help create flourishing communities once again. This will happen as churches and leaders hold fresh hope, draw upon their historic strengths, redefine ministry in the future, and become a partner in creating new pathways to a thriving community.

PART 3
Together

12

PROACTIVE CITY PLANNING
FOR CHURCH PROPERTY TRANSITIONS

Kurt Paulsen

Here is a recent headline in our local newspaper: "Another Madison Church Hopes to Sell Its Building for Housing Development Project."[1] The church property is 3.6 acres, strategically located along an arterial road with public transportation, adjacent to an elementary school, near thousands of jobs, and in an ethnically diverse area of the city desperately needing affordable housing. The current building is only ten thousand square feet and dates to the 1960s. The proposal would provide space for the church to continue its worship and provide community services (legal clinics, financial literacy programs, etc.) along with over one hundred affordable housing units.

As a first impression, what's not to love? A multiethnic church maintains its presence in the neighborhood and better uses its underutilized parcel in a strategic location, and affordable housing for a range of incomes is built where urban planners say it should be—near schools, jobs, and transit. City plans and funding clearly

---

1. Dean Mosiman, "Another Madison Church Hopes to Sell Its Building for Housing Development Project," *Madison Wisconsin State Journal*, August 16, 2022, https://tinyurl.com/2mdvjufv.

identify the need for more affordable housing, and the city will get the redeveloped parcel back on the tax rolls to fund services and infrastructure in the area.[2] In our expensive city, affordable housing developers have difficulty securing adequately sized and sited parcels for redevelopment at reasonable prices.

This church property transition, announced just as I was writing this chapter, is in the earliest stages and likely won't see occupancy until at least 2025. When the church announced their proposal, this likely reflected the outcome of years of internal conversations, discernment, and strategic planning and an agreement to partner with an experienced affordable housing developer.

But now the public planning process begins. There will be many—and long!—neighborhood meetings, plan commission meetings, meetings with city staff, reports, revised site plans and architectural renderings, public hearings, and ultimately a vote at city council.

Urban planners see these property transition proposals all the time. My first instinct (since I regularly drive by the site) was to check the comprehensive and neighborhood plans and the zoning ordinance. The plans show that parcel as "low-medium density residential," and the current zoning (SR-C1) allows places of worship and single-family detached homes as permitted uses by-right.[3] Because the proposed redevelopment is not consistent with current zoning, the church and the developer will need to go through an "entitlement" process—rezoning the parcel, possible amendment to the comprehensive and neighborhood plans, site

---

2. Current plans are for the developer to acquire ownership of the parcel and to lease the first floor back to the church. Because the property would have commercial land uses and not be owned by the church, it would likely not be exempt from property taxes.

3. Schools, day care, libraries, community centers, etc., are conditional uses in the district. Uses permitted by-right are approved by the plan commission without a public hearing or neighborhood meeting if they meet the other standards in the ordinance. Conditional uses require public notice, a public hearing and approval by plan commission. Rezoning requires a public hearing and approval by the city council. The details vary by city and state.

plan approval, design review, and all other city approvals such as traffic/parking, lighting, and landscaping. Every single one of those approvals occurs at a public meeting, some of which may involve a public hearing or public comments.

Neighboring property owners will get their say, as will the area's city council member. In some cities, entitlement processes can be completed in under a year, but in other cities the process can take years and still not be successful. The affordable housing developer also intends to apply for city and county and state funding sources, each with their own separate requirements, meetings, and decision makers. At every stage, a no vote could kill the project. Without zoning approval, they can't apply for housing tax credits and city funding, and without funding, the development would not be financially feasible.

Property transitions like this happen all the time, in big cities and small towns. Neighborhood demographics and property values are always changing. Disinvestment, abandonment, blight, gentrification, displacement, redevelopment, NIMBYs, traffic, parking, affordable housing—these issues regularly dominate local news, local politics, planning, and neighborhood conversations.

Church properties are certainly not immune from these forces.

Whenever any property owner—including churches—wants to change the use of a building or parcel or alter the buildings or site plan, this requires a public planning process. It is a "planning" process (city planning departments, zoning, design, entitlements, etc.) that is "public" (public meetings, neighborhood reaction, NextDoor posts, newspapers, anger, suspicion, and potential conflict). We don't want churches to fear this public process (because there are successful examples in this book), but we also don't want churches to be naïve about how potentially challenging this process can be.

A church may have built up lots of neighborhood goodwill and even political deference. But once they propose to alter their property, people's attitudes can change. A church may have agreed, "Let us start building!" (Neh. 2:18), but Sanballat the NIMBY and his friends might get angry and try to oppose and stop the work (let the reader understand).

For every "successful" case study we observe or imagine—a holistic, inclusive, community development process where cities and neighbors and church property owners work together to create a mutual plan that benefits all stakeholders—we see more cases where the process breaks down or turns acrimonious, where neighboring homeowners thwart needed housing or community services, or where longtime lower-income neighborhood residents feel displaced, powerless, or not listened to by the city or the developer.

The possibility of thousands of church property transitions offers exciting opportunities for "planning world" and "church world" to advance shared values such as providing affordable housing, expanding community services, remedying past injustices, and lifting up the voices of the marginalized and vulnerable. But church property transitions could easily become like most other urban property transitions as sites of conflict or mistrust.

In this chapter, I offer some thoughts on the public planning process involved in church property transitions. I define a property transition to be a change in the primary use(s) of a parcel(s) or a significant alteration of the existing buildings (including removal and redevelopment) or significant changes to a property site plan. Church property transitions occur when the current principal use of the property is as a church[4] and the property is owned by a church or a nonprofit. I will begin with a discussion for urban planners about how and why they should prepare for church property transitions, and then will discuss how churches can engage with the public planning process.

For Urban Planning: Why You Should Plan for Church Property Transitions

In many religious traditions, one begins with confession, so here's mine: even though I am an urban planning professor who re-

---

4. The issues I discuss could equally be applied to all religious property, including mosques, synagogues, temples, etc.

searches and teaches urban property and finance issues, I was initially dumbfounded when Mark Elsdon explained the concept of this book. I remember face-palming and blurting out, "My goodness, of course! Why have I never heard of this before?!" Although churches may have been talking about this for years, I suspected that most urban planners have not thought much about church property transitions, except for case-by-case examples.

So, I first wanted to find out what our profession thought about the issue of churches and property transitions. I did a complete text search of the main professional publication for planning (*Planning Magazine*) for the past five years and the main academic journal (*Journal of the American Planning Association*) for the past ten years.[5] In our leading academic journal, the word "church" (or any variant) does not even appear in the last ten years. Not once. In the professionally oriented publication—distributed to tens of thousands of local government officials every month—there were no articles or even brief news items related to church property issues. None. There are some brief mentions of the role of African American churches' history in community development (e.g., Abyssinian Baptist Church) and the civil rights movement. There is one brief mention of a church redevelopment in Saratoga Springs, New York, but no details. To be fair, the professional magazine frequently recognizes that churches are deeply involved in their communities in providing spaces for community meetings, substance abuse counseling, homeless shelters, feeding programs, etc., and that churches are ideal places to hold community outreach and engagement meetings. But nothing about church properties, except for the legal and regulatory issues involving the First Amendment, and property tax exemption.[6]

5. Of course, that means I missed: Nadia Mian, "'Prophets-for-Profits': Redevelopment and the Altering Urban Religious Landscape," *Urban Studies* 45, no. 10 (2008): 2143–61. Dr. Mian is a contributor to this volume and kindly pointed out this reference.

6. Most planners are familiar with the RLUIPA, the Religious Land Use and Institutionalized Persons Act (42 U.S.C. §§ 2000cc, et seq.), which governs many zoning decisions regarding churches. There is fre-

Because "planning world" and "church world" would otherwise appear to have little connection, the purpose of this chapter is to try to offer pathways of partnership and conversation between both. I hope that some of this information can help church-world better understand local government planning to be proactive in connecting with your community and neighborhood stakeholders. I hope to convince planners and local governments of the need to proactively engage with churches and neighborhoods regarding potential church property transitions.

CHURCH PROPERTY TRANSITIONS ARE UNIQUE

Why are church property transitions a unique category for planners? There are at least five reasons.

First, zoning for churches in cities is influenced by a federal law, the Religious Land Use and Institutionalized Persons Act (RLUIPA).[7] RLUIPA is designed to protect religious land uses from discrimination in local zoning (and historic preservation) ordinances and prohibits land use ordinances that impose a "substantial burden" on religious exercise or "unreasonable limits" on religious land uses within a jurisdiction. Under RLUIPA, most cities allow churches in residential zones, either as a permitted by-right use or as a conditional use. However, because they are in residential areas, church property transitions or redevelopment that includes "commercial" land uses like multifamily housing can provoke neighborhood resistance. The "church" use of the

---

quent discussion of a recent Supreme Court case, *Reed v. Town of Gilbert*, 576 U.S. 155 (2015), which dealt with First Amendment issues of sign ordinances. Reed was the pastor of a church that sued Gilbert concerning their sign ordinances.

7. 42 U.S.C. §§ 2000cc, et seq. The information presented here is for general informational use and does not constitute legal advice. For more information on RLUIPA, see the US Department of Justice informational page: https://tinyurl.com/yc7vwdfm (accessed August 16, 2022). Many states have statutory or constitutional provisions that provide additional rights and protections for religious land uses.

property vis-à-vis the zoning ordinance is protected by RLUIPA (and possibly state statutes and constitutional provisions), but the proposed "commercial" use might not be. When the "use" of a property is proposed to change and the proposed new "use" is not a "religious use," the change will be treated as any other private or commercial land-use transition in the public planning process.

Of course, everything in the preceding paragraph is generic, and the specific facts of any case or ordinance will be determinative. To the best of my knowledge, the federal and state case law on the topic is evolving and unsettled, and there are no definitive cases that would provide unambiguous precedents. Churches considering property transitions will need experienced legal counsel for any of these potential issues. In the Madison church proposal described above, the church may believe that providing affordable housing is a religious exercise, motivated by the abundance of biblical commands to love, serve, and welcome the marginalized and vulnerable—the widows, orphans, strangers, and the poor.[8] However, the principal "use" of the property will be the "commercial" use of multifamily residential, which is likely not a protected "religious" land use and will likely be evaluated under the planning and entitlement process the same as any other multifamily building proposal.[9]

Second, most churches have unique architecture. While not every church is Gothic with stained glass windows, church architecture is often distinct and designed to signal the type of activities that occur in the building. In many neighborhoods, the unique architecture of churches contributes to urban design, sense of place, and character of the neighborhood. Even when a church building is not protected by historic district regulations, the potential loss

8. Cf. Nicholas Wolterstorff, "Justice in the Old Testament/Hebrew Bible," chapter 3 in *Justice: Rights and Wrongs* (Princeton: Princeton University Press, 2008).

9. In this particular case, the developer/owner of the affordable housing component is a for-profit entity rather than a nonprofit entity, which would not qualify for the property tax exemption in Wisconsin. See Wis. Stat. 70.11(4a).

of the church architecture may be undesirable for planners and neighborhood residents. The contribution of church architecture to urban design, however, also mitigates against economically viable reuse: vaulted ceilings, stained glass, and large sanctuaries are ideal for worship services but less conducive to office or housing uses without significant costs. Planners need to consider the trade-offs of preservation with the financial obligations that imposes on aging buildings and the economics of new uses.

Third, churches generally occupy prominent and strategic locations, often along major arterial roads or on significant corner lots. As a general principle, urban planning departments map and identify locational and suitability criteria for areas that are likely to experience redevelopment or are better candidates for redevelopment. Those criteria generally include the parcel size, proximity to higher capacity transportation facilities, and the location of the parcel relative to established neighborhoods. There is substantial overlap between property features that are suitable for redevelopment and the location of many church properties. Cities should, therefore, consider updating or revising their redevelopment strategies and policies to potentially include current church properties.

Fourth, a church property transition is a unique process compared to commercial or profit-oriented transitions. Congregations are likely unfamiliar with the public planning process and therefore may need attention and support from the city to accomplish their mission-driven goals. Both planners and churches are (or should be) committed to social justice and inclusive community processes. The opportunity to work with willing property owners committed to these values means a real opportunity to advance city goals. The trade-off is that congregations may not have the experience and technical capacity of experienced for-profit development teams, and so may need additional support and technical assistance.

Fifth, the incumbent church property already provides a wide range of community services and social capital infrastructure that would potentially be lost if the property is simply redeveloped and the church moves. As part of a neighborhood planning process, cities might consider what services are currently provided by churches (and other nonprofits that might use church facilities) and prepare for the impacts if churches no longer exist in some areas of the city. All nonprofits (including churches) need revenue to maintain their level of programming and services. Cities should consider that some form of income-producing property may be necessary to maintain churches in neighborhoods with the capacity to continue service provision. If not, the quality of life in the neighborhood may decline, which could require the city and taxpayers to provide more services.

Proactive Planning by Municipalities

I know that every city planning department is already overworked and its staff underpaid, and yet I'm suggesting additional work and responsibilities? Hopefully, the information in this book convinces planners and local governments of the positive possibilities of helping to manage church property transitions and what could be lost if proactive planning is not undertaken. As the other chapters make clear, these property transitions are going to happen even if cities are not prepared. In that spirit, I make three suggestions for this planning.

First, a city should consider convening a forum or work group of interested religious groups (or nonprofits generally) that might be considering property transitions. Working with and through established church associations, this group could share best practices, provide information and education, and strategize together. Such a forum could be a reasonably low-cost way (in terms of staff time) for staff to reach out and learn about potential redevelopment projects.

Second, a city planning department could consider a dedicated process team or staff team to provide technical assistance to churches that are considering property transitions. The idea is that by creating a way for property owners to meet with and work with staff as early in the process as possible, staff can provide guidance on the process and recommend steps to engage with neighbors and other stakeholders.

Third, planners should consider evaluating and updating their neighborhood plans or redevelopment plans to consider which church properties are potentially going to experience a property transition in the coming years. This proactive planning can make the process transparent and can ensure that the city's priorities, policies, and funding are aligned.

FOR CHURCHES: HOW TO ENGAGE WITH THE PUBLIC PLANNING PROCESS

Churches considering a property transition need to understand how the city's current plans and zoning ordinances will constrain what they can do with the site and will need to be prepared to engage in dialogue and outreach with their community and nearby neighbors. This is a complicated undertaking, and the key to any good property development process is to assemble an experienced team of professionals to guide you through the process. Churches need to take the time to assemble a team they can work with and trust. After internal agreement to proceed, I recommend churches establish a steering committee to speak for the church and interact with the development team. As the steering committee begins to meet, it is better to seek the advice of development experts sooner rather than later.

Churches need to have honest internal and external conversations. Once you decide to undergo a property transition, you are in the property development and commercial real estate business. It is entirely possible (as the case studies in this volume demonstrate) to engage in that type of business and the public planning process with integrity while maintaining focus on mission. Possible, but neither easy nor automatic.[10]

10. RootedGood offers resources like their "How to Develop Well" tool that is a good starting point for churches considering property development. rootedgood.org.

Let me be honest from my experience: a high-quality design, planning, and development team that can navigate the complex internal relationships (within the church), the complex external relationships (with the city and with the neighborhood), and the complex lateral relationships (with contractors, architects, engineers, financiers, etc.) is worth its weight in gold. Without a good team, you won't get a quality outcome. But that level of experience and expertise does not come cheap because experienced firms and developers are in high demand. Many firms have concerns about working with institutional clients like churches because of the "too many cooks in the kitchen" problem or the perception that churches require too much "hand-holding" through the process. Many firms might feel that churches won't have adequate financial reserves to pay a consultant through the concept development and entitlement phase.

Any church undergoing this process needs to understand how all of the participants on the development side actually make their money or get paid.[11] After all, "the laborer deserves to be paid" (Luke 10:7). Almost every real estate deal is accomplished through a partnership structure, an agreement as to who owns what, who provides funds (and at what time), who gets paid, when, and how. Who receives cash-out at closing, and who guarantees the debt or note? Some participants get paid up front, and some are paid as they perform work (fee-for-service), while others get "paid" with an equity (ownership) stake in the project. Each modality of getting "paid" on a deal has different tax consequences. Will the church hire an owner's representative (who gets a portion of the development fee)? Does the church need or want ongoing revenue from the project, or does it want/need an up-front payment for the land? How does the project "pencil out" for all parties at the

11. The usual disclaimer: "This information is for informational purposes only and does not offer any technical, legal, or financial advice. Anyone involved in complex real estate transactions should seek the advice of competent and licensed professionals including (but not limited to): engineers, real estate brokers, accountants, and attorneys."

beginning of a project, and who bears the risk if something goes wrong? Who owns the property and who could claim any property value appreciation in the long run?

I ask these difficult questions so that churches enter the process with eyes wide open. You don't know the answer to these questions, and if you think you do, you don't. The only exception would be if an experienced professional belongs to your congregation who will volunteer expertise in a fiduciary manner and not participate financially in any deal. But churches should be careful about using congregants in this way, because of potential conflicts of interest and trust issues.

Ways to Partner with a Developer

The choice of a developer or development team might be the most important choice a church can make. There are two main options for partnering with a development team. At the earliest stage, a congregation could hire (either on a fee-for-service basis or as a portion of the future development fee) a consulting firm or an "owner's representative" to advise and guide them on the process, to sketch out preliminary development concepts, and to be a fiduciary to protect the church's interests. An experienced consultant or representative would help the church decide on potential programming of the site and what is possible (financially, technically, and politically). This person would then help the church negotiate an agreement with a developer (directly or through an RFP [request for proposals]).[12]

Alternatively, a church could enter a partnership with an experienced developer up front, and the developer would then internalize the architecture, engineering, site planning, and entitlement process costs within the eventual developer fee. The advantage of working with experienced developers is that they already have good relationships with architects, planners, and en-

12. Chapter 14 in this volume (by Philip Burns, Jill Shook, and Andre Johnny White) describes advisory services like this in greater detail.

gineers and have experience with the city to know what types of projects are possible. By partnering with a developer early on, the church is off-loading a lot of the design and planning process to the developer. The advantage of this is the developer's expertise. The disadvantage is that experienced developers tend to like to stick with the same concepts that have worked before and may not have the patience or the creativity for something different or unique. If a church is not "paying" a developer on a guaranteed fee-for-service for this predevelopment work, that means the developer is taking on additional risk that would be reflected in the development fee.

A key question becomes whether a congregation wants to "decide" about the site programming (land uses, density, affordability level, parking, green space, etc.) ahead of time and shop that concept to a developer or whether the congregation wants the developer to help guide them through the site-programming decisions. This all can and should be negotiated with the developer or consultant so that everyone's expectations are accounted for. For example, a church may decide to maximize the economic return of their parcel to fund an alternative site or their other programs. Or a church may decide that targeted affordability restriction for the lowest income brackets is most important. Those values and concepts need to be communicated to the development consultant or developer and clearly articulated in any agreements. As the process enters the public planning phase and designs/programs are challenged or changed, a church needs to know what it is willing to compromise on and what it is not willing to change. But trust is also needed because unexpected problems will arise. In any negotiation and partnership, there is always change and unplanned contingencies. Trust and communication are essential in any relationship. Churches need to understand that even mission-driven developers need to make a financial return on their investment, and developers need to understand that church clients are unique in their mission-first approach to property development. Churches should interview potential development team members to find out their experience and willingness to work with them.

A second question is how committed the congregation is to a specific vision or design when it bumps up against the entitlement process. For example, if a church is strongly committed to developing their property for affordable housing but the property is in a single-family neighborhood whose homeowners oppose the project, how much negotiation/compromise is acceptable? Even when we believe that NIMBY opposition to affordable housing by incumbent homeowners is unjust and reflects racial or class bias, we recognize that incumbent homeowners are a powerful constituency that influences city council votes.

Churches need to decide ahead of time (with their partners) how much and what type of engagement, listening, and dialogue to undertake with the neighboring property owners and residents. Should the church itself conduct this engagement, or should the development partners or consultants? Should the church reach out to the local city council representative or ask the representative to hold a neighborhood information and discussion session early in the process? Does announcing plans and intentions—in good faith—early on just give neighbors more time to organize opposition? If the opposition gets nasty or misrepresents the proposal or expresses racist sentiments in public meetings or social media, how does the church want to respond? A church can strategize and learn from other cases and their development partners but must be prepared to address this public conversation.

For Us All: Public Planning in Good Faith

Redevelopment proposals, affordable housing, and property transitions in already-built neighborhoods are contentious because all of us are situated or embedded within meanings shaped by the market and economics (prices, property values, rents, taxes, return on investment, interest rates, supply and demand, etc.) and meanings affected by our moral and political values (justice, fairness, equity, remedying past injustices of racial segregation, etc.). If you listen carefully to debates and public hearings about urban planning, you'll hear both types of language, and we often talk past each other. And we must recognize that decision-making power and voice in land-use decisions is not distributed equally or fairly.[13]

I wish there were some evidence or argument emerging from either social science research or theology or ethics that can provide clear and unambiguous answers. We know from theology that all human decisions, whether individually or in groups, are a complicated entanglement of good motives and selfish motives. All participants in the public planning process are influenced by their own economic and property interests. We tend to assume that we judge our own motives and others' motives correctly and with fairness, while others' judgment of us is biased and clouded.

A church might intend to produce affordable housing to serve those most vulnerable or at risk of homelessness or those who have experienced racial segregation and injustice. This intention is rooted in good motives and spiritual discernment and reflects a heart for justice. To implement that vision, the church partners with a developer to build a multifamily building on its property. To the neighbors, however, this intention might be interpreted as "greedy" or an unjust interference with their own sense of the neighborhood. Incumbent homeowners may think their motives to oppose the project are good and rooted in protecting the neighborhood that has nurtured them and their children. But their motives may be perceived as exclusionary and selfish by folks proposing the affordable housing.

Over the years, I've seen so many public meetings where both proponents and opponents of the project appeal to moral values that, on their face, are good values. But their visions of what should (or should not) happen on this parcel or in this neighborhood are completely contradictory. Politics may be the art of compromise, and economics may be the art of negotiating a mutually

13. See Katherine Einstein et al., *Neighborhood Defenders: Participatory Politics and America's Housing Crisis* (Cambridge: Cambridge University Press, 2020), for empirical research demonstrating that participants in the public planning process are disproportionately whiter, older, of higher income, and more likely to be homeowners than the general population.

advantageous deal. But when deeply held values are in opposition to each other, the public planning process feels messy and frustrating, and we muddle along, and no one really feels good about the process.

The social science research side of urban planning understands that local real estate politics (and that's what this is) are driven more by economic interests than by "values." Those whose stated political values tend toward the left with a commitment to inclusion and justice still show up to public meetings to oppose affordable housing and redevelopment within their own neighborhoods. Those whose stated political values tend toward the right with a commitment to free markets still show up to public meetings to oppose changes to the zoning ordinance to allow more development and investment. Opposition to more intensive property transitions occurs in red cities and blue cities. People's interests in preserving the value of their property are more influential to decision making than are stated moral or political values. We shouldn't necessarily expect people to be able to dialogue in good faith when unstated economic interests are at stake. Churches that engage this conversation need to do so "in good faith" (double meaning intended).

With that in mind, I wish I was smart enough or wise enough to offer advice on how to have conversations with neighbors who oppose the church's plans. The process will be messy and unsatisfying. That's one of the deepest conundrums of our field of urban planning right now: we don't have any clear rules that tell us who should get to decide these things. My main area of research is in housing, and we know that housing is really expensive in places where people want to live because zoning and planning processes make it hard (if not impossible) to build more housing. If every established neighborhood gets to veto any property transition in or near their neighborhood, we will never build enough housing within the city for all incomes and all families who would want to live here. Should developers and property owners be able to transition their properties to more intensive uses over the objections of the neighbors? To many within planning and community development, that feels wrong because it prioritizes individual profit over community concern. On the other hand, if we think that communities should be able to control property transitions within their neighborhood, that becomes a tool for middle- and upper-class neighborhoods to exclude, segregate, and protect their property values.

This is the process and conversation churches enter when they decide to engage in a property transition. The answer from "planning world" is mostly "process." We still believe that when planning departments, neighbors, and property owners can engage in a thoughtful, proactive, iterative, cooperative process of discussion and listening in good faith, we can increase the likelihood of a better outcome for all.

13

CHANGING THE (ZONING) CODE TO BUILD BONDS BETWEEN CHURCH AND STATE

Nadia Mian

Pastor Doolittle was praying for an answer. The congregation wanted to build affordable housing on the church parking lot, but zoning regulations were making it difficult for the project to proceed. According to the ordinance, the plan they submitted to the planning department did not have enough parking spaces for the proposed development. In San Diego, California, the number of parking spaces on church property was tied to the linear feet of pew space in the sanctuary. Even though the congregation's size had declined significantly in recent years, the zoning regulations were still requiring a large number of parking spaces be included in the proposed project.

Clairemont Lutheran Church was founded in 1954 in the Clairemont neighborhood of San Diego, one of the first planned communities in the United States. The congregation built the church themselves by laying the bricks for the main fellowship hall. A community church focused on addressing the needs of the Clairemont community and San Diego, the congregation offered many support groups and community programs, including Alcoholics Anonymous, senior companion programs, Boy Scout troops, literacy and English as a second language classes from the county. They also hosted a German school. Reflecting the diversity of the community—approximately 21 percent of which was born in Latin America—the congregation hosted one of the first Spanish-language ministries in the synod.

Like many communities in America, Clairemont struggles with the rising cost of housing for purchase and rent and limited housing stock. Located on the southwest corner of a major intersection, the church sits across the street from a major commercial center. To its east and west are single-family homes. With a population of approximately eighty thousand residents, and a median household income of approximately $85,000, the area has quickly become unaffordable for many residents. The median value of owner-occupied housing units is approximately $600,000, and the average rent for a two-bedroom apartment is $2,200.[1] How could Clairemont Lutheran be a part of the solution and provide respite for their neighbors?[2]

In addition to the community programs they offered, the church partnered with San Diego's Interfaith Shelter Network to provide for people in need through rotational shelter services, that is, area churches provide shelter for unhoused people on a rotating basis for a few weeks at a time. One year, the families who had been staying at the church were unable to find permanent places to stay. It was unclear how the Interfaith Shelter Network could help these families stay intact and not end up on the street. Congregation members were concerned about the situation and how difficult it was for the families to find housing. How could they help the families who were facing homelessness? What was the role of the church, and what had God called them to do?

This experience prompted the congregation to pursue an affordable housing development on their property to help alleviate the housing crisis in their community. As pastor of the neighborhood

1. For these figures, see Census Reporter, at https://tinyurl.com/yzas8uyp.
2. This case study used interviews and archival research as sources. Interviews with the pastor of Clairemont Lutheran Church, select members of the YIGBY Team, and Brian Schoenfisch from the San Diego Department of City Planning were conducted from September to November 2021.

church, Pastor Doolittle felt deeply connected to the Clairemont area. The congregants were from the neighborhood, the church programs were for the community, and he was committed to making connections with others in the area. Even non-church-member residents of the community would sometimes stop by to talk to him. Pastor Doolittle believed in helping people figure out what God has called them to do and fulfilling their potential. He wanted the church to be a space where people could think about and explore what that meant to them. For him, it meant bringing the church and the community together to serve the greater good. The members of Clairemont Lutheran felt called to do this work.

The church had previous experience with property development and affordable housing. In the 1980s, Lutheran churches in San Diego wanted to work together to build a thirteen-story senior center. Clairemont Lutheran began acquiring properties around the church for the cooperative venture, but the development project fell through. The church used some of the properties they purchased to expand their parking lot and rented the other properties out—some at market rate and some at more affordable rents. However, those rental properties were occupied. The community needed more affordable housing units.

The congregation decided to renovate the 1950s fellowship hall that was in need of repair. They thought that tying affordable housing to the renovation project and including housing as part of the new proposed fellowship hall would speed the development through the approvals required by city hall. However, regulations made it difficult to include housing as part of that project. As Kurt Paulsen notes in chapter 12, the "planning world" and "church world" do not often collide partly due to the separation between church and state. As church properties transition, there needs to be better communication and conversation between the two parties.

In their initial exchange with the city, the congregation learned that the housing portion of the project was tied to parking and zoning regulations. The lot was zoned for two separate uses, single-family housing and commercial. Part of the lot was zoned for housing, but not multifamily housing. Another part was zoned commercial, and the city was not going to rezone the entire parcel. The city also wanted to designate the fellowship hall as a historical property. The historical significance of the church became a point of contention between the city and the church. The congregation did a historical analysis of the church and did not find that the building was historically significant. The city did not agree with the report and wanted the church to commission an environmental impact evaluation to back up its claim, which the congregation did not want to do. According to San Diego building regulations, if a development does not exceed by 10 percent the current space, no environmental impact report is necessary. The congregation's original plan of adding a third floor with housing to the fellowship hall had to be eliminated because that would change the square footage of the building and require the environmental impact report. This changed the amount of space they would have available for the fellowship hall, and so the two projects—building affordable housing and renovating the fellowship hall—became separate. The church then decided to build affordable housing on their parking lot, but that reduced the number of parking spots available. Regardless of whether parking spaces were needed, the zoning regulations were tied to the amount of pew space, and a large fellowship hall required a large number of parking spaces even if the congregation had declined and those spaces were not being used.

The initial exchange between Clairemont Lutheran Church and the city had not gone as well as they had hoped. As the congregation was coping with the parking and zoning regulations, Monica Ball, a local realtor and homeless advocate, was working with Yes in God's Backyard (YIGBY), a group advocating building affordable housing on church property. The congregation and the group would eventually end up working together to change zoning regulations in San Diego. Pastor Doolittle's prayers were about to be answered.

BRIDGING THE DIVIDE BETWEEN CHURCH AND STATE

The United States is experiencing an affordable housing crisis. There is a shortage of almost 7 million units of affordable housing for extremely low-income households, and approximately 70 percent of such households spend more than half their income on rent.[3] Churches can help alleviate this shortage by constructing affordable housing on their property. A study conducted by the Terner Center at the University of California at Berkeley found 6,298 potentially developable parcels of religious land in five counties in California.[4] As religiosity declines in America, many church parking lots remain empty during the week and are not fully utilized on Sunday. That land could be used for the greater good to build affordable housing or for other community uses.

Houses of worship have always been part of the fabric of a neighborhood, and historically communities were built around the church. If a congregation wants to build housing or community facilities on their property, they will need help with zoning and planning approvals, applying for government funding, applying for bank loans, and building internal capacity to undertake development projects. However, the divide between church and state makes building relationships with municipal staff and other stakeholders difficult. As church assets are in transition, so is the relationship between congregations and city officials. That relationship needs to change if church properties are to survive. If cities need space and partners to build affordable housing and community facilities, then churches need to be considered as stakeholders in the development process. This relationship building can be used to benefit both the house of worship and the city.

Pastor Doolittle believed that doing these development projects was a way of evolving and moving beyond traditional models of worship and pastoral care. He asked, "How do we look to the future and see where God is taking us as church evolves and as we evolve as God's people? What does it mean to be a church?" Pastor Doolittle argued that this evolution also meant that the church

3. "The Problem," National Low Income Housing Coalition, 2022, https://tinyurl.com/mv2b7r4z.

4. Daniel Garcia and Eddie Sun, "Mapping the Potential and Identifying the Barriers to Faith-Based Housing Development," Terner Center for Housing Innovation, May 2020, https://tinyurl.com/mwmd2z8z.

needed to move beyond relying on tithes and diversify their income portfolio. Being a church also meant taking a hard look at finances and thinking about where the money comes from. Clairemont Lutheran received some income from renting out church classroom space to the Head Start Preschool program—a national program. He argued, "We need to be aware of how we fund church, how we maintain our church property, how we're able to reach out to our neighborhood. We need to be aware of how worship changes, to continue to involve young people who are much more tactile and participatory than previous generations."

The triangulation of caring for church property, funding the church, and serving the community could be a driving force for congregations who want to move forward and think about their properties in a different way. Serving the community meant working with secular organizations, including politicians, to serve a common goal—in this case, affordable housing. The following section highlights the exchange, challenges, negotiation, and solutions between Yes in God's Backyard (YIGBY), a group representing houses of worship in San Diego, and the City of San Diego planning department.

YES IN GOD'S BACKYARD!

At the same time that Pastor Doolittle was struggling with zoning regulations, Monica Ball was looking for a church that needed her help. As a realtor in San Diego, she spent her days showing clients million-dollar homes, and in her spare time, she was serving the homeless. After years of working with the nonprofit organization Urban People Living Faith in Trust (UPLIFT), doing outreach to homeless individuals, conducting assessments, and helping provide other services, Monica was frustrated with how the problem of homelessness and a lack of affordable housing was being handled. There had to be a way to provide affordable housing that did not take years to build and was cheaper than the traditional model. She also believed that the faith community needed to be involved when community resources and public money were allocated for social services and when decisions were being made. Faith community properties could help solve the homelessness and affordable housing crisis.

It was during a lunch meeting with the local tax collector, Dan McAllister, that the seeds for YIGBY (Yes in God's Backyard) began to grow. Monica was airing her frustrations with expensive land acquisitions in San Diego County, high property values, the affordable housing industry, and the tax credit financing system. McAllister suggested looking more closely at properties owned by the faith community in San Diego County. He sent Monica a list of 1,100 parcels based on land-use designation that were identified as houses of worship. At the time, Monica was also a part of Catalyst, a philanthropic organization focused on social investing in San Diego, and Funders Together to End Homelessness, a subgroup of Catalyst. It was during this period that Monica met Tom Thiessen, the former president of the regional task force on the homeless. Monica presented her idea to Tom, who had faith that it could work. They called the new model of faith-based affordable housing Yes in God's Backyard.

With all the challenges that congregations face, from declining attendance to increasing property maintenance costs, many churches look for ways to use their buildings and property in a different way. Municipalities, especially in high-cost cities like San Diego, struggle to provide affordable housing. The YIGBY model provides another way to look at the intersection of faith-based development and affordable housing. If the problem with affordable housing is that construction is expensive, financing overly complex, and the development process time-consuming, then those elements would need to be simplified. The YIGBY model aimed to reduce costs by using land donated from the congregation, modular construction, social impact investing, and construction loans. In high-cost cities like San Diego, land is expensive, so having the congregation donate land would significantly minimize costs. Having a faith-based institution as a community partner was also beneficial, because trust was already established with the community, thereby reducing neighborhood opposition. In

California, modular construction was already preapproved, which also reduced costs. The completed unit is then trucked to the site. Many houses of worship do not have the expertise to go through a development project, and so the YIGBY team of cross-sector professionals would also aid in the design, finance, construction, and management of the project.

Monica and Tom presented the YIGBY concept to both the Catalyst and Funders Together to End Homelessness team. Andy Ballester, a cofounder of GoFundMe and member of Funders, was inspired by YIGBY and backed the idea financially. Monica and Tom also presented the YIGBY concept to over one hundred faith communities in the San Diego area and received an overwhelming positive response. However, YIGBY was theoretical. What was needed was a church where the group could test the model and create a proof-of-concept project. In addition to her volunteer work with UPLIFT and Catalyst, Monica represented UPLIFT on the Downtown Planning Council as the Social Issues Subcommittee chairperson. An architect on the Council introduced her to Pastor Doolittle. His church had been struggling with their planning application because of parking regulations. They did not have enough parking for the proposed development project, even though their current parking space was mostly empty. It was Monica's hope that Clairemont Lutheran could be the pilot project YIGBY needed to understand the actual challenges a church faces when undertaking a development project.

REFORMATION ... OF LAND USE REGULATIONS

In urban planning, zoning is a way of separating areas in a community based on the type of use to guide the growth and development of the city. Historically, the purpose of zoning was to control the expansion of the city and to keep noxious uses from encroaching on one another. For example, for public health purposes, housing and industrial uses were separated. However, zoning was also used to segregate communities from one another on the basis of race and class. To preserve white, middle- and upper-class neighborhoods, zoning regulations limited the size of lots, the height of buildings, and density. This kept the suburbs unaffordable for many low-income residents of color.[5]

Religious institutions were not exempt from land-use regulations, and the zoning classifications for a house of worship vary. Some are classified as "special use," "community facility," "religious institution," "house of worship," or "conditional use." With these classifications come restrictions on what can be built on religious-owned property. The Religious Land Use and Institutionalized Persons Act (RLUIPA) was enacted by Congress in 2000 to keep municipalities from placing an undue burden on religious institutions because of land-use regulations.[6] Since the inception of RLUIPA, municipalities have become more apt to work with religious institutions to address their development concerns.

When the YIGBY team began speaking with Pastor Doolittle and the congregation, it became clear that they needed to work with the city's planning staff to solve the zoning issues. It has been approximately four years since the congregation started their development application, and they were frustrated with the delays. At a cocktail reception Tom Thiessen was able to speak with San Diego mayor Kevin Faulconer and explain the YIGBY model. The mayor was excited about ideas for building affordable housing on faith property. Tom explained that he needed to speak with people in the planning department to get help with some issues that Pastor Doolittle and Clairemont Lutheran Church were having in getting their project approved.

Pastor Doolittle and the YIGBY team shared with the planning department their concerns about zoning regulations that hindered faith-based affordable housing development. In meetings with city council members and staff, they asked Pastor Doolittle: What were the hurdles with the current code? What would he do to change the regulations? The group discussed the challenges facing houses of

5. E. Talen, "Zoning and Diversity in Historical Perspective," *Journal of Planning History* 11, no. 4 (2012): 330–47.

6. "Religious Land Use and Institutionalized Persons Act," US Department of Justice, accessed February 15, 2023, https://tinyurl.com/yc7vwdfm.

worship and property development, including outdated parking regulations. Pastor Doolittle asked, "Why were churches required to have a different number of parking spaces than any other gathering business? Why is it more stringent for us than for anyone else?" Being able to discuss with city staff the larger problems with planning regulations as opposed to specific issues with the application provided a platform for how to overcome those challenges.

Having a group of professionals as part of the YIGBY team was also instrumental in navigating the relationship with local governmental officials and staff and coming up with a solution. YIGBY's team consisted of a cross section of professionals from real estate, planning, development, affordable housing advocacy organizations, and faith-based institutions. The team reached out to Brian Schoenfisch, a manager in the Housing, Policy and Implementation team. Brian's team regularly worked on solving problems with planning applications, so when the YIGBY committee approached him about Pastor Doolittle's issues, they were ready to listen and reform the relevant regulatory barriers. Solving these regulatory problems could help create affordable housing units in a community where land was scarce and expensive. It would also help the city meet its regional housing needs allocation. Since 1969, the state of California has required each municipality to plan for the housing needs of its residents at various levels of affordability. This planning process is called a regional housing needs assessment and is then used to adopt a local housing plan for each city or county.[7]

Brian and his team went over the zoning codes and realized that the parking requirements for churches were outdated. They pulled the plans, analyzed the codes, and looked at the obstacles and reviews that were conducted. They put together a list of all the churches across the city, and in dialogue with the YIGBY team, discussed how at least three thousand units across all those sites could be built. They figured out which part of the zoning code was problematic: the ordinances from the 1960s, when there was a

---

7. Regional Housing Needs Assessment, 2022, https://tinyurl.com/mr46akvt.

very different model of suburban development and more people attended church and were driving their cars to services on Sunday. The number of parking spaces required by a church was attached to the linear feet of pew space. However, with fewer people attending services, many parking spaces were no longer needed, which meant empty parking lots and a lot of underutilized property.

The Housing, Policy, and Implementation team, with transportation and engineering staff, figured out a better parking formula. In transit-oriented development areas, churches wanting to build affordable housing on their property would have no minimum parking requirements.[8] In other areas, the parking requirement would be reduced. The YIGBY team offered their suggestions to the proposal and then discussed those suggestions with their faith community partners, who also gave their advice. It was through this dialogue and recognition of the challenges and solutions that zoning regulations were realized.

Changing zoning codes was not an easy task and required more than just individual churches approaching the planning department. The YIGBY team consisted of an organized network of people who were involved in development, including affordable housing developers, consultants, and market analysis professionals. YIGBY also represented faith groups across the city of San Diego, which informed the government that they represented a wide group of constituents. When the planning department was ready to present their code changes to city council, the YIGBY team brought faith groups, pastors, and congregants to council meetings to voice their support, which was important for those measures to be adopted. A coordinated team effort between elected officials, city staff, and faith-based housing advocates paved the way for churches to develop affordable housing on their property.

---

8. In transit-oriented development areas, smart-growth neighborhood development is focused on creating a compact, walkable, dense community with a mix of land uses such as housing, commercial, and recreational uses located in and around rail stations and transit corridors so people can more easily commute to work and other areas.

Building Bonds

As church assets are in transition, so is the church's relationship with the community. A long-standing church building that is being torn down or converted to housing or a community use changes the character of a neighborhood and requires approval from local government. That approval generally comes in the form of a change to the zoning regulation.

In San Diego, outdated parking regulations prevented houses of worship from building affordable housing on their property. Clairemont Lutheran Church worked with a local group, Yes in God's Backyard (YIGBY), who advocated on their behalf to change those laws. The YIGBY team challenged local zoning regulations and discussed solutions with planning department officials. As a result of those exchanges, the San Diego planning department came up with solutions, and the zoning bylaws were changed. As a result, religious institutions in San Diego County are now permitted to construct affordable housing on their property.

Conversations with those outside the church contribute greatly to the dialogue that needs to take place between houses of worship and secular organizations. For Pastor Doolittle, working with the YIGBY team as well as secular organizations was instrumental in moving the development project along. Congregations that require a change in land-use designation to develop their property need to foster their relationship with politicians, local government staff, stakeholders, and neighborhood residents to navigate the planning and development process. This is done by drawing on existing connections and reaching out to people who live in the community and organizations and institutions that are important to visions and goals of the congregation and the development process. This could include local groups such as historic preservation commissions, housing advocacy organizations, planning department staff, city council members, residents, other houses of worship, and so forth. Reaching out to someone could be as simple as calling or sending an email to ask for a meeting. These meetings are an opportunity to present one's case before being heard by the zoning board or city council. They also give the planning department a chance to understand how current regulations are problematic for development and to work on addressing those changes for the common good.

Pastor Doolittle credits connections with those outside the church for helping move his development project forward and for changing zoning regulations. As he reflects, "Maybe God is using me in this particular moment to do something greater than I could ever imagine."

14

THE REAL ESTATE ADVISORY TEAM

Philip Burns, Jill Shook, and Andre White

There are many possible outcomes when a church decides to re-develop their property. Some are good. Some are disappointing. Consider these two stories.

A Portrait in the Lobby

Trinity Presbyterian Church had dreamed the dream. Responding to their neighborhood's systemic disinvestment and abandonment, they had filled their hearts with a vision of quality housing, community gardens, and a revitalized community they could be proud to grow old in. This would happen through a new mixed-use project with fifty-eight units of senior affordable housing on church property, generating community development and church renewal. Rev. Johnson had worked hard on the project for years, preaching and teaching about the social and community dimensions of the gospel, and now the congregation would greet his frequent references to the project with hearty Amens. During coffee hour, they would privately speculate which church members would get the apartments.

As the framers and concrete pourers gave way to the painters and cabinetmakers, Community Builders, the developer, made its first mention of the word "lottery" on page 18 of a monthly project status report given to the church. A few months later, the church secretary took note—"What exactly was to be given away in the lottery, and who could participate?" Rev. Johnson and the elders anxiously discussed the issue. The developer had implied, during the negotiations to acquire the property, that the church's elderly members would be the first ones eligible to rent units. The reality only surfaced later. Apartments in the new affordable housing development would be opened to the public and their residents chosen by lottery, and the seniors from the church would have to compete for housing like every other applicant.

In the end, 986 applications were received for the initial lottery. None of the church's members were ultimately selected. The church had donated its land for zero economic consideration and invested $35,000 of its own money in the project because of a false understanding that the church's members would have first opportunity to lease apartments in the building. Instead, all they had received was a portrait of Rev. Johnson in the lobby.

IS THAT THE ONLY OPTION?

The Congregational Church of Eden Highlands had been known for decades in their small but influential community for their principled stands on social justice. Their board of trustees, composed of professors, real estate agents, and nonprofit executives, had always enjoyed finding ways to care for those on the underside of their otherwise exclusive town—the unhoused, street musicians, hotel maids, nannies, and gardeners. And yet, ministry could not continue in the same way forever. The church had been declining for decades, and in three years the operating fund would be depleted and the church would cease to exist. For the church to remain in the community for the long term, their mission would have to be redefined and property monetized. The trustees were faced with a question of faith—would they pursue affordable housing development that truly embodied their values for the community, or would they sell for McMansions or a high-end hotel?

Complicating this decision was the town of Eden Highlands's notoriously strict zoning code, which required a conditional use permit (an action that required an up-or-down vote by the city council) for all construction of apartments. And the town was tightening these codes even further in response to a strong movement of angry citizens gathering petitions for a ballot measure to require a citywide vote before allowing any apartment, condominium, or hotel project.

The trustees reached out to a commercial developer, friendly to the church, to discuss their options and agreed to perform a feasibility study. After a few months, a lengthy volume came back stating that single-family homes were the most viable option, with a hotel as a risky but lucrative alternative. The developer ruled out affordable housing, citing the city's conditional use permit requirement and stating that it would not provide sufficient operating income to save the church. Having engaged his firm's architects and engineers, the developer sent the church a bill of $150,000 for the feasibility study; however, he said he would conveniently forgo payment if the church would let his firm build the project.

A couple of days from signing on the dotted line, the president of the trustees frantically sought out a team of affordable housing advisors for assistance. This group guided the church in an inside-outside advocacy strategy for a reimagined church campus with the majority of the land earmarked for an affordable housing development. The trustees used their existing relationships and respect they had earned to hail elected officials to meetings and site tours. At the same time, the advisors wrote letters to the State of California leveraging its housing element process to challenge the validity of the conditional use permit requirement. The strategy ultimately worked and obligated the town to allow a minimum of 75 units on the site.

This allowed the trustees and advisory team to consider four options: an easy-to-permit luxury single-family option; an affordable option that would preserve the sanctuary and demolish the education building; the reverse of that option (preserve the education building and demolish the sanctuary); and a final option to wipe the entire site clean and replace it with affordable housing and a modern gathering place physically expressing the church's desire to become a "spiritual center" welcoming expressions of faith from a variety of religious traditions. After the advisory team helped the church evaluate the financial, physical, and political pros and cons of each alternative, the preferred affordable housing alternative was selected. They created a request for proposals (RFP) to pitch to potential affordable housing developers. Four excellent proposals were received, top among them a well-known, for-profit, affordable housing development firm that committed almost $10 million in milestone payments to the church for an affordable housing development of from 75 to 100 units.

Stepping into a Gap

These stories represent some of the extremely varied scenarios and outcomes that can happen when churches step into redevelopment of their property. However, the heartbreak of Trinity Presbyterian and the success of the Congregational Church of Eden Highlands illustrate the key role that an advisory team can play for churches. Since 2019, the authors of this chapter, who are experienced professionals, have been working as a team to advise congregations in Southern California interested in having affordable housing built on their property. This chapter lays out some of the key principles that we have learned through our work with the congregations mentioned above and from conversations with similar teams across the United States.

If you are a leader of a local church seeking to redevelop your property, it is our sincere recommendation that you would seek out assistance from an impartial advisor before reaching out to a developer.

And if you are a denominational or parachurch leader, or professional in the real estate, design, or planning fields, it is our prayer that you would consider forming such an advisory team for your area.

A TEAM COMES TOGETHER

Something was stirring in Jill Shook's heart when she and Phil Burns met at a little sushi boat restaurant in Pasadena, California, in the summer of 2019. As an urban missionary and cofounding director of Making Housing and Community Happen (MHCH), Jill had dedicated her last twenty years to organizing churches to advocate to local officials for affordable housing projects and just housing policies, including the big win that she and Phil had just achieved: convincing the city council to strengthen the city's inclusionary zoning ordinance, to now require 20 percent of all new housing units built in the city to be affordable. As of 2022, that one ordinance has produced over one thousand affordable units at no cost to the city. Other MHCH advocacy efforts have contributed to a 56 percent reduction in homelessness since 2012. But with average market-rate rents edging up to $3,000 a month, much more was needed.

As they met to discuss what might come next, Jill shared how she found herself imagining a team that would support churches to create affordable housing on their unused land. Back in 2006, she had written a book[1] exploring how congregations across the country are addressing the affordable housing crisis, not only through advocacy but also through development. Was it time to make this also happen in Pasadena? If so, churches would need the assistance of a team of professionals, and she believed Phil could lead it.

Once a Peace Corps volunteer in rural Guatemala, Phil was no stranger to new efforts that would be bottom up, incremental, driven by passion, and dependent on faith. Just two years prior, he had taken over a planning and urban design consulting firm

1. Jill Shook, *Making Housing Happen: Faith-Based Affordable Housing Models*, 2nd ed. (Eugene, OR: Cascade, 2012).

when his boss retired, and now had the opportunity to move the company in a new direction. As Jill explained her dream for a team to support churches in affordable housing development, he recognized that God seemed to have been preparing him as well. But they would need one more important set of skills—a person with affordable housing development expertise.

Andre White had worked in the affordable housing development field for fifteen years. From the Mitchelville neighborhood on Hilton Head Island, South Carolina, the first self-governed community of formerly enslaved persons in American history, Andre was the grandson of an important community leader who had given him a spirit of service and a thirst for justice. Much to his grandfather's delight, Andre had achieved extraordinary success far beyond the community, working on Wall Street, attending Harvard, landing jobs at the top real estate development firms, and moving to California. Yet even as he worked in affordable housing in Los Angeles, something about the work rang hollow to him. As typically the only African American member of the development team, Andre would be asked to manage deals whenever there was an African American landowner—often, a church. Land prices, terms, procedures, and risks would be negotiated, but it was clear to Andre that a tremendous imbalance of knowledge allowed his firm, and many others like it, to take advantage of churches. This stirred in Andre a passion to educate churches and ensure them a fair return for the use of their land. When Jill invited Andre to join the Congregational Land Committee, God had prepared his heart to jump in. At the same time, he made the leap of faith to leave his firm and establish himself as an independent development consultant, advising landowners involved in affordable housing transactions.

Since summer 2019, the three of us have worked as a Congregational Land Committee that advises congregations interested in building affordable housing on their campuses. Others joined, too: another faith-based advocacy organization (LA Voice), a Methodist minister, an organizer/theologian, and another affordable housing developer and finance expert. Motivating all of us is a love for the church and desire to help it thrive in its mission. The call for churches to provide affordable housing on their land is not only a response to a contemporary problem but an application of the biblical theme of land use that can be traced from Genesis to Revelation.[2] It is deeply missional. And it is also feasible—there are public and private financial resources and an established industry of developers who are able to convert a church's vision into actual, completed projects—but assistance is needed to navigate that process effectively.

Our typical process (see the figure on p. 226) begins with putting out our shingle; inviting congregations to workshops to identify interested congregations, then initial one-on-one-meetings; then inviting one clergy and one lay leader from an interested congregation to a required training, which provides an introduction to affordable housing, including understanding local housing needs, the development process, project types, and a theology of housing and land use. If congregations finish the cohort with solid commitment and strong feasibility for a project, they then sign professional services agreements with our advisors and move into more intensive stages. A feasibility study is prepared that includes several options for the conceptual design and layout of the development, the potential population it will serve (seniors, families, youth, the unhoused, special needs, etc.), and the types of housing (bungalow courts, high rise, low rise, mixed use) that can potentially be funded along with other financial considerations. During the congregation's discernment phase, these options are ultimately whittled down to a preferred option, then shared with others who may need to sign off on the project in the future, such as denominational bodies and city planning staff or city council members. Ultimately a final concept is produced and included as the basis for a developer RFP, which the advisory team produces, along with desired terms of the agreement; the RFP is then sent to potential high-quality professional affordable housing developers, proposals are received, and interviews conducted. We help con-

2. See Shook, *Making Housing Happen*, chap. 2, "Ownership Land and Jubilee Justice."

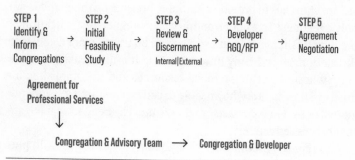

THE PROCESS

gregations evaluate their choices for the final selection of a partner and negotiate ultimate agreements.

We have found an overwhelming interest among Southern California congregations; in the three years that we have worked together, about seventy churches have requested assistance (despite our limited outreach) and we have worked in depth with nearly two dozen.

Getting Help:
Selecting and Working with an Advisory Team

Partnering with developers is an essential for many reasons. Real estate development, and affordable housing in particular, is an extraordinarily complex endeavor; without specialized professional experience, a church will very rarely be able to navigate it and access the multiple competitive funding sources that are usually required to put a deal together. Another challenge is property management: many churches already spend far too much time and energy maintaining their spaces and leases; managing a large housing development that requires income-qualifying residents is on another level. Financial risk is another major consideration that can be alleviated with a partner.

Since partnerships are necessary, the role of an advisory team is to help structure a fair partnership that would build and operate a project that provides benefits to people in need, creating win-win-

wins between churches, developers, and communities. From this experience we have discerned four principles of engagement with advisory teams that we feel are key to achieving successful projects.

Principle #1
Churches need competent and sympathetic advisors who guide them in envisioning, partnering, and executing development projects without a conflict of interest.

The stories of Trinity Presbyterian Church and Congregational Church of Eden Highlands illustrate the perils of engaging in development without advisors, or with advisors who have ulterior motives. A team that listens well to the desires of the church and represents them, not the developer, empowers the church and guards against deceptive practices. Churches are wise to heed Jesus's command to be "wise as serpents."[3] We have institutionalized this through a conflict-of-interest policy.[4] More broadly, we recommend that a church seek an "owner representative" as well as specialized legal counsel throughout the development process to be adequately protected.

Principle #2
Churches should be empowered to help their vision become reality as well as meet their needs and interests.

Sadly, it has been our experience that too many church property deals do not reflect the vision of the congregation. Yet churches hold the one irreplaceable asset in the deal—the land. They have the power to cast a vision and place parameters around the project

3. Matt. 10:16.
4. See our policy at https://tinyurl.com/4zvbzjvf.

that ultimately gets built. Before engaging a developer, a church should be asking questions such as, How would a housing development reflect our core values and mission? Who do we most want to serve? How is God leading? What are the needs in the community? How might a new housing project enhance church programs? How would our church facilities and programs evolve if there was a new project? Is there a specific dollar amount the project needs to generate to maintain church operations?

Although it may seem that such a process works against a developer's interests, in our experience developers are often grateful when the church is clear on what they want and retains an advisor. In some cases, developers have even referred congregations to us. Without a methodical, prayerful discernment process within the congregation, with sufficient knowledge of feasibility and options, the decision-making process can become messy with rumors and bad feelings that can ultimately kill a project or victimize a church. To avoid such outcomes, an advisory team serves as facilitator, structuring discussions and processes that enable clear and effective decision making. Once a church is clear, developers are happy to get involved in a process that is much more certain, even if they receive potentially less favorable terms from the deal.

Principle #3
Rather than knocking on doors, an advisory team should allow congregations to seek out advisory services.

We made the decision early on not to reach out to congregations but to have them come to us. Because of the frequency and history of bad development deals like Trinity Presbyterian's, there is often a great lack of trust between churches and developers. This is especially true of African American churches and other congregations of color. When advisory teams cold-call congregations, they open themselves up to being perceived as just another group that wants to take advantage of the church's property.

Instead of knocking directly on different congregations' doors, we employ a variety of methods to identify interested congregations. Most important are preexisting relationships and word-of-mouth referrals. It helps that several of our committee members are clergy and work as organizers and networkers among churches. We also speak on panels and in workshops, and with denominational bodies, and hold occasional webinars and events, all of which allow interested congregations to reach us.

Principle #4
There are no cookie-cutter solutions that work for all churches.

So many congregations own land in American metropolitan areas that there is a strong desire to identify a scalable solution to the problem, or a single prototype that can be rapidly constructed. Yet experience indicates that many factors influence each site—size, zoning, adjacent land uses, political will, local funding availability, changing construction costs, market factors, and funding criteria, not to mention the mission and idiosyncratic preferences of each individual church or leader—that ultimately render each project rather unique in the end. Consider a recent list of projects being worked on by our team: a 35-unit, privately funded bungalow development for independent seniors; an 89-unit five-story tax-credit family project with a relocated preschool; a 499-unit high rise with 20 percent affordable units and storefront sanctuary; and a 52-unit development for unhoused and disabled seniors split across two noncontiguous sites on the same block.

PROVIDING HELP:
CREATING AN EFFECTIVE ADVISORY TEAM

If you are excited about creating an advisory team in your area to assist churches, here are a couple of steps to get started: First, pray and develop a vision for what this could look like in your city, region, or denominational jurisdiction.

Second, get plugged in with us (the authors in this chapter) and others across the country to learn and provide support.

Third, network with other followers of Christ to identify people who might have the heart and the skills to contribute to an advisory team. Advisory team members should have a desire to serve the body of Christ, be committed to social and racial justice, be team players, and demonstrate an understanding and empathy for people of faith from different denominations, theological perspectives, and racial and cultural backgrounds. The history of housing policy in the United States is fraught with racism, so a racial justice emphasis, including racial diversity among the advisory team members, is crucial. The team can further apply racial justice through efforts like setting minority-owned contractor goals for the development partner to meet.

Some team members will likely need to be compensated for their work, but flexibility may be warranted, as the effort will initially feel like a start-up business. Professionals who are willing to dedicate a limited percentage of their time to the project or "semi-retired" professionals may be a good place to start. Ultimately, however, you may need people who can dedicate many hours to the work, and who are expert in their fields.

While all on the team support each other, team members have essential and unique roles. The team needs one or two members who are plugged in with the community and have many relationships with churches, who can inspire trust by virtue of their name or organizational affiliation. They often provide theological resources, including preaching, teaching, and facilitation as necessary, to guide churches and strengthen their resolve in key moments of what can be an arduous development path. They may also organize events.

A second essential role on the advisory team is the planner/designer. Given the type of work and workload required, this role could be played by a single person, several planners, or a firm. The planner/designer's role is to understand zoning and entitlement strategies and be able to produce site plans and conceptual visualizations that accurately reflect zoning constraints, quantify the number of units that would be built, and set internal and external expectations for how the church property might look after development, especially including modified church spaces. Having an urban planner on the team may also open up the opportunity to advocate for structural solutions to zoning barriers that projects routinely face. In 2021, a faith-based coalition in Seattle successfully advocated for a zoning amendment that allowed a religious congregation with otherwise restrictive zoning to build affordable housing. Our committee has followed with three similar amendments in Southern California cities, with seven more with written commitments to do so.

The final key role on the team is the real estate/affordable housing advisor, who handles all the financial and "deal" aspects of advisory services. Affordable housing operates very differently than other real estate classes, so it is necessary to find someone with many years of direct experience with affordable housing, ideally who has relationships with developers and investors in the space.

Finally, consider different funding and contractual relationships. Advisory team groups across the country are experimenting with different business models and methods of compensation. Many have the goal of being self-sustaining; however, to our knowledge no one has achieved it yet. The primary reason for this is that the type of advisory services that we have described fit within the "*pre*-predevelopment" stage of a project. Predevelopment, undertaken by a developer after it has site control, can often be financed by banks and other conventional sources. However, pre-predevelopment typically is considered too high-risk for conventional investment.

One obvious source of funds is the congregation itself. With a typical advisory, cost for one church ranges from $15,000 to 40,000, or higher if additional studies such as market or community impact studies are required; however, many churches are not ready to make the investment. Another potential source is a pool of developers. However, that source is fraught with potential conflicts of interest.

Depending on the advisory team's financial situation, the team may be able to defer compensation until a deal is reached (this is known as taking on a project "at-risk"). The team can stipulate as a condition of the RFP that the selected developer reimburse the team for the work it has provided to the church prior to developer selection. For publicly funded projects, the developer is able to pass on cost for the advisory work to the public funder. However, this model carries significant risks for the advisory team, requiring that the team be very selective as to which churches it partners with, since many churches will not reach fruition; it also requires operating capital to sustain the team before funds start flowing in.

Denominations, either at the national level or through middle judicatories, could be a promising source of funding. They could hire an advisory team to provide services on their behalf to congregations within their service area. Teams should be mindful, however, that the interests of denominations and individual congregations are not always aligned. An advisory team working for a denomination should consider if the congregation is subject to a process that could result in closure. This could result in tension and mistrust unless there is a clear understanding and conflict of interest policy. Advisory teams should also strive to respond to the needs of the local community, which may be overlooked by denominational authorities.

The field, however, is ripe for philanthropy. With relatively modest investments, philanthropies can contribute to the production of affordable housing units that cost many times their investment. Foundations across the country are beginning to fund this type of work, making advisory services available to congregations free of charge or at very low cost.

In Mark 10:51, Jesus asks blind Bartimaeus, "What do you want me to do for you?" Developing property is an amazing opportunity for the local church to answer that question. Advisory teams can empower churches to envision a feasible new use of property that blesses communities and churches, pouring new life into ministries.

15

MAKING THE MOST OF THE CHURCH AND DEVELOPER PARTNERSHIP

Tyler Krupp-Qureshi

What would it mean, as a developer or a church, to (re)develop sacred space within a prophetic tradition, rather than to maximize profit? The question isn't so far from the one Mark Elsdon has rhetorically posed for this collection, *Gone for Good?* What would it mean for churches and developers to (re)develop sacred space responsive to the Good, with a capital *G*?

This is one way of understanding what the prophets were up to, living a life hyper-responsive to the Good, otherwise called God. An adequate response to such a question would require an unusual coming together of serious theological reflection with the very practical world of real estate development. As a real estate developer with little formal theological training, I'm not well positioned to bring these threads together. That said, I'll risk a start, with the hope of provoking others who know more to join a conversation.

What follows can be divided into two parts. Part 1 attempts to frame a clear choice between (re)development that maximizes profits and development oriented toward the Good. I believe there is always a choice to be made. Part 2 distills some suggestions or "lessons" from my concrete experiences attempting to redevelop church property for the Good. My hope is that taken together, the two parts will simultaneously provoke reflection on what development oriented toward the Good might mean, and also help those navigating actual development processes to steer away from pitfalls.

PART 1: PROPHETS OR PROFITS?

First, a word about why I'm quite confident there is a choice to be made between developing for the Good, within what I'm calling a prophet tradition, and developing for profits. There is a certain faith, or market ideology, which we're all more or less swimming in, in the United States, that would have us believe that the pursuit of profits is not only compatible with the good but the best means available for attaining it. Or at least the least bad means. We are told that private market actors, acting on the motive of profit maximization, properly regulated, balanced off against one another, will generate results that are in the common interest. Quasi-mystical concepts such as the "invisible hand" are used to sustain this faith.

Two points, one conceptual, the other empirical. First, I would suggest that in no other domain of our lives would we accept the logic of a common good arising mysteriously from the attempt to maximize private benefit. Imagine such a logic in the context of a marriage, a family, a household, a sports team, etc. Most of us would reject this logic out of hand as absurd and destructive of the common good in those contexts. Why do we accept it at the broader social level?

Second, at the practical level, perhaps we hold the view that the common good does enter the private market, either at the level of politically accountable regulations and policy that restrain and shape private actors, or in the setting-against-one-another of multiple private actors with different interests. The realm of real estate development is a nice test case for this possibility. My own experience as a real estate developer has seriously undermined my belief that (regulated) market dynamics subject to public pressure, left to their own functioning, are conducive to the common good.

One cannot underestimate the extent to which real estate developers and the broader real estate industry operate on a pure profit maximization motive without much further intentionality. This isn't to suggest that all actors in the industry are pure profit maximizers, but my experience is that this is a sound default starting assumption, to be proven wrong in exceptional cases. It's safe to assume that even the best actors are ultimately "two-pocket" operators, ruthlessly maximizing profits within the bounds of the law in the business environment, perhaps with the intention of steering those profits to a social good at a later time.[1] Business and social good are kept separate, with a rationalizing ideology that assumes somehow pursuing profits is good for us all.

One of my very favorite capital partners, a genuinely good person, a person of faith who gives back generously to the community, exemplifies this. He owns a used-car business that literally buys beat-up vehicles, fixes them, and sells them at twice the price (with warranty) to poor folks who are too much of a credit risk for conventional lenders. Arguably he's providing a social good, but it's hard to overlook the level of usury and exploitation at work in this business. The same partner recently made an investment in multifamily apartments in the South, where buildings are constructed, and sold and resold, in a very short time frame, while increasing rents as quickly as possible. The return on the investment is strikingly high. For him, these investments are fungible or interchangeable, abstract numbers on a spreadsheet that generate returns. After having spent a year of my life building an apartment building for this group, while giving them the final tour of the project, I realized the building was literally a number on a spreadsheet

---

1. See Mark Elsdon's book *We Aren't Broke: Uncovering Hidden Resources for Mission and Ministry* (Grand Rapids: Eerdmans, 2021) for more on "two-pocket" thinking.

to them. There was zero interest in the actual reality of the asset generating the return.

Public regulation and policy at best constrain bad outcomes. City planning, zoning regulations, and building codes will tell a developer what uses are permissible and impermissible on a site and how large a building can be, and provide some minimum criteria for safety. After those minimums are met, policy is broadly neutral (or even punitive) on whether the developer attempts to attain higher levels of safety, sustainability, or other social goods.

We might think while public regulation is meant to rule out the bad, perhaps the common good emerges within that framework, through the democratic process, public input, and the balancing of private actors against one another. I had hoped this was true before I began working as a developer. On the face of it, there's something plausible about the notion that the "common" good could emerge through a gathering up of a wide range of different voices. In practice, having navigated many such public processes where competing private interests are set against one another, it's hard to maintain faith that the common good is emerging. The felt experience is not that of aggregating toward a common good but rather of a power game, in which private groups, speaking from their own interest, press their own narrow agenda as far as their power will allow while compromising only when necessary. Though private actors will rationalize their own private interest as representing the collective interest, it's usually revealed in the process that no one is really deliberating from a broad perspective of what would be good for the whole. Outcomes usually reflect prior balances of power more so than any intentional compromise aiming at a common good.

In summary, my own experience is that there is an intentional choice to be made, by developers and churches, as to whether they will develop for the Good (within the prophetic tradition), or whether they will develop within the profit-driven market. Unfortunately, neither public regulation nor community involvement can be relied on to deliver the Good or relieve us of responsibility for this basic choice.

Prophetic Development?

If we can't rely on regulated profit seeking to produce the Good, what then might it mean to consciously choose to develop while oriented toward the Good? What might it mean to intentionally develop within a prophetic tradition and orientation? I'd like to try on two different ways of thinking about this question. First, each of us may locate ourselves within a *particular* faith tradition, within a specific prophetic tradition, that guides us through any particular life circumstance, including (re)development of sacred (church) property. I situate myself within the Islamic tradition, and as I've moved into development work, I've tried to grapple with what my faith tradition asks from me, both in specifics and also in spirit. I'll leave it to others situated within the Christian faith traditions to discern what possibilities the tradition calls for in a property (re)development context. Setting aside what any particular faith tradition might entail for prophetic development, I'd like to ask, from a broader perspective, what prophetic development *as such* might require, and what it would require in the specific context of (re)development of sacred space. What might it look like to stand on sacred church space, with a prophetic orientation, and ask, what does the Good/God call for here, now?

Who are the prophets? What does it mean to live and act generally in a prophetic spirit? The prophets are those who live in relation to God and who are intermediaries between God and society. The prophets listen to/for God's word and speak that word to society. What does it mean to live in relation to God, to listen to God's word? Negatively, it means not to listen to the doxa and conventions of society or the voice of one's own ego. Positively, it has the sense of opening up to a listening grounded in the real, to the mysterious source from which we arise and return. Alternatively, it has the sense of listening attuned to the "whole" (the Holy), in the broadest manner possible. We are to imagine ourselves standing in a particular place, setting aside convention and egotistic wants, asking what is aligned with the mysterious source, the "whole" from which we arise and return.

Imagine ourselves standing on church property, envisioning the redevelopment of that space. What is called for here? What is a church in the broader whole of human life nested in the whole of creation? Clearly it is "sacred space." What, though, is the place of sacred space, in human life, in creation as a whole? Can we allow the whole creation, God's creation, to speak to us? What is truly needed in this place at this time? As part of the creation, our needs will count, but so too must the needs beyond our own, the needs of all creation.

Sacred space is a space designed to invite contact and relation with God. Designed in architecture, but also in ritual, liturgy, and habit. Can relation to God happen outside formally designed sacred space? Outside collective ritual and liturgy? Of course. What is lost, though, when individuals are left to relate to God outside consecrated space(s)? Here one would need to consider the very nature of faith and the place of communal space in sustaining faith.

Sacred space is a space that invites us into relation to God in the sense of inviting us, communally, to ask questions we don't normally ask together: "What does God require of us?" Alternatively, what is the Good? Or, "What does the whole need?" Granted, God-talk doesn't suit everyone's taste, but where else in our community is there a space devoted to setting aside our competing interests and inquiring into our shared highest good? A good potentially outside our own understanding and will. Are we so sure something isn't lost when such questions lose their home? Can a community center, nonprofit, or brew pub host such conversations as a way of being together? Perhaps. But perhaps not automatically.

PART 2: LESSONS FROM A DEVELOPER

Moving from the philosophical to the practical, I offer a narrative overview and distilled lessons from five separate church redevelopment processes I've been involved with. I share these experiences with the hope that they might facilitate more value-driven, mission-aligned development in the future.

The Church and Developer Partnership

Lesson 1
*Churches sometimes care about more than money.
Conversations around shared values and vision potentially
open possibilities while merely transactional conversations can
close them. It is incumbent upon both developers and churches
to invite wide-ranging conversations that consider monetary
and nonmonetary concerns.*

My initial exposure to church redevelopment came my first week on the job. Sitting as a junior observer in the boardroom of a half-billion-dollar real estate investment firm, I witnessed two very senior developers pitch a young pastor and four older working-class congregants on the idea of buying air rights to a church parking lot to construct ninety units of market-rate apartments adjacent to their 150-year-old church. The church was offered a million dollars and a brand-new underground parking lot for air rights on top of a mostly vacant, mostly unused, poorly maintained surface parking lot. I was privy to the preparations prior to the pitch, which consisted mostly in figuring out the precise dollar amount that would be offered such that the church couldn't possibly refuse. There was some attempt to anticipate nonmonetary concerns, such as preserving the view corridor to a recently completed mural and providing sufficient open space between the church and the apartments. To clinch the deal, we even threw in a contemplative walking labyrinth on the open space between sites. Armed with a flashy full-color rendering of the building we hoped to build, an offer price they couldn't refuse, and some token nonmonetary concessions, the senior developers and architect launched into their presentation. It was met from the very beginning with cordial politeness and awkward silence. In the end, the pastor thanked the group for the presentation and a few congregants asked about parking during winter months. One congregant, familiar with past projects of the developer, suggested the proposed apartments looked more like a prison than a place someone would want to live. Not exactly the enthusiastic response the developers were looking for. An hour later the room dispersed, and the developers never heard back from the pastor or the congregants again.

The developers were left with a genuine sense of confusion and befuddlement. Why would a church turn down a million dollars and a new parking lot? The group speculated about inertia and an aging conservative congregation and wrote it off as dysfunctional church politics. Fast-forward a few years later, however, and the story becomes more interesting. People familiar with the congregation suggested that church leadership and congregants were in fact very open to doing something with their underutilized parking lot. It was suggested that a conversation exploring shared values might have been more effective than a polished pitch emphasizing monetary payoffs. Then only recently it was publicly announced that the church had entered a formal partnership with a new community center and music venue across the street that supports minority artists, allowing them use of their parking lot in perpetuity. The church received a refinished parking lot and some share of parking revenue in exchange. It's hard to estimate the precise dollar value of this arrangement, but I'd guess the present value of the improvement and parking revenue to be less than $200,000. The church left nearly $800,000 on the table for a partnership that spoke to them in some other way.

Lesson 2
Sometimes churches only care about money. But the development process involves trade-offs and risks that churches may not be aware of and that developers may exploit.

Another encounter with church redevelopment began with a call from the priest at a local Catholic church. The church had a large property, including adjacent buildings that were formerly a Catholic school that were soon to be vacant. The church no longer had the resources to maintain the buildings and wanted to create a fund for long-term maintenance of the church by selling excess property.

At our first meeting we listened carefully as they outlined their situation, their needs and expectations. Having learned from our prior experience that churches sometimes care about more than money, we were prepared to explore more value-aligned, creative possibilities. We asked about affordable housing, community gardens, community space, and more generally what might inspire the church and congregation. The invitation to explore creative possibilities was met with indifference. We were told that so long as we had a "sin filter" on commercial tenants, the church was genuinely neutral on possible redevelopment uses. We asked if congregants would have higher expectations. We were told that the congregation would follow the decision of church leadership, and there was no need to explore value-based possibilities with the congregation. We left with a mandate to propose projects that would maximize economic value for the church. As for-profit developers, we know how to do that, so we came back with two proposals, one maximizing market-rate residential on the site they had requested, another proposing to double the density by developing every open piece of land around them that wasn't their church building.

After nearly a year of internal church discernment process, in which very different proposals from three developers were being considered, we received a short email indicating the discernment process had come to an end, and the decision was . . . make us your best cash offer. The request struck us as odd. We're used to that logic generally in the marketplace, but it doesn't usually take a year of discernment process to get there! From the outside it appears that after a year of talking, the only concern that survived was to maximize sale price.

Having made our highest price cash offer and awaiting a decision from the church, we're well aware that this is a competition we may later regret winning. The winner will be given the opportunity to navigate a complex, lengthy, likely politicized, highly uncertain process to attain results that could much more easily be achieved on a nonchurch site. We're aware of this dynamic and have decided to move forward nonetheless. This is partly based on our historical relation to the neighborhood and confidence that we are uniquely situated to navigate the complex process, but also based on our ability to write contingencies into our offer that shift most of the risk on to the church. As the church pursues the highest cash offer in what they see as a conventional straightforward development process, it's clear they aren't aware of the risks involved in their particular process. This lack of awareness is likely to result in them overlooking nonmonetary factors that are probably more important in selecting who will develop their site. It's also likely to blind them to the ways that developers will attempt to externalize the risk onto the church.

Lesson 3

Everyone involved with church redevelopment needs to have a clear understanding of how these properties differ from others and that those differences will add layers of complexity, delay, and cost. If this is not well understood, risks are increased, time and resources are jeopardized, and mutual frustration and demotivation may result.

Another adventure into church redevelopment began with an informal conversation at a bar. The church pastor and a few congregants were gathered at the bar adjacent to their small seventy-five-year-old neighborhood church. They recognized one of our property managers at the bar and mentioned that they were looking for someone to help them redevelop their church site. Two days later we all gathered on Zoom to hear more.

The church had been slowly losing congregants and no longer had the resources to maintain their building. They had decided to sell their property and join with another congregation a mile away. For the past five years they had been in conversation with nonprofit developers to build affordable housing on their current site. Two separate nonprofit developers took on the project, only to back out after years of work. They were coming to us, for-profit market-rate developers with many projects in their neighborhood, because they needed a quick, more certain path to exit their property. We moved quickly to get site control without much due diligence, confident we could sort out the details in a neighborhood we were very familiar with. We soon discovered church properties (at least in Madison, Wisconsin) are not like other properties.

Where we work, the difference primarily has to do with how underlying zoning and future land-use plans intersect. Very often neighborhood churches are in low-density single-family neighborhoods. Their church status often results in a special zoning for their property, in this case an "institutional zoning." Because of the proximity to single-family neighborhoods, the underlying default zoning is often very low residential. Rezoning of low-density sites to higher-density sites is not uncommon, and in many cities future land-use plans call for higher density, especially along transportation corridors, making rezoning straightforward. But in this case, and it turns out in the case of churches all across the city, planners had never contemplated church property becoming something else. Absent future land-use plans anticipating church departures, the default reflects municipal density preferences from the era when the church was built.

The effect of this is twofold: first, it enshrines antiquated visions of appropriate density, and second, it makes rezoning to higher density extremely challenging and politically fraught. Conventional for-profit developers, with other available projects, having done their due diligence, may not take on an average small to medium-size neighborhood church redevelopment process because it is too difficult. It is often easier and more time-efficient to pursue projects in less complex contexts than church redevelopment. Unless congregations and cities shift this dynamic, churches needing to redevelop may find reluctance by established developers to take on their projects.

The process is even more complicated if a church is disconnected from the neighborhood. They may discover that the neighborhood is not at all sympathetic toward their need to leave or redevelop. Ironically, even though neighbors may not be congregants, because the church functioned as a quasi-public space the neighbors may actually imagine the property to be quasi-public property, subject to their determination of its next best public use!

Back to the church that taught me this. A year and half later, after more than a dozen neighborhood meetings, hundreds of emails, and emotionally charged social media posts, our group navigated this complex process to entitlements for a thirty-two-unit market-rate apartment building. The process reduced the density that we initially proposed and reduced the offer price the church received. Neighborhood relations were polarized, resulting in shifting friendships and at least two families selling their homes and leaving the neighborhood. Committed progressive public officials questioned whether they wanted to continue serving in office.

In this case, ultimately the church received their compensation for the property, and the project is proceeding. But the general sense was that neither the neighborhood, the developer, nor public officials would relish repeating that process again, and some other, perhaps better options were left on the table. Creative possibilities often take time. Short time horizons leave little room for creative outcomes. Start imagining possibilities early.

Lesson 4
While purely market-based conditions will often support new church space or money for the church or mission-aligned alternatives, doing more than one is harder.

The last church redevelopment project I'd like to share is an ongoing one. Two congregations that recently combined and have resources from the sale of one congregation's property are exploring options for the redevelopment of their shared remaining building. The church is clear that their existing building is badly in need of repair, and they'd rather rebuild than repair an aging facility.

As part of the rebuilding process, the church intends to create a new worship space that also serves the broader community as a community center. There appears to be interest in also building a mission-aligned housing component on top of the new worship space, both to generate long-term resources for the church and to meet the housing needs of the community. They are well advised by nonprofits and incubator groups that are helping them think through a range of options based on what others have done elsewhere. I came into discussion with them, as a market rate for-profit developer with whom they had a prior relation, interested in exploring creative possibilities. It became clear immediately that the economics of the site, absent creative outside resources, would allow for a new church space or affordable housing, but not both. The church is not ready to give up on worship space, so the default option from a market-rate developer is likely to be three to four stories of market-rate apartments serving young professionals on top of new worship space. While that possibility hasn't been ruled out, everyone wants something better.

Wanting more mission-aligned creative options, the church has continued to talk with other players in the community, including the alderperson, city staff, nonprofits, and the local community land trust. Creative ideas have emerged through this process, and we are getting closer to some actionable options. But the most creative options will require some additional financial or land subsidy either in the form of government funding, impact investment, philanthropic money, or all of the above.

Lesson 5
Possibilities exist in conversation, and new conversations give rise to new possibilities. Cities and planning departments have a special role to play.

At some point the separate players in the above example found each other and formed a broader, very informal discussion group to begin thinking through what might be done, together, on this particular church site, but also on other church sites generally. A few things have become clear in this informal discussion group.

First, actionable mission-aligned options are unlikely to emerge in siloed conversations. Second, actionable possibilities arise when conversation is expanded to simultaneously include a broad range of stakeholders. Complementary capacities need to be mobilized for creative solutions. And third, magic happens when all parties transparently express their hopes and concerns and imagine together possibilities that speak to these hopes and concerns.

To be sure, even in this best-case scenario, when all the parties are gathered— value driven and mission aligned and creatively imagining possibilities together—there remain tensions and potential impasses to be navigated. These tensions could be characterized as classic first-actor paradoxes. Everybody is willing to act in a cooperative way but needs someone else to move first to generate trust and cooperation.

The developers (for profit and nonprofit) need the city or politicians to create an incentive framework that favors creative solutions and reduces uncertainty. The city needs to know that if they create such an incentive structure, which unlocks higher value on church sites, that the churches and developers will choose to "leave money on the table" and pursue mission-aligned projects for the public benefit rather than attempting to capture the higher value. Churches need concrete options and reduced uncertainty from both the city/policy makers and the developers. The for-profit developers need the value alignment of nonprofit developers to interact with church mission and city visions of the public good. Nonprofit developers need for-profit developers to expedite the process and navigate uncertainty by mobilizing market resources and relationships. Luckily, the nature of collective action first-actor problems is such that any one actor has the power to break through them! It takes a leap of faith, trust, and a principled and value-driven stand around which others can let down their guard and collaborate. Who in the church redevelopment process is ready to take this leap of faith and principled stance? Might we not expect this from faith-based institutions such as churches?

It's clear that redevelopment of church property is a unique historical opportunity to create mission-aligned projects for the public good on a very large scale. The confluence of mission-driven property holders (churches) needing to transition property quickly and market-rate developers not being able to facilitate those transitions due to uncertain zoning/regulatory frameworks, means politicians and planning staff are in the driver's seat to extract public benefit in exchange for new zoning frameworks. How often do planning staff find themselves in a situation where a large amount of property in need of redevelopment is held by potentially value/ mission–driven property owners that can't easily be redeveloped by profit-seeking developers? I'll leave it up to the planning and policy experts to reflect upon the incentives, but clearly with the right incentives large amounts of property can be transitioned for the greater good.[2]

And a secret
Value is brought into being in relation, through the development process. Churches need to know how much value is being created and claim a portion of it.

I still recall the awe I felt the first time I saw a pro forma and the financial modeling that developers do to figure out how profitable a deal is. Within that modeling there is a genuine moment of magic, where developers, in concert with bankers, conjure value into being in a developer's fee and then share faith that this conjured value will materialize as real in the future. For example, on

2. See chapters in this book by Kurt Paulsen and Nadia Mian for more about how cities can have an effect on what sorts of projects get built.

a $10 million project there will be something called a developer's fee of about $750,000 that magically appears. Developers and bankers won't be transparent about this process of magic and faith, to clients, politicians, or the public, as it would raise genuine questions about who is in fact creating the value and who might have a claim on it. Developers will claim this value as their own, based on the risk they purport to be taking and the skills they bring to the process, without which development wouldn't happen. But as I hope I've made clear, the development process is essentially relational and collaborative, and the value created is essentially relational. Developers and bankers can't create value outside of relationship with other stakeholders. Likewise, the risk entailed by the development process is relational; no single party holds it. Churches too will bear much of the risk of development, and they hold the property without which development would not be possible.

Churches need to know that development can't be done by developers alone. Churches should claim a portion of the value that is created in development. Ask for financial transparency from developers. Ask that they share their modeling and pro formas. Be certain that they are sharing the same pro forma with you that they are sharing with bankers. Anytime a developer proclaims what is or isn't feasible in a project, ask to see the numbers. And ask for part of that developer's fee to be returned to the church or put back into the project to increase affordability or make the project better.

A NEVER-ENDING CONVERSATION TOWARD THE GOOD

As a multifamily apartment developer who is quite familiar with the ways of life and the sorts of conversations that our projects invite, it saddens me to imagine filling sacred space, and the collective orientation toward a shared highest good, simply with market-rate apartments. Spaces removed are not easily restored. Christians in America have been the stewards of the vast majority of sacred space embedded in our neighborhoods and communities. As the Christian flavor of inquiring after the highest Good ebbs and flows, as congregations shrink and grow, might there not be an obligation to sacred space as such? What might it mean for Christian congregations, acknowledging their particular historical role as stewards of sacred space in America, to transition sacred space as sacred space? What might it mean to transition sacred space in a way that keeps alive, in particular places, a never-ending conversation oriented toward the Good, the Whole, beyond?

Of all the players getting involved in this game of property development, churches are the best positioned to lead in the direction of Good. Developers will want to build on your property. But only churches can truly shape the conversation toward Good on your property. You need to lead us. Please lead on.

16

OBSTACLES AND OPPORTUNITIES FOR PHILANTHROPIC PARTNERSHIPS WITH CONGREGATIONS IN TRANSITION

Mark D. Constantine and Elizabeth Lynn

Foundations, especially those with a grounded commitment to local communities, could be crucial partners for congregations that are in transition or decline and considering what to do with their buildings and lands. But are foundation leaders aware of the accelerating transition of religious properties in the communities they love and serve? If so, what questions are these leaders asking about the changes under way? What obstacles and opportunities present themselves? What partnerships between foundations and congregations might emerge in this time of transition for so many congregations across America?

In the fall of 2022, we asked these questions of selected philanthropic leaders and synthesized what we heard into a series of philanthropic perspectives and possibilities on the transition of religious properties.

SETTING UP THE CONVERSATION

In selecting conversation partners, we reached out to leaders who work at foundations serving states and communities in the South

253

(Arkansas, Florida, Louisiana, Mississippi, North Carolina, South Carolina, Tennessee, and Virginia). The role of religion in community life varies by region in the United States, and a more extensive study would surely discover significant differences in the way philanthropy as a sector relates to faith-based organizations and congregations. For this first foray, however, we chose to stay south, in an area that one of us (Mark Constantine) knows well, having served foundations in Florida, North Carolina, Mississippi, and Virginia since 1990, and the other of us (Elizabeth Lynn) has lived in since 2018.

We spoke with eight leaders in all, some of them foundation presidents and others program officers. The foundations they represent serve a mix of rural communities, small and midsize cities, and massive metropolitan areas.

A little additional context about these eight philanthropic leaders: First, they are all people of significant gifts and profound commitments. Often, they are former grantees who bring on-the-ground knowledge and passion to their work. They care deeply about the communities they serve.

Second, they do not dismiss the importance of religious institutions in communities. Most have a personal relationship to a specific congregation and a deep appreciation of the importance of religious and spiritual life for human flourishing and well-being.

At the same time (like other organizational leaders), these philanthropic leaders are accountable to specific constituencies and are charged to advance institutional mission and aims. The line of accountability is usually to the foundation board, as the keeper and interpreter of the guiding values and strategic plan.

Also, like other organizational leaders, philanthropic leaders engage with specific conversation partners as they develop their understanding and approaches. One set of conversation partners are grantees, who often dwell at the center of staff attention and help shape philanthropic imagination; another set includes elected officials, public health and community development leaders, grassroots and civic leaders, and leaders in the financial sector.

A third and crucial set of conversation partners is other philanthropic leaders, who connect regularly through philanthropic support organizations, known more familiarly as PSOs. These PSOs may be affinity based (Grantmakers in Health, for example), or they may be geographically based (Philanthropy Southeast, for example).

In short, if there is no focused discussion about an issue in these circles of influence, accountability, and mutual support, foundation leaders can understandably miss what is happening and its potential impact on the very communities they love.

And this, it seems, is what is happening with the phenomenon of religious properties in transition.

STARTING THE CONVERSATION

Through our interviews we hoped to explore the topic of religious properties in transition. However, we began by asking more generally *what these leaders see happening to religious life and organizations in the communities that they care for and serve through their grant making.*

As we talked, it struck us that the answer to this question often depends on the personal experience and relationships of the leader. Most see what is happening in American religion through the lens of their own congregation or religious life, rather than as a larger societal shift with direct implications for the communities they serve or their own grant-making strategies.

Likewise, all are anecdotally aware of church buildings being sold or repurposed, but for the most part they do not perceive these transitions as significant for the communities they are in, or as part of a larger story, beyond reflecting religious preferences (mainline churches selling to nondenominational churches) or demographic shifts (White churches selling to Hispanic churches). Indeed, several of the anecdotes we heard were of properties the leaders pass on their daily drives.

One interviewee who was aware of trends in religion, and had previously been in ministry, was particularly attuned to changes in the religious landscape. He is also in regular conversation with other foundation leaders in his metropolitan area and region. Reflecting on the situation with us, he described the problem of religious properties in transition as "a crisis hidden in plain view." "[It] just doesn't enter people's minds yet. It's kind of like this is a crisis . . . hidden in plain view. Unless you're a church person and have some history with a congregation, or follow church news in any way (which most people don't), they just know these are buildings that have always been part of the architecture they drive past. I don't think people understand the fiscal crisis that churches are in."

Why is there a gap between foundation leaders and congregations, such that the changes under way are like a crisis hidden in plain sight? Our interviews point to two closely related challenges—indeed, almost different sides of the same coin. Many congregations are not in conversation with funders. And many funders aren't talking about religion.

NOT AT THE TABLE

Part of the challenge lies with the fact that many congregations are not in regular conversation with local funders. Church leaders are not at those tables, real and metaphorical, where they might talk with philanthropists and other community leaders about the challenge of properties that no longer serve mission and ministry, sparking imagination and partnership for the good of the community.

Data suggests that many foundations are not comfortable funding faith-related organizations—a problem highlighted by the philanthropic advising group Bridgespan in its 2021 report, *Elevating Faith-Inspired Impact in the Social Sector*. In the report, based on an analysis of social-sector spending in six representative cities, Bridgespan found a marked disparity between the percentage of services provided by faith-related organizations and the percentage of foundation dollars received by these organizations. While faith-related organizations accounted for 40 percent of social safety net spending in the six cities, they represented only 12 percent of social safety net funding from the fifteen largest private foundations.[1]

1. Jeri Eckhart-Queenan, Peter Grunert, and Devin Murphy, "Elevating

Allison Ralph, director of Aspen Institute's Faith and Philanthropy Initiative, suggests a few reasons for this "faith gap": "Religion in America is a complex topic, studded with the minefields of our personal and societal hurts. Institutional funders may have concerns about the constitutionality of funding faith-inspired organizations, worry about faith-inspired grantees' willingness or ability to separate worship from service delivery, or be concerned about partnering with organizations or communities whose stances on social issues are at odds with their own. While philanthropy wants to have an impact on [the] common good, these and other worries get in the way of funder-grantee partnerships."[2]

We heard some of these concerns from philanthropic leaders we interviewed. The president of one foundation put it bluntly, right up at the top of our conversation: "I have to tell you from the beginning that the —— Foundation, which is the only philanthropy show in town in our little county, made the decision not to provide religious funding. In fact, we avoid it because our donor did not want to fund religious activities per se. Even though she was active in her church, she didn't want her foundation to fund [religious education]." The same foundation funds faith-related organizations engaged in social service, but only if they serve all people regardless of faith background and do not seek to convert, a criterion that has to be carefully monitored and sometimes renegotiated as leadership changes. "The best example is a free medical clinic on the campus of an Episcopal church. When people come into the . . . clinic for help, the . . . volunteers and employees don't say, 'Have you accepted Jesus Christ as your Lord and savior?' They say, 'Where does it hurt?' And that's why we are happy to fund the . . . medical clinic that sits on the campus of a church."

By point of contrast, she talked about an after-school program that had received funding in the past but took an evangelical turn

---

the Role of Faith-Inspired Impact in the Social Sector," Bridgespan Group, January 28, 2021, 9–10, https://tinyurl.com/2zj9ryzu.

2. Allison K. Ralph, "But What If They Preach? A Guide for Funding Faith-Inspired Grantees with Boundaries and Integrity," Inclusive America Project, September 2021, 5, https://tinyurl.com/43mfpw9h.

with the hiring of a pastor as its new executive director: "[It] became ... a Christ-centered thing, which is fine, but they wanted
their high school students to write a paper on what Jesus means in
my life. And I had to say, 'I'm sorry, we can't fund you all any longer because we think that what you do is important for everybody
not just the Christians.'"

Another foundation officer told us that, even when churches
engage in mission work, the work doesn't necessarily address the
deepest problems in the community: "We don't invest in the religious mission of churches..., we'll only invest in the work that they
do that's community focused. There are so many problems in the
community: affordable housing, health, general welfare, youth opportunity ... the list is endless. And flooding resilience, mitigation
concerns, septic problems for people that are low income, internet
broadband access.... Most churches aren't doing that work."

There were exceptions to the we-don't-work-with-churches
rule, even within the small set of interviews we conducted. One
of the significant exceptions comes from a philanthropic leader
who represented a foundation that works primarily in Black communities in the South. Her foundation has historically worked with
religious partners, because the Black churches are, simply, "the
ones that are there." They are anchor institutions in their communities, with relationships to city leaders and capacity to access and
deploy federal funds. They are essential social service providers.
This leader has not observed closures among these churches, and
she also noted that their footprint is so small that their property
is not of interest to developers: "Some of it, I think, is probably
the way that the neighborhoods are. These churches are not taking up a significant amount of area in the first place. And so that's
probably why, if anything, it was once a Baptist church and now
it's got a Spanish language congregation. But a lot of re-use of the
buildings into condos and things of that nature, you don't see that
here. I think it's fair to say, those churches are not that large."

Another exception came from a program officer who works in
rural communities in the South. Again, in these areas, the churches
are still the anchor institutions, "the ones that are there." As she
remarked: "I have ... heard less of people leaving [church], at least

in the areas that we are in. In fact, I've seen folks talk more about how they are using their space for other services, the community garden, the food pantry, or the little pantry outside. In some of our communities the church is still a hub."

The same officer also works with urban immigrant and refugee communities. There, too, she notes a different approach: "In areas where more immigrants or refugees live, we have partnered with religious associations . . . and have used congregational outreach . . . because there's not (or at least it's been explained to me by my friends in the immigrant community) the nonprofit infrastructure in a lot of the communities . . . which our refugees or immigrants are coming from. And so really, they only rely on the faith community, or the church community, to provide social support."

Several leaders also noted that the pandemic had fostered relationships with religious leaders and their communities, as foundations looked for partners to support vaccine distribution in Black and Brown communities. In one case, a vaccine-distribution partnership between a foundation and a religious leader led the way into deeper relationship, and the pastor is now serving on the foundation's board—a first, in many years. As the foundation president notes,

> He did drive-through testing in the parking lot of his church. He helped other pastors in the tri-county pastoral group do similar things at their churches. And almost every single day that vaccination center was open, he was standing outside . . . , instructing people how to fill in the screening information that they needed before they got in the doors to do their vaccines. He was a force to reckon with. And I think because he was so well recognized by the rest of our board for the work that he had done, it made it much easier for us to invite him to serve on the board.

In short, there were many variations on our theme—as many variations, almost, as there were interviews! This lifts up the need for much more research, qualitative and quantitative, to understand the range and patterns of relationship between local foundations and religious organizations/communities.

ISSUES, NOT INSTITUTIONS

Alongside these variations and expressed concerns, we heard something else at work that may be a significant factor keeping foundations and congregations apart. Foundations are increasingly interested in funding issues over institutions. And congregations understandably have a hard time not seeing themselves as inherently valuable institutions to be supported for their own sake.

The shift from funding institutions to funding issues is, in many ways, a generational one. Whereas members of the "Silent" or World War Two generation were drawn to supporting institutions (often through regular and unrestricted gifts), more recent generations are increasingly cause oriented, looking for ways to leverage impact on specific issues (often through program and restricted gifts). These donors seem less interested in supporting institutions for their own sake and perpetuity.[3] The same trends can be perceived in foundation giving. Whereas an earlier foundation might have centered its grant making around a commitment to specific types of institutions (colleges, libraries, art museums, and congregations, to name a few), contemporary foundations are increasingly orienting their grant making around cross-cutting issues within a community or zip code (equity, place making, community health, to name a few).

Congregations may well have trouble making this shift. Birthed in "the age of association," to quote Dwight Zscheile of Luther Seminary, and constructed on the once-solid financial foundation of annual pledges and estate gifts, congregations naturally see themselves—and seek support for themselves—as institutions whose perpetuity is a good in itself.[4] This, perhaps most of all, may be why they aren't in the grantee mix or at the table.

One of the philanthropic leaders with whom we spoke offered a powerful case in point. The foundation he works for had been

3. Dick Feldman et al., "The Millennial Impact Report: Ten Years Looking Back," Achieve, 2019, 4, https://tinyurl.com/4zv3d2cb.

4. Dwight Zscheile, "From the Age of Association to Authenticity," Faith+Lead, August 11, 2021, https://tinyurl.com/mrj4fx47.

established to nurture a group of institutions that the original donor (a member of the Silent Generation) had supported by check in a few select years before her death. Many of the institutions that made that list were churches. For years, the foundation offered a building maintenance fund to those eligible churches to help them repair and restore their buildings. The result, as our interviewee noted, was that over time some church buildings in the same geographical area were in excellent condition while others lacked resources to invest in maintenance or upgrades—a differential that had little to do with membership levels or community impact.

More recently, this foundation has redefined its mission in terms of several core issues, including place making and equity. The church building fund has been discontinued. It doesn't contribute, after all, to the goal of equity. As the program officer put it to us: "If we provide restoration grants [for these churches], the question becomes, 'how are we being equitable in a community that has so many other churches, especially minority congregations that would see no support?' . . . and the simple truth is that we don't have endless amounts of capital."

Instead of the building restoration fund, new opportunities for issue-based funding have emerged. But, in the view of this program officer, the churches struggle to relate to this issue-based approach. While they may in fact foster place making and equity in their communities, they are unsure how to engage with an issues-oriented funding approach—how to shift away from thinking institutionally, even as foundations do just that.

Again, there are exceptions to these patterns:

- Some foundations maintain a commitment to supporting specific kinds of institutions, including congregations (perhaps in part because of their understanding of the intent and wishes of their original donors, who saw themselves as beneficiaries of institutions and their philanthropy as an opportunity to support those institutions).
- Likewise, some congregations are engaging in issues-based partnerships with funders and other partners. For example, Jennie Birkholz describes how partnerships between founda-

tions, health-care systems, and rural congregations foster community health in her chapter in this volume.

These exceptions offer powerful examples that could benefit both foundations and congregations. But the exceptions prove the rule. In many communities, congregations are not in regular conversation with local funders.

RELIGION, WHAT?

There is a flip side to this communication gap as well. Just as congregations are not talking to funders, funders aren't talking about religion with any regularity.

Our interviews suggest that, for the most part, philanthropic leaders are not talking with others in their organization or field about religion. Because politics has moved so firmly upstream of religion in American society, conversations about religion are potentially polarizing and are often avoided. This general veil of silence over the topic of religion extends to boards and sometimes staff, and it is also true in philanthropic support organizations, or PSOs, in which staff and trustees meet and talk about common concerns across organizations. Religion is seldom—if ever—on the agenda these days, which is something of a contrast to previous eras. For instance, in the 1980s, the Council on Foundations had a program devoted to philanthropy and the Black church, and PSO conferences put the topic of faith-based partnerships on the occasional agenda. Not so today. As one foundation leader remarked: "In terms of [my PSO], there has not been a recent conversation that we've had, either at the board level, or at a workshop or training that I've been to, that is specifically focused on working with people of faith, or congregational work.... We've talked about corporate partnerships, and private/public partnerships, and we are thinking deeply about government impact.... I can't think of hardly ever [talking] about faith communities and philanthropy working side by side."

Another foundation leader noted the same silence in her philanthropic leadership circles and wondered if it doesn't sprout from a misunderstanding about the separation of church and state. "I have to say I've not had a lot of conversation along that line with my other colleagues, and certainly not in our CEO learning group.... I think part of that is because there is still some degree of this separation of church and state (which by the way, I find wholly terribly misinterpreted from its original writing). That has not been a huge topic of conversation. I think if I were to enter into that conversation, I would be curious as to how my colleagues view it."

A third interviewee was struck, upon reflection, by the lack of talk about the ongoing transition in religious properties among local philanthropic leaders, leaders with whom he is in frequent conversation. He wondered whether part of the challenge might be that the trustees of most of his city's foundations attend churches that seem to be very stable; they do not sense the change happening because—again—it is not happening in their own congregation.

In short, on the basis of our interviews, it appears that, as increasing numbers of congregations confront questions of closing their doors and disposing of or repurposing their properties, they are not talking with local philanthropic leaders about the potential impact of these transitions on the common good—and philanthropic leaders are not talking with each other about it either. As one such leader observed, "I don't really know that folks in philanthropy are thinking about this . . . or seeing how they might fit into it."

If the closing of congregations and transition of church properties constitute a crisis, then, it is, for many in philanthropy, "a crisis hidden in plain sight."

FROM CRISIS TO OPPORTUNITY

But it may also be an opportunity hidden in plain sight.

Foundations are deeply concerned today about numerous challenges facing their communities, and three seem especially front of mind for the leaders with whom we spoke: the need for child care, senior care, and affordable housing. All three require *space*—and all three could potentially align well with the mission and desired legacy of religious communities.

If that is the case, how can connections be fostered in a timely way, for the benefit of all?

Perhaps some clues lie in the last of our interviews, with a program officer whose foundation has maintained a commitment to supporting Methodist congregations in North Carolina, in a straight line from donor intent to the present day. From its earliest years, the foundation had supported the maintenance of church buildings. Over time, it has added investments in congregational development, clergy health, and community impact, along with a focus on rural churches.

Several years ago, driven by the foundation's commitment to churches and their buildings, the program officer found himself staying up at night worrying about the deferred maintenance on those buildings. He conducted an audit of Methodist properties in one part of the state, with help from a faith-related community development corporation (CDC). The program officer had anticipated as much as $30 million in deferred maintenance costs among these properties. But as the audit proceeded, another picture came into view.

> I just wanted to see, is that $30 million in deferred maintenance enough, accurate? And what we found out is that we had $1.4 billion in tax value of land . . . 2,400 buildings . . . 15 million heated square feet . . . 7,650 undeveloped acres of land . . . and the utilization of this 15 million heated square feet was about 8 percent of what was available. So then [it] became, "Oh no, we don't have a $30 million worth of deferred maintenance issue, what we have is a $1.5 billion, 15 million heated square foot opportunity." . . .
>
> And that's what this audit shifted. I went from, "Oh no" to, "Oh my goodness, what are we going to do with all this?"

Working through the faith-related CDC, the foundation began to support efforts to help congregations repurpose their properties in ways that align with their mission and legacy. One church is converting its property into a new church-start ministry for women and children in transition, with a shelter and affordable housing, and the congregation will continue its worshiping life in that space. The campus of another church that is closing will become a site for therapeutic development for children with autism, and the sanctuary a bakery and coffee shop that will employ young people with special needs. A third church is turning its space into a farm-to-table restaurant that provides work to underemployed and unemployed people.

As the program officer notes, some of these places won't be worshiping congregations, but there will be ministry, a way forward that honors and names the good that has gone before, and an opportunity for new good to emerge—for the church people as well as the community. Indeed, the program officer shared that what had started as *worry* about the property has become *wonder* at the people, who can do amazing things if helped to see their situation differently:

> Once the people, the congregants, . . . decide that closing is not the last nail in their coffin—once they realize that they can build a legacy and make a contribution to their community through everything that they built up over 50, 100, 200 years—you tap then into their creativity. And if you think about all the creativity and all the energy and all the wisdom that's out there, in all of these congregations, the building assets are only a fraction of what we have. We have people that are brilliant. And to turn them loose, you've got to nudge them. You got to get them out of the building. You got to get them into the community. You got to get them having conversations. But once they do, amazing things can happen.

PARTNER OR PERISH

The North Carolina foundation presents a special case, since it has a long-standing relationship with Methodist congregations and religious support organizations in its own state. But how can other foundations and congregations start to work together on these "opportunities in plain sight," if they are already not in relationship? Where to begin?

Congregations might practice thinking about themselves not as institutions that need to be sustained in perpetuity but as stewards of extraordinary community assets (human and financial) that can be put to new use addressing pressing proximate issues in partnership with others. Looked at through this lens, do new opportunities for partnership appear? How might local funders get to know these congregations as potential partners and hear the questions they are asking about the future of their properties? What roles can funders play in gently nudging religious leaders to frame their realities in a new light and see the possibilities?

Foundation leaders, in turn, might start talking about religion again, with attention to what is happening to religious organizations and properties in the communities they care about. As we have noted, every community is different: the challenges and opportunities presented by religious properties in a rural area will not be the same as those encountered in the high-value real estate market of some cities. But PSOs, which convene diverse kinds of foundations on the common ground of region or affinity, offer opportunities for conversation that can benefit from these kinds of differences.

If foundations are going to engage with congregations, though, they will ultimately need to help their boards understand how this work aligns with mission and goals. As one of our interviewees put it, not mincing words, "It really has to start at the board education level. Because philanthropic leaders . . . don't make a move without the nod and approval of their board." Her board, she suggested, would need data to make the case, and would also need to be able to see a strong tie-in with the foundation's strategic plan: "I could go to my board and say, 'These five churches are contributing $50,000 worth of services to the community. Let's match that dollar for dollar, $50,000.' Maybe I could get them to consider a discretionary grant to do that, but it would all have to get tied back to our strategic plan. It starts at the strategic level, with deep board education."

Another possibility, suggested to us by a foundation leader, would be to convene foundation trustees within a particular metropolitan area around this issue. He wisely suggested drawing on recently retired religious leaders in the area, who have strong ties to and credibility with those trustees, to convene the conversation, aided by good data and some powerful examples of what might be done. In the view of that interviewee, it would take just one leader in a network of trusted peers to catch fire on this issue and show the way.

SPARKING DREAMS

If we learned anything from these interviews, it is that simply raising the issue of congregations and religious properties in transition with philanthropic leaders sparks genuine interest and imagination. When asked what questions they were left with at the end of our interview, two colleagues at one foundation showed the philanthropic possibilities that might emerge.

The foundation's executive director, who also serves in a key board leadership role at a philanthropic support organization, said: "This conversation has brought up the thought that . . . we've not talked about it with our board as much as we could or should. And also, from my PSO chair hat, I'm asking how to engage [the PSO] board in this conversation, too, and that that's maybe a piece that we've been missing."

And her colleague, a program officer who works in rural as well as urban areas, said, "It makes me want to dream." Her dream, she added, would be "to have this beautiful retreat place for folks to go, and be cared for, that work in nonprofits. . . . It would be really special to have a healing place, for people doing the work in nonprofits, but that could be anywhere. But if there's a beautiful space that's already promoting things like mercy, and love, and healing, and redemption, let's go there, right?"

Right!

CONCLUSION

MAKING MORE AND BETTER SOUP

Mark Elsdon

As the contributors to this book have so clearly laid out, we are at an important moment in the history of the Christian church in America that has wide-ranging implications not only for people of faith but also for the social fabric of our communities. There is significant risk that the wide-scale transition of church property will leave us with less support for the most vulnerable, greater inequality, fewer spiritual resources, and other deep losses. But there is also a great opportunity to think about the mission of church in a more expansive manner, to make greater use of church property to serve our neighborhoods, and to extend the light of God's grace in beautiful ways that are very, very good.

So where do we go from here? What themes have emerged? What next steps can be taken to encourage more good to emerge as a result of church property transitions? As a reader, you will have developed your ideas on these questions. I will share a few thoughts to conclude this book.

In my introduction I likened property development to the story of stone soup. Different partners put their individual ingredients into the pot to make something that is better than the sum of the parts. The following are five key ingredients that, if contributed, will help us together make better, and more, soup for the benefit of our communities and the glory of God.

Support for Pre-Predevelopment

As the stories in this book illustrate so well, good property transitions and development require intentional, prayerful, and thoughtful discernment. Too often the first step churches and leaders take when considering selling a building is to "call a realtor," or when developing property, it is to "hire a developer." Those are important steps in the process—at the right time. Most churches need to step back, however, and do the more important pre-predevelopment work before taking those steps. Many churches in our RootedGood Good Futures Property and Enterprise *Accelerator* have thanked us most profusely for helping them *slow down* and prepare well for this work. (Perhaps we need to change the name of the program!)

The term "predevelopment" typically refers to the process of doing a feasibility study, creating an early pro forma (financial projection), commissioning initial architectural or site drawings, and so on. But most churches need to back up and start with more fundamental, and arguably more important, questions before engaging in predevelopment.

Pre-predevelopment is the process of getting ready to do something new with a church property. It starts with a focus on mission, understanding the needs and assets in the community around a church, considering business models and demand, and connecting all of that with the passions, gifts, history, and theological commitments of the church. This work helps a congregation develop a new ecclesial imagination. It may involve learning from existing projects or models, but rarely can a model be simply applied to a new setting. Good property development is very contextual.

Property developers tell me that churches who haven't done the pre-predevelopment phase well are rarely ready to move to predevelopment and beyond. Just as the real work for preparing for marriage happens in the months and years prior to the wedding day, the pre-predevelopment work is where the church prepares for its new future. This step cannot be skipped if we hope to have good outcomes.

But churches need help with this process. Organizations like RootedGood, Partners for Sacred Places, Making Housing Happen, the UCC Building and Loan Fund, and others can provide consulting and resource assistance to churches to do pre-predevelopment. At RootedGood we learn from our work with churches and turn that learning into tools and resources like our guide, "How to Develop Well," that assists churches in this pre-predevelopment process. The authors in this book are excellent guides along the journey.

In addition to good partners, the next two ingredients are needed in order for pre-predevelopment work to happen: time and space, and funding.

What pre-predevelopment work is needed in your context in order to create the most good with church property?

TIME AND SPACE

In my work with churches, and in the stories I hear from others, there is a strong sense that many are running out of time and space to do the creative, innovative, and collaborative work that is needed to create the most good on church property. Churches are rushing into decisions because money is running out, leaders are wearing out, or both. By the time churches make decisions about their property, leaders are finding it to be too little, too late. They are also often surprised to find out that thoughtful property development, or even intentional sale, can take many years to complete. I've heard church leaders say, "We just wish we had a longer runway to figure this out."

One response to this is for denominational leaders and others with influence to encourage churches to begin conversations about their property earlier than they might first expect. If a congregation wants to leave a legacy when they are gone, or reimagine their ministry in a community, ideally they will start that work five to seven years (or longer) before they expect to close on a sale or want redevelopment to be complete. Starting early keeps options on the table that will disappear if decisions are made as the lights are turned off or in a final desperate move.

Another way to create time and space for congregations and leaders to do this work well is for foundations and other philanthropic organizations to provide bridge funding that "buys time." In most cases, even a fragile group of people in a congregation will do a better job envisioning the repurposing of their property than denominational leadership or a real estate agent will after the church has closed. Providing funding to extend the runway could lead to better decisions and better outcomes.

A third approach that could provide more time and space is for a "holding company" to purchase church property in order to hold on to it and then work with local leaders to decide how to best dispose of it or repurpose it for good.[1] This could in essence be a form of church land banking, much like how cities buy up strategic property and then hold it for future development when the right time, purpose, and partner come along. Such an entity would likely need philanthropic funding to start up but then over time could be funded by the development and sale of the properties in its portfolio. Another alternative that would relinquish church control but let other vital stakeholders have time and space to make decisions for community good is to donate or sell church property into a local community land trust or give land back to indigenous peoples.

What other ideas can you think of to create time and space for this important work to take place?

NEW FUNDING

There are two types of new funding streams needed to support the most effective sale and repurposing of church property: (1) grant funding and (2) concessionary investment financing.

It is fantastic when churches that have ample funding think proactively and missionally about how to do deeper and wider ministry with their buildings and properties. The reality is that many churches begin these conversations when money is tight.

---

1. Eileen Lindner proposed this idea at a gathering of this book's authors in October 2022.

A lack of sustainable funding is often the impetus to explore new options with their building or property.

This means that the very churches that need the most time, space, and assistance often have the least ability to pay for those things. This is where grant funding from foundations, donors, and denominational structures can help. Grant and donor money can provide gap funding in order to buy time and space. It can help churches hire the partners and consultants that they need to assist them. It can pay for the tools and resources that churches need to purchase in order to do good pre-predevelopment work. Grant funding is also needed on the research and development side and to support the organizations that help churches when churches themselves cannot pay what it costs for such assistance.

After pre-predevelopment work has been done well and a concept is ready to be developed and funded, concessionary investment financing can be a game changer. One of the major factors that limits how creative and "good" a development project can be is the cost of financing the development. For example, a multifamily housing project being built on church property may have to be rented out at market rates in order to cover the costs of traditional financing or investor expectations. But if impact investors are willing to take lower rates of return, that same project could be offered at lower rents in order to make it affordable and therefore contribute more to addressing community needs.

As another example, a project financed with concessionary money could afford to put the land into a community land trust, thus ensuring permanent affordability and community ownership where traditional investor expectations would not allow for such a community-beneficial approach.

Church institutions own billions of dollars of invested assets that are mostly invested very traditionally. We could deploy those assets as patient, concessionary investment capital to develop church-owned property for the good of our neighbors and our mission.[2] As developer Tyler Krupp-Qureshi explains, impact in-

---

2. For much more on this idea, see my book *We Aren't Broke: Uncovering Hidden Resources for Mission and Ministry* (Grand Rapids: Eerdmans, 2021).

vestment can improve the quality of the broth that goes into the soup of development, thus leading to a much tastier and more satisfying meal for everyone.

What could concessionary impact investment financing do to improve development projects in your neighborhood? What sources of funds are you connected with that could be deployed to create a tastier soup?

PATHWAYS TO BETTER DEVELOPMENT

A fourth ingredient that will lead to better soup for everyone is engagement from government and civic leaders to help create pathways to better development. When churches start considering selling or redevelopment, they are often not aware of the legal limits imposed on the development process. As Kurt Paulsen and Nadia Mian explained in their chapters, zoning restrictions, parking minimums, planning overlays, financing incentives, and other carrots and sticks have an enormous impact on what kinds of development can, and cannot, be done.

Cities and municipalities have an opportunity to review how their existing regulations and incentives will influence the sale and development of church properties in their jurisdiction. They can add, remove, or amend such restrictions and incentives to encourage the kinds of development that will enhance the community and discourage the kinds of development that will not support flourishing. For example, as has been noted in this book, many cities are facing an affordable housing crisis. Church properties are often ideally situated to be redeveloped into affordable housing and may be some of the only infill property left to develop. But unless zoning and other regulations are updated, many churches will not be able to develop their properties into affordable housing.

Cities that want more affordable housing can create pathways to that outcome that involve churches. Communities that need more early childhood education and day care can create pathways that encourage churches to create centers that meet that need.

Neighborhoods that have no fresh food stores can create pathways that make it possible for churches to open grocery co-ops.

This transition in church property is only going to happen on this scale once in a lifetime (or even more rarely). It will almost certainly involve multiple church properties in a city, not just one or two. The disappearance of church property and the community support services it provides will leave serious gaps in the social fabric of many cities. Now is the time for government and civic leaders to get ahead of this issue and use the levers they have to create pathways for good development.

What government regulations need to be changed in your community in order to open the way for better development?

HOPE AND CREATIVITY

The fifth, and most important, ingredient we need added to the soup going forward is hopefulness. So much of the conversation around church property is filled with loss and sadness. And there is much to mourn, for sure. When our beloved church closes or the building is sold, there is deep grief and loss. We should allow ourselves, and our communities, the space to properly remember the past and grieve our losses.

But this is also a moment of extraordinary opportunity. The Christian story is one of death and resurrection. Of new life. And a new future.

Shifting the primary use of a church property from Sunday services to coworking space that creates community is not failure—it is transformation. Supplementing income and mission activity by turning an unused education wing of a church into a grocery co-op that addresses a neighborhood food desert is not failure—it is innovation. Closing a congregation after many years of fruitful ministry, tearing down the church building, and repurposing the property for affordable housing is not failure—it is rebirth. We may grieve the changes. We should celebrate the past. But let us also look forward to new life and what God will do through us next.[3]

As we've sampled through the stone soup of this book—letting go of property can be freeing, relinquishing control can be life giving to others, giving land back can be deeply healing, and redeveloping can be restorative. Repurposing church property is a chance to do something new. It allows us to think differently, see more vividly, listen more deeply, and love more fully. It is an opportunity to take the good news outside the Sunday worship service. The transition of church property is one of the largest issues facing the church today. It is also one of our greatest opportunities. Yes, churches, buildings, and property will be gone. Of this there is no doubt. But when we all contribute ingredients, in partnership together, I am incredibly hopeful that new and good things will emerge. They will be gone for GOOD.

Where do you find hope in the stories in this book? What is next for you?

3. Elsdon, *We Aren't Broke*, 88.

ACKNOWLEDGMENTS

First and foremost, I am incredibly grateful for the contributors to this book, who have shared their insights, experiences, and myriad gifts with me and the readers of this volume. In addition to the words they share in these pages, these authors are doing incredible and important work around the country to bring about more good in our world. I am humbled, inspired, and grateful for their partnership on this project.

I thank the folks at Laity Lodge and the H. E. Butt Foundation in the Texas hill country for hosting the contributors and other guests at a Gone for Good symposium in October 2022. At that gathering, writers became friends, and together we encouraged each other with vision and next steps for the future of church property transitions. The symposium, and the many good things that emerged from it, was a highlight of the process of putting this book together. We are grateful to the Baltimore-Washington Conference of the United Methodist Church, Covington Investments, the Lake Institute on Faith and Giving at Indiana University, the Presbyterian Foundation, Springtide Research, Thrivent Financial Services, and the Wesleyan Investive for sponsoring the symposium and making it possible. And we could not have pulled the gathering off without the help of the folks at the Impact Guild in San Antonio who managed the logistics, transportation, and hospitality for that special time.

I am blessed to work for two organizations that are incredibly supportive of me as a person and this project: Pres House and

RootedGood. My board and staff team at Pres House provide the support and flexibility that make a project like this possible. And I cannot overstate how vital my colleagues at RootedGood have been to bringing this book about. They encouraged me to pursue the project at the beginning, cleared space and time for me to work on it, envisioned and pulled off the Gone for Good symposium, and engaged in hours of conversation about the subject that has shaped the book and my thinking. I consider Shannon, Mark, and Tito honorary contributors to this book alongside those whose words are on the pages. Thank you!

I am grateful for the many conversation partners, experts, and practitioners who are doing work related to church property throughout the country, some of whom I've met, many of whom I haven't. Your work is so important. I'm especially thankful for the community and relationships that have formed among the Faith Properties Professional group that emerged from Faith+Finance and the Ormond Center at Duke Divinity School. Our regular online conversations over the past couple of years helped shape my thinking, and the work of each of you encourages me to press on.

Thank you to Andrew Knapp, Tom Raabe, Jenny Hoffman, Sarah Gombis, and the rest of the team at Wm. B. Eerdmans Publishing for entertaining the idea for this book so soon after *We Aren't Broke* was published, and for guiding me and these pages throughout the process all along the way. Thank you to Coté Soerens, who not only wrote an excellent chapter but also did the beautiful illustrations found throughout the book.

Finally, I'm thankful for all the pastors, church leaders, and church buildings that have touched me and my family over the years. Twenty years from now, some of them will be gone. But the mark they have left will remain. God has worked through you, and for that I am grateful.

In the end, nothing in my life compares to the pride and joy I have in my spouse, Erica, and our daughters, Emma and Sophie. Thank you for supporting "another book!?" I love you.

CONTRIBUTORS

JENNIE BIRKHOLZ, MHA, is the principal of Breakwater Light, a consulting firm that partners with diverse organizations to improve the health and well-being of others and where they pray, play, learn, work, and live. Jennie served in the community behavioral health and substance-use disorder field for over fifteen years before becoming a national consultant. She earned a bachelor of science in psychology from Texas A&M University and a master of health-care administration from Texas State University. She loves audiobooks, walking her dog in the rain, and making sand castles on the beach with her family.

DAVID BOWERS is vice president and mid-Atlantic market leader for Enterprise Community Partners, Inc. He also serves as the senior advisor for Enterprise's Faith-Based Development Initiative. His work includes facilitating affordable housing and community development transactions and policy implementation in collaboration with public and private sector stakeholders in the Baltimore and Washington, DC, metropolitan areas. David earned his bachelor's degree from the University of Virginia and his master of divinity degree from Howard University. He is an ordained minister and a founding member of the Greater Washington chapter of 100 Black Men.

PHILIP BURNS, AICP, is managing principal of the Arroyo Group, an urban design and planning firm based in Pasadena, California. Philip has worked with cities and congregations in a variety of ways to design more equitable, vibrant, and sustainable communities, including supporting over fifteen religious congregations in the process of envisioning, advocating for, and implementing affordable housing on their campuses together with the other members of the Congregational Land Committee of Making Housing and Community Happen.

MARK D. CONSTANTINE is senior vice president of community investment at Dogwood Health Trust, which exists to dramatically improve the health and well-being of all people and communities in the eighteen counties and Qualla Boundary of western North Carolina. Mark has authored two books and holds a PhD from the University of North Carolina at Chapel Hill, an MBA from the Fuqua School of Business (Duke University), and a Master of Theological Studies degree from Duke Divinity School. He serves on the Board of Partners for Sacred Places and is a past board member at Episcopal Relief and Development.

JOSEPH W. DANIELS JR. is the lead pastor of the Emory Fellowship in Washington, DC. He is a nationally sought-after preacher, teacher, and speaker on the topics of congregational, community, and economic development. He and the Emory congregation recently facilitated the construction of a $59 million, ninety-nine-unit affordable rental housing, commercial, and community development project called the Beacon Center. Joseph coaches and consults leaders and nonprofit organizations desirous of revitalizing congregations and communities through his company, the Ananias Consulting Group, LLC.

PATRICK DUGGAN is the executive director of the United Church of Christ Church Building and Loan Fund (CBLF). CBLF is the oldest church-building society in the United States and has financed more than four thousand church real estate projects in 168 years.

Patrick was ordained to the Christian ministry in 1989 and obtained full ministerial standing in the United Church of Christ in 1995. He earned a bachelor of arts degree from Harvard University and a master of divinity and doctor of ministry degrees, both from New York Theological Seminary. He served as senior pastor of the Congregational Church of South Hempstead/United Church of Christ from 1995 to 2023.

MARK ELSDON lives and works at the intersection of money and meaning as an entrepreneur, nonprofit executive, author, and speaker. He is the author of *We Aren't Broke: Uncovering Hidden Resources for Mission and Ministry*. Mark is cofounder of Rooted-Good, which supports catalytic and innovative church leaders working on property development, money and mission alignment, and social enterprise; and executive director at Pres House and Pres House Apartments on the University of Wisconsin's Madison campus. Mark has a bachelor of arts in psychology from the University of California–Berkeley, a master of divinity from Princeton Theological Seminary, and an MBA from the University of Wisconsin School of Business. He is an ordained minister in the Presbyterian Church (USA) and lives in Madison, Wisconsin.

ASHLEY GOFF is the pastor at Arlington Presbyterian Church (PC[USA]) in Arlington, Virginia, and ordained in the United Church of Christ. Her family has origins in southern and central Ohio, going back to parts of Europe. Ashley graduated from Union Theological Seminary in New York City, where she fell in love with the art of liturgy and the ways of organizing community. She lives with deep gratitude for several communities that have formed her along the way: Denison University, the Jesuit Volunteer Corps, the Open Door Community, Rikers Island jail in New York City, and Church of the Pilgrims (PC[USA]).

JIM BEAR JACOBS was born in St. Paul, Minnesota, and is a member of the Stockbridge-Munsee Mohican Nation, an American Indian tribe located in central Wisconsin. He has degrees in pastoral studies and Christian theology and has served various churches as youth minister, adult Christian educator, and director of men's ministries. Presently he is parish associate at Church of All Nations Presbyterian Church. Jim Bear is the director of Community Engagement and Racial Justice for the Minnesota Council of Churches and the creator and director of "Healing Minnesota Stories," a program of the Minnesota Council of Churches dedicated to ensuring that the Native American voice is heard in areas where it has long been ignored.

A. ROBERT JAEGER is president and cofounder of Partners for Sacred Places, America's only national nonprofit organization dedicated to maximizing older religious properties as assets for both congregations and their communities. He is author or coauthor of *Sacred Places at Risk*; *Conservation of Urban Religious Properties*; *Sacred Places in Transition*; and *Religious Institutions and Community Renewal*. Robert is the founding editor and a columnist for *Inspired* magazine and is the editor of *Sacred Places* magazine.

TYLER KRUPP-QURESHI is a principal and development lead for Threshold Development Group. A social entrepreneur, educator, and community developer with more than twenty years of experience in small business and higher education, he is interested in how the built environment can support sustainable and thriving community. Tyler has a master of science in real estate from the University of Wisconsin–Madison. A student of law and philosophy, he also has undergraduate and graduate degrees from Yale University, the University of California–Berkeley, and the University of Wisconsin–Madison.

EILEEN LINDNER is a Presbyterian minister who has served congregations in Illinois, New York, and New Jersey. She holds a ThM and PhD from Union Theological Seminary in New York. She served on the staff of the National Council of Churches of Christ, USA, as director of research and finally as deputy general secretary. There she was editor of the *Yearbook of American and Canadian Churches*, the single largest database for denominational life in North America. At the National Council of Churches she was the primary investigator for two landmark studies, one documenting the extent of church-housed child day-care programs and the other a national survey of congregationally based health-care programs.

ELIZABETH LYNN has founded and led several programs designed to expand moral imagination for civic engagement, including the Center for Civic Reflection and Valparaiso University's Institute for Leadership and Service. Through her writings she has contributed to contemporary understandings of philanthropy and the humanities in American life. Currently, Elizabeth leads Shifting Ground, an initiative of Lake Institute on Faith & Giving that is focused on deepening conversation about the changing landscape of faith, philanthropy, and community. She coauthors the weekly blog *Digging a Deeper Well* with her husband, Mark Ramsey, for the Ministry Collaborative.

NADIA MIAN is senior program director at the Ralph W. Voorhees Center for Civic Engagement and a lecturer at the Edward J. Bloustein School of Planning and Public Policy at Rutgers University. Nadia holds a PhD from the New School, and a master's in environmental studies, in which she specialized in urban planning, from York University in Toronto, Canada. She previously taught at New York University, the New School, and Columbia University, where she was managing editor of the journal *City & Community*. Her latest research examines how faith-based institutions are using their property to build affordable housing and at the same time advocate for and change land-use, zoning, and housing policy.

KURT PAULSEN is a professor of urban planning in the Department of Planning and Landscape Architecture at the University of Wisconsin-Madison. His teaching and research focus on housing, affordable housing finance and policy, land use, and municipal finance. In addition to his published academic research, he has authored two Dane County housing needs assessments, has chaired the City of Middleton Workforce Housing Committee, and does economic impact analysis research for WHEDA (Wisconsin Housing and Economic Development Authority). Kurt is a member of the American Institute of Certified Planners (AICP).

JILL SHOOK is cofounder of Making Housing and Community Happen with her husband, Anthony Manousos. After serving as a campus minister, coordinating teams from Berkeley to Harvard to serve in developing countries to do sustainable community development with and by the people, Jill moved from Mexico to Pasadena to learn from Dr. John Perkins. She cofounded STARS, an after-school program, and saw how segregation and the high cost of housing was a root of poverty, and how affordable housing was breaking that cycle. Jill is the author of the book *Making Housing Happen.*

COTÉ SOERENS is an urban revitalization strategist and innovator working to create democratic spaces through place making. She has led a number of initiatives in her neighborhood aimed at fostering equitable development in South Park, Seattle, such as Resistencia Coffee, the Barrio Building, and Reconnect South Park, an initiative seeking to decommission a highway that cuts South Park in two, reclaiming forty acres of public land for equitable development. Coté drew the illustrations found throughout this book.

ROCHELLE A. STACKHOUSE is the senior director of programs for Partners for Sacred Places, a national nonprofit working with faith communities as they steward older and historic buildings. She was ordained in the United Church of Christ in 1982. A graduate of Princeton Theological Seminary, she has served churches of varying sizes as senior, solo, interim, and transitional pastor in Michigan, New York, New Jersey, Massachusetts, Pennsylvania, and Connecticut. She received a PhD from Drew University in liturgical studies and has taught at numerous seminaries, most recently Yale and Lexington.

Contributors

KEITH STARKENBURG was born in northwest Iowa and spent most of his youth in Rapid City, South Dakota, on the edge of the Black Hills. He serves as associate professor of theology at Western Theological Seminary and director of the Vita Scholars Program, an accelerated BA/MDiv program with Hope College. He has published articles and essays on the theology of Karl Barth, the eschatology of creation, as well as the theology and ethics of place. He is currently working on a book that presents a biblical and theological case for land reparations in Turtle Island/North America.

ANDRE WHITE is a real estate advisor with Mitchelville Real Estate Group. He was born and raised in a Gullah community on Hilton Head Island, South Carolina. Since late 2003, Andre has worked on real estate transactions that exceed $1 billion in total value in California, Massachusetts, Connecticut, New York, Texas, Colorado, and South Carolina for for-profit, nonprofit, and public entities. He holds a master's degree from Harvard University with an emphasis in the development and investment of housing and a bachelor's degree in business from South Carolina State University.